MEN ALIVE

STOP KILLER STRESS WITH SIMPLE ENERGY HEALING TOOLS

by **Jed Diamond, PhD**
author of *The Irritable Male Syndrome*

ACCLAIM FOR JED DIAMOND'S
MENALIVE

"You *need* to read this book, whether you think you do or not. Dr. Diamond is a brilliant, caring professional. He is one of the world's leading experts in men's health. I have been a health care professional for many years and learned so much from Jed's book myself. You will have multiple *aha* moments as you read. The *aha* moments will lead to practical positive changes in your life. It has in mine."
—**Alexander Loyd**, PhD, ND, author of *The Healing Code*

"In this wonderful book, Jed Diamond lucidly explains the major challenges facing men in navigating their way through this most critical period of human history. More important, he shows us how to address the hazards and opportunities in ways that are new, creative, and highly effective. It will change the way you think about the life you have been given and empower you to find greater fulfillment in it."
—**David Feinstein**, PhD, coauthor of *The Promise of Energy Medicine*

"*MenAlive* is more than a book. It is a complete tool kit for relieving stress and bringing about lasting health. It changes the way we look at ourselves, each other, and the world."
—**John Gray**, PhD, author of *Men Are From Mars, Women Are From Venus*

"After decades of intense men's work together, Jed knows what men need. Being a great pioneer he immerses himself in new 'tools' until he finds what works. Jed offers the precious gift of his hard-won wisdom for us to care for our own body, mind and soul.

—**Bill Kauth**, Co-founder of The ManKind Project, author of *Circle of Men* and *We Need Each Other: Building Gift Community*

"Jed Diamond's book dispels two myths. One, that as time passes we will inevitably develop age-related aches and pains that we will simply have to live with. The second is that 'energy healing' is complete nonsense. These myths cause us to pay unnecessarily for pills and doctors when fresh air, sunshine, and a barefoot walk in the grass can make us feel much better. This book introduces practical personal energy tools with which to feel better longer and save money at the same time."

—**James L. Oschman, PhD,** author of *Energy Medicine: The Scientific Basis*

"The problem with simple energy healing tools is that they seem just too simple! If you can find it in you not to scorn simplicity, you may get a world of help from Jed Diamond's new book."

—**Eric Maisel, PhD,** author of *Rethinking Depression*

"*MenAlive* is a wonderful and easy-to-follow guide for stress reduction in men. It helps create awareness to address challenges in new and effective ways, which will lead to self-empowerment and positive changes."

— **Rollin McCraty, PhD,** Director of Research, Institute of HeartMath

"Dr. Diamond's new book is not only packed with information but offers powerful solutions. One of Diamond's gifts is his ability to write books that help men change their own lives while helping women understand men at deep, empowering levels. This book is needed...a must-read if you are growing through the stresses and strains of a lifetime (and who isn't?). I highly recommend this book to all men—and to the women who love them."

— **Michael Gurian**, author of *Leadership and the Sexes* and *How Do I Help Him?*

"Jed Diamond's remarkable book is full of insights, tools, and touching truths. It is a great open window into a man's soul, stresses, and strains. I highly recommend it to both men and women."

— **John Lee,** author of *The Flying Boy and The Half-Lived Life: Overcoming Passivity* and *Rediscovering Your Authentic Self*

"*MenAlive* is a veritable compendium of the most readable and understandable information related to energy healing that starts at the beginning historically, weaves through time, takes the reader systematically to the present, and then discusses the four simple energy healing tools in depth, which are the centerpiece of this book. If you only buy one book this year, make it *MenAlive*, and buy one for every man in your life and every woman who loves them!"

—**Jackie Black, PhD**, author of *Couples & Money: Cracking the Code to Ending the #1 Conflict in Marriage*

"Diamond has researched the entire field of energy healing, found out what really works, and applied it to specific issues that men face—such as stress, irritation, and depression. He doesn't stop there, however. He sets out a series of practical techniques that any man can learn and use to de-stress, relax, and heal. If you're a man, learn these tools. If you're a woman, buy this book for your man."

—**Lion Goodman**, Director of Men's Programs, The Shift Network

"As a long-time leader in the men's movement and author several books that inspired me, once again Jed brings an important new set of tools for men to grow with."

—**John W. Travis**, MD, MPH, Co-author of *Wellness Workbook*

"Two facts are indisputable: Baby Boomers are aging, and they're aging into a time of life fraught with greater risks of disease and decline. Further, a significant number are health and wellness oriented, and these explorers are more than willing to go beyond traditional medical paradigms to discover how to become healthier and less dependent on conventional treatment modalities. Jed Diamond has picked exactly the right moment to give them the gifts of energy healing."

—**Brent Green,** author of *Generation Reinvention: How Boomers Today Are Changing Business, Marketing, Aging and the Future*

"Dr. Diamond's wondrous synthesis of theory and practice allows us to understand the true nature of what ails modern mankind and empowers us to recreate our health. This book moves us from the sick-care model of the solid atom to a true health care model based on dynamic energy fields. Read it and be all you can be!"

—**Gregory J. Nicosia, PhD, DCEP**, Immediate Past President, Association for Comprehensive Energy Psychology

"Jed Diamond has created an extraordinary book which allows men to access both physical and emotional vitality. In a sea of self-help books geared towards the female demographic, this books stands out as a practical and effective guide for men to learn more about self-healing techniques which have been proven to really work."

—**Clint Ober**, coauthor of, *Earthing: The Most Important Health Discovery Ever?*

"This book is a must-read for all men and the women who love them. Jed Diamond's pioneering work will change the way men view their health."

—**Carole G. Stern**, President, Association of Comprehensive Energy Psychology

"An invaluable resource and guide for men who struggle with their life, health and negative emotions—and consequently in their love relationships."

—**Martin Ucik,** author of *Integral Relationships: A Manual for Men*

"MenAlive illuminates key challenges blocking men from shifting into more mature masculinity, and provides equally key tools for succeeding. We men owe it to our loved ones, our spheres of influence, and most importantly ourselves, to take *MenAlive* to heart."

—**David Gruder**, PhD, DCEP, author of *The New IQ (Integrity Intelligence)*, ManKind Project Elder, Founding President of the Association for Comprehensive Energy Psychology

MenAlive: Stop Killer Stress with Simple Energy Healing Tools
Copyright © 2012 by Jed Diamond
Published by Fifth Wave Press
www.MenAlive.com

Library of Congress Cataloging-in-Publication Data
Diamond, Jed
1. Men's health 2. Energy medicine 3. Stress relief

Includes notes and index

Diamond, Jed
MenAlive: Stop Killer Stress with Simple Energy Healing
Tools / Jed Diamond

ISBN: 978-0-911761-00-9

Printed in the United States of America

ALSO FROM JED DIAMOND, PHD

<u>Books</u>

Mr. Mean: Saving Your Relationship from the Irritable Male Syndrome

Male vs. Female Depression: Why Men Act Out and Women Act In

The Irritable Male Syndrome: Managing the 4 Key Causes of Depression and Aggression

The Whole Man Program: Reinvigorating Your Body, Mind, and Spirit After 40

Surviving Male Menopause: A Guide for Women and Men

Male Menopause

The Warrior's Journey Home: Healing Men, Healing the Planet

Looking For Love in All the Wrong Places: Overcoming Romantic and Sexual Addictions

Inside Out: Becoming My Own Man

How to Connect with Me

For more information about books and other resources, or if you need help dealing with the stresses in your life, I invite you to visit me at http://MenAlive.com.

I'd enjoy hearing from you. Send an email to MenAlive@ MenAlive.com and sign up for Team MenAlive, which is a book owner list, so I can send you new information, videos, and updates.

Let's start a conversation. Say "hi" on Twitter @MenAlive-Now or use the hashtag #MenAlive to share your insights and examples. Discover how others are using the concepts you'll read about.

You can also join us on Facebook at http://Facebook.com/ MenAliveNow/ for more tips and ongoing dialogue.

MENALIVE: STOP KILLER STRESS WITH SIMPLE ENERGY HEALING TOOLS

JED DIAMOND, PHD, LCSW

"The cell is a machine driven by energy. It can thus be approached by studying matter, or by studying energy. In every culture and in every medical tradition before ours, healing was accomplished by moving energy."

—Albert Szent-Györgyi, Nobel Laureate in Medicine

ACKNOWLEDGMENTS

This book is the culmination of work over the last forty-plus years, and there are many more people to thank than I have space to do so here. More than just a helpmate, my wife, Carlin, has been a loving presence and partner. She has supported my work from the beginning and I want to honor her here. She was practicing energy healing long before it became popular.

In addition, three groups of people deserve special mention:

1. Leaders in the field of Energy Healing.

David Feinstein, PhD, who challenged me to write a book on energy healing for men. His wife, Donna Eden, who inspired me when I read *Energy Medicine for Women* after buying it as a gift for my wife, Carlin.

I've also learned a great deal from Patricia Carrington, Dawson Church, Gary Craig, Blair Dunn, Charles Elder, John Freedom, David Gruder, Sue Johnson, Lindsay Kenny, Bruce Lipton, Alex Lloyd, Carol Look, Michael Mayer, Rollin McCraty, Caroline Myss, Gregory Nicosia, Clinton Ober,

James Oschman, Lynne McTaggart, Betsy Muller, Candace Pert, John Petersen, Robert Schwarz, Stephen Sinatra, Carole Stern, Greg Warburton, and Martin Zucker.

2.   Leaders in the men's health field.

Peter Alsop, Jean Bonhomme, Robert Bly, Malcolm Carruthers, Will Courtnay, Gordon Clay, Stephen Dinan, Warren Farrell, Brent Green, Lion Goodman, John Gray, Michael Gurian, Ron Henry, James Hillman, Bert Hoff, Steve Imparl, Thomas Joiner, Bill Kauth, Sam Keen, Howard LaGarde, John Lee, Tom Matlack, Michael Meade, William Pollack, Mark Schillinger, Justin Sterling, Rich Tosi, and John Travis.

3.   Those who helped bring this book into being:

Mike Aplet, Tony Black, Hal Zina Bennett, Josh Bowers, Rosamond Crowder, Kirsten Ellis, Ian Fitzpatrick, Jeff Franklin, Betha Gibson, **"Gold Diamond" Supporters (Dianna and Tim Browning, Carlin Diamond, Brad Dunne, Denis Sutro, David Terrell, Judy Whelley, Lawrence and Elaine Yundt),** Leon Greef, Wulf Heinigen, Angela Hennek, Aaron Nelson-Moody, David Newman, Whitney Parks, Ken Petron, Tom Plunkett, Tom Porpiglia, Geoff Pomeroy, Kathy Regan, Amanda Rice, Lucille Rock, Rani Saijo, Suzanne Sifuentes, Sherryl Soukup, Dickey Weinkle, and Mary Zellachild.

AUTHOR'S NOTE AND SPECIAL BONUS

The practices, ideas, and suggestions in this book are not intended as a substitute for medical or psychological attention. When considering applying these methods to various health-related issues, please consult with your medical doctor, psychotherapist, or other appropriate health care professional.

Scan this tag using you smartphone, or visit http://MenAlive.com/JedWelcome, for a personal message from me.

Not familiar with tag technology?

Throughout the book, you'll find these symbols called QR codes which are electronic gateways to supplemental material and examples included in the text. There are several QR code readers available and you may already have one on your smartphone. If you don't, then via your mobile browser visit http://get.beetagg.com to download a free application.

Once you've downloaded Tag, just open the application, take a picture of the tag using your phone camera, and you are immediately transported to the related information.

Reading a book is great, but it's also nice to hear the author speak. I've created an on-line course called Men Alive: Stop Stress and Live Free that will help bring this information to life. You can learn about the course and sign up by going to:

http://www.entheosacademy.com/courses/MenAlive-Stop-Stress-and-Live-Free

or take a picture of this tag using your smartphone.

I enjoy hearing from you. Let me know how the book has helped, questions you have, comments, suggestions. Go to www.MenAlive.com/Feedback

CONTENTS

INTRODUCTION
How to Get the Most Out of the Book

I grew up in a family that relied on things you could see, touch, and take apart. My mother was the office manager for a company called Tubular Structures, which made solid scaffolding out of pipe—the kind you see big burly men climbing up and down as they paint houses and fix upper-story windows. My stepfather was a welder, carpenter, and all-around handyman. This was a mechanistic world, a clockwork universe, where separate objects could be assembled and where things were more important than feelings. My family believed in hard science and taught me to distrust anything that couldn't be measured.

But there was another side of my family story we rarely spoke about. My biological father was a writer, poet, and stage actor. In the years following my birth, he struggled to find work and support his family. Stresses in his life mounted, and when I was five years old he tried to commit suicide. He was sent to a mental hospital for treatment. Growing up, I tried to understand what had happened to him. My mind couldn't grasp the idea that he had been taken down by a mysterious "nervous breakdown" that I couldn't see and no one seemed to be able to explain. Looking back, I realize that two competing forces shaped my life:

(1) The world of things we can engage and manipulate with our five senses: the "tubular structures" of the world.

(2) The world of energy and spirit that can cause "nervous breakdowns" as well as inspire writing and beautiful poetry.

Energy healing enables us to bridge these two worlds. As you'll learn, it allows us to deal with problems at the physical level as well as those that are caused by emotional and spiritual disturbances. It has taken a long time for me to accept my relationship with energy healing. Even after I knew it worked, I couldn't quite believe it. I needed a scientific explanation for *how* and *why* it worked. I wanted to be sure energy healing wasn't just New Age snake oil that promised to cure anything and everything, but really did very little.

Energy healing is based on the supposition that illness results from disturbances in the body's energies and energy fields and can be addressed via interventions into those energies and energy fields. It is one of five domains of "complementary and alternative medicine" identified by the National Institutes of Health (NIH). David Feinstein and Donna Eden, two of the most widely acknowledged experts in the emerging field of energy healing, say that conventional medicine, at its foundation, focuses on the biochemistry of cells, tissue, and organs. **Energy medicine, at its foundation, focuses on the fields that organize and control the growth and repair of cells, tissues, and organs, and on ways of influencing those fields.**[1]

Although there is still a lot we need to learn, I believe the scientific foundation of energy healing[2] is solid enough to share what I've learned thus far. I'm convinced that we can now stop the stresses that are killing so many men and their families. These simple tools are deceptively powerful, so powerful that we no longer have to rely solely on "experts" to keep us healthy. Using the tools of energy healing, we can regain control of our own lives. We can embrace the wisdom of William Ernest Henley, who said, "I am the master of my fate: I am the captain of my soul."

This book is meant to guide you through the process. I'll be with you every step of the way, sharing what has worked for me and what has worked with friends and clients. Though this book is focused on men's health, it is not just for men. Women, too, are concerned about the health of the men in their lives. I've included the results of the latest cutting-edge scientific research that demonstrates the value of energy healing in dealing with the most difficult problems we face today. I've shared the tools that I've found to be most useful and effective, but there are Internet links and endnotes for further study once you learn the basics.

Energy Healing: The Mind/Body Connection

My first experience with energy healing occurred shortly after I graduated from UC Berkeley in 1968. My wife and I had found a wonderful house in Pinole, a rural suburb in the East Bay, across the bridge from San Francisco. Our neighbors had horses they let us ride whenever we wanted to. Life was wonderful.

The first summer in Pinole, we invited our closest friends from college for a visit. They had a four-year-old son who was cute as a bug and adventurous. While we recounted stories of success, the little boy wandered off and climbed under a fence into the horse corral, where a skittish horse kicked him.

By the time the boy's father reached him, he was screaming in anguish, with a red welt rising on his forehead. His mother immediately comforted the boy with her words. She calmly told him that she was there and that things would be all right. She held one hand about three inches above his head and passed her hand back and forth over the wound. While she did this, the boy's father called for an ambulance. The boy seemed to relax and eventually stopped crying.

I wondered how waving her hand over the boy could be helpful. She kept her hand moving slowly and said, "It's energy healing." I nodded as though I understood. She turned her attention back to her son. I rolled my eyes and looked at my wife, thinking, "We love her, but what she's doing is *nuts*."

Well, things turned out okay. The boy was checked at the local hospital, and there didn't seem to be any permanent damage. My scientific mind concluded that he must not have really been hurt. I relegated energy healing to New Age mumbo jumbo and forgot all about it. Much later, I learned that solid science had demonstrated that healing the energy body could help heal the physical body. Over the years, I've tried a number of different energy healing practices. Not all of them worked for me, but the four I describe in the book have proven themselves over time. I have found these four to be the easiest, the most effective, and the most scientifically grounded.

Options for Using This Book

If you're skeptical, that's fine. It's good to have a prove-it-to-me attitude. All I ask is that you keep an open mind and an open heart as you learn more about the power of energy to heal. Whatever you think about the field of energy healing, I suspect you'll agree with me on the following:

- **We can no longer afford to get sick.**

Our current medical system is not working well for many people. It's too expensive and not effective enough in treating the chronic problems most of us face today.

- **It's better to prevent problems than to treat them.**

Stress is at the root of many of our medical problems. If we can reduce stress, we can improve our health.

- **Treating humans as though we are machines doesn't work.**

Our modern world separates us from ourselves, from each other, and from the earth. Our medical practices treat a thousand separate problems, but they often neglect the whole person. We need to have better choices. There must be a better way.

There are a number of ways you can approach this book:

1. Start at the beginning and go to the end.

Many people like this approach. You take it in sequence, one step at a time.

2. Go directly to the tools section and put them to use.

In Part II of the book, I describe the four most effective energy healing elements. You can read this section and apply them to the issues in your life. There's a saying in the energy healing field: "Try it on everything." Although I offer specific examples in this book of how these tools can be used, they have proven themselves for a variety of issues.

3. Start with the issues section.

In Part III of the book, I address the issues of most concern to men. You can learn more about an issue such as pain, midlife sexuality, or anger, and then try out various tools to see how they work on the problem that is most concerning you.

Notions that may be particularly helpful are in bold lettering so you can easily spot the gold. Of course, these are just the nuggets I think are important. You'll undoubtedly want to have a highlighter or pen available to mark your own.

One Caution

If you're like me, you may find these tools work so well that you'll have trouble believing them. Perhaps your skeptical mind will jump in to tell you to stop using them, even when they are working for you. In a world where we are taught that real medicine is costly, time-consuming, and painful, we have a hard time believing in practices that work *and* are inexpensive, quick, and painless. **Just remember, some things *are* just too good to be true. Others are *just plain good*.** These techniques are still new, and there is a lot more to be learned. But there's no reason to wait any longer to get started.

We can all learn from each other's experience, and I genuinely enjoy hearing from people. Contact me through my website at www.MenAlive.com. Let me know how these tools work for you.

PART I:
THE COST OF STRESS AND THE PROMISE OF ENERGY HEALING

CHAPTER 1:
THE HAZARDS AND BLESSINGS OF BEING MALE

It isn't easy being a man today, though many of us try to hide this fact. We are told that males are the privileged sex and boys have it better than girls. We learn that real men are tough, take care of their own problems, and don't complain. After all, what could we have to complain about? Social scientist Thomas Joiner, PhD, tells us, "Men make a lot of money and have all the accompanying privileges and power. This has been so for millennia. Men are over-represented in each of the following categories, just to name a few: those earning over $100,000 per year; Fortune 500 company CEOs; and U.S. presidents, state governors, and senators."[3]

I'm assuming that you (and most of the men reading this book) don't fall into any of those "privilege and power" categories. But for all of us, regardless of our wealth or position, the stresses we face can be deadly. A recent report states, "Males experience higher mortality rates than females at all stages of life from conception to old age."[4] Suicide is the most extreme indicator of the stress men feel today, particularly in men over forty. **According to the National Centers of Disease Control and Prevention, 34,598 people killed themselves in**

2007 (the last year for which full statistics were available)— **and 27,678 of them (80 percent) were male. Eleven times that number attempted suicide.**[5] I felt the reality of these statistics at a very young age.

I still remember the terror I felt when I heard my father had an "accident" and was taken to the hospital. I was five years old, and he was forty-two. I didn't learn until years later that he had tried to take his own life, but even as a small child I was aware of the stresses he felt as an out-of-work writer trying to support his family. When I was forty, I came across a journal he had written during that critical time of his life. He describes his mounting frustration, anger, and despair as his hopes and dreams began to fade:

June 4

Your flesh crawls, your scalp wrinkles when you look around and see good writers, established writers, writers with credits a block long, unable to sell, unable to find work; yes, it's enough to make anyone blanch, turn pale, and sicken.

August 15

Faster, faster, faster, I walk. I plug away looking for work, anything to support my family. I try, try, try, try, try. I always try and never stop.

November 8

A hundred failures, an endless number of failures, until now, my confidence, my hope, my belief in myself has run completely out. Middle-aged, I stand and gaze ahead, numb, confused, and desperately worried. All around me, I see the young in spirit, the young at heart, with ten times my confidence, twice my youth, ten times my fervor, twice my education. I see them all, a whole army of them, battering at the same doors I'm battering, trying in the same field I'm trying. Yes, on a Sunday morning in early November, my hope and my life stream are both running desperately low, so low, so stagnant, that I hold my breath in fear, believing that the dark, blank curtain is about to descend.

As a midlife man myself, I felt my father's pain as his self-esteem slowly eroded away, the fear and frustration of trying to support a family taking its toll and the tide of shame beginning to envelope him. Six days after his November 8 entry, he tried to kill himself.

Though he survived physically, our lives were never the same. Over the last thirty-five years, I've treated more and more men who face stresses similar to those my father experienced. The economic conditions and social dislocations that contributed to his feelings of shame and hopelessness continue to weigh heavily on men in today's battered economy.

As psychologist Herb Goldberg reminds us in his book, *The Hazards of Being Male*, **"The male has paid a heavy price for his masculine 'privilege' and power."** He writes, **"He is out of touch with his emotions and his body. He is playing by the rules of the male game plan and with lemming-like purpose he is destroying himself—emotionally, psychologically, and physically."**[6]

Three Critical Stages Where We Lose Men

In order to reclaim our health and wellbeing, we have to overcome our denial and take a hard look at the reality of our lives. When I think about men's health, I often think of my father. He loved baseball, but he would never watch it on television. He always preferred listening to it on the radio. I think he liked bringing his own imagination to the words and picturing the action in his mind. When I think about the crisis in men's health, I picture a baseball field. To be successful in the game of baseball, you have to touch all three bases and make it home. If life were like baseball, I believe we're losing too many men before they can make it around the bases and back to home plate. I believe we are losing men at three critical stages of their lives.

Too many young men don't ever make it to first base. The stresses of young adulthood lead to accidents, alcohol and drug abuse, and violence. We lose young men before they've had a chance to truly live. Many midlife men have trouble letting go of their youth. They try to stay forever young. They deny their age, refuse to make the turn at second base, and end up alone in left field. Older men often give up on life and become isolated, depressed, and withdrawn. They aren't able to make the turn at third, and they end up dead in the dugout.

When I've talked with men over the years, they often feel powerless to change their lives. This surprises women, who often see men as having most of power. In his book, *Why Men Are the Way They Are,* gender researcher Warren Farrell helps us better understand why men and women often have a different experience of power and powerlessness. He says, "When a woman is divorced, has two children, no alimony, no child support, and no job experience—that is her experience of powerlessness. When a man is in the hospital with a coronary bypass operation caused by the stress of working two jobs to support two children his former wife won't let him see, and he feels no other woman will get involved with him because of those very circumstances—that is his experience of powerlessness." Farrell concludes, "Both feel loneliness. The flip sides of the same role make both sexes feel powerless."[7]

It doesn't have to be that way. We can change the restrictive roles that harm men and women. Men are not destined to get sick and die before their time. Men can have wonderful and productive lives. But in order to live long and well, we have to recognize the stresses we are under and take a hard look at our current state of health.

The Reality of Men's Health Today

The Men's Health Network (MHN) is a national nonprofit organization whose mission is to educate men and their families about the state of men's health today and how it can be improved. MHN details the "silent health crisis" of men as follows:[8]

Life Expectancy Gender Gap.

In 1920, the life expectancy gender gap was only 1.0 years. By 2011, men are dying four to six years younger than women.

Leading Causes of Death.

Men have a higher death rate than women for all ten of the leading causes of death: heart disease, cancer, injuries, cerebrovascular disease, chronic lower respiratory disease, diabetes, pneumonia/flu, HIV infection, suicide, and homicide. We all die of something, but if you're a guy, you are more likely to get a serious disease and die from it than are women.

Heart Disease.

Almost twice as many men as women die of ischemic heart disease, the leading cause of death by far for both men and women. This year, more than four hundred thousand men will die of heart disease, 25 percent of whom will be under age sixty-five. More than fifty thousand men will die of a stroke. Of course, the death rate for women compared to men goes up as they get older, but that's because there aren't as many older men. Too many of us have already died.

Cancer.

Fifty percent more men than women die of cancer. This year, more than seven hundred thousand men will be diagnosed with cancer, and nearly three hundred thousand will die of it. Over the course of a lifetime, half of all men will get cancer at least once.

Homicide.

We know men are more likely to kill others than are women. A research study[9] showed that, although women comprise more than half the U.S. population, they committed only 14.7 percent of the homicides during the study interval. Many people don't know that, although men do most of the killing, they are also most likely to be *victims* of homicide.

Over the ten-year study period, 215,273 homicides were studied, 77 percent of which involved male victims and 23 percent involving female victims.

The study noted that men are more likely to be killed by someone outside the family, while women are more likely to be killed by their spouse or intimate acquaintance. In contrast to men, who killed non-intimate acquaintances or strangers in 80 percent of cases, women killed their spouse, an intimate acquaintance, or a family member in 60 percent of cases.

Depression and Suicide.

Suicide is the ultimate indicator of despair, and men suffer at rates more than four to seventeen times higher than women. Not only do men commit suicide at rates much higher than women, but they kill themselves indirectly as well. Psychotherapist Terrence Real, author of *I Don't Want to Talk About It: Overcoming the Secret Legacy of Male Depression*, says: **"Hidden depression drives several of the problems we think of as typically male: physical illness, alcohol and drug abuse, domestic violence, failures in intimacy, self-sabotage in careers."**[10]

Most people know that men are more likely to commit suicide than women. But most are not aware of how much more likely men are to kill themselves or how our risk differs with age. "The suicide rate is four times higher among males than females overall," says Dr. Will Courtenay, author of *Dying to be Men: Psychosocial, Environmental, and Bio-behavioral Directions in Promoting the Health of Men and Boys.* "Suicide rates for males range from two times higher among children aged ten to fourteen to more than seventeen times higher among adults aged eighty-five or older."[11]

Even in the armed services, where we tend think of men dying in battle, suicide is a major problem. "To our knowledge, for the first and only time in human history, a country at war—the United States—lost more of its service members in a month to suicide than to combat," says Dr. Thomas Joiner. "That occurred in early 2009."[12]

All my life, I've felt the reality of men's pain, from the time my father tried to commit suicide when I was five to the struggles with depression I've had in my own life. These statistics tell an important story: at every age, including when we are young, men are much more likely to commit suicide than females. That is a tragedy for everyone: men, women, *and* children.

Randolph Nesse, MD, and colleagues at the University of Michigan examined premature deaths among men in twenty countries. They suggest that as many as 375,000 lives could be saved in the U.S. alone if male mortality rates were brought into line with those of women. **Being male is now the single largest demographic factor for early death, the study concluded. "If you could make male mortality rates the same as female rates, you would do more good than curing cancer."**[13]

Why Men Live Sicker and Die Sooner

Some people have come to believe that men don't live as long or as well as women simply because...well, because we are men. There's an assumption that our problems are built into our genes, and there's nothing we can do about them. But recent research has shown there are things men do, or fail to do, that affect our health. Of course, we're talking generalities here—most men compared to most women. Some men engage in more healthy practices than some women. But on the whole, our health practices leave a lot to be desired. Men's health researcher Dr. Will Courtenay describes the following behaviors in his book *Dying to be Men*:[14]

They Have Less Healthy Lifestyles.

Men and boys, in general, have less healthy lifestyles than woman and girls, and they engage in far fewer health-promoting behaviors. For example, men are more often overweight than women, and they have less healthy dietary habits. They eat more meat, fat, and salt and less fiber, fruits, and vegetables than women. They have higher cholesterol and blood pressure, and they do less to lower them. Men use fewer medications, vitamins, and dietary supplements. They also sleep less, and less well, and they stay in bed to recover from illness for less time than women.

They Engage in More Risk-Taking Behavior.

Men and adolescent males engage in more reckless and illegal driving and they drive drunk more frequently than women and adolescent females. They also have more sexual partners than women and engage in significantly more high-risk physical activities—such as dangerous sports and leisure-time activities—and physical fights. They are also more likely than women to carry guns or other weapons, and they engage in more criminal activity.

They Often Have Problems with Drugs and Alcohol.

Compared to women, men use more alcohol and other drugs. More men than women use tobacco products, and they have more dangerous patterns of tobacco use. Although not everyone who uses drugs or alcohol becomes addicted, men are more likely to continue using even when they experience negative consequences. As one man told me in counseling, "My drug of choice is *more.*" For him, like many men who become addicted, "too much is never enough." I believe addiction is the disease of lost self-hood. Addicts are looking for pleasure and escape from pain in all the wrong places. Like confused homing pigeons, they seek the safety and security of family and friends, but they fly 180 degrees in the wrong direction.

They Misperceive Their Susceptibility to Risk.

Men are consistently less likely than women to perceive themselves as being at risk for illness, injury, and a variety of health problems. Despite being at greater risk from drug and alcohol use, for example, males of all ages perceive significantly less risk than females associated with the use of cigarettes, alcohol, and other drugs. With rare exceptions, people who think they are invulnerable take fewer precautions with their health—and thus have greater health risks—than people who recognize their vulnerability.

They Are More Likely to Be Victims of Physical Abuse and Violence.

Men and boys are more likely than women and girls to be the victims of physical abuse or violence. For example, nearly half of men nationally have been punched or beaten by a person—in most cases by another man. We often think that sexual abuse happens only to females, but 5 percent of boys (compared to 10 percent of girls) report having been sexually abused. Many believe that male sexual abuse is under-reported. Among adolescent boys nationally, those who have been sexually abused are more likely than those who were not abused to report poor mental health, and they are twice as likely to smoke or drink frequently or to have used drugs.

They Are Less Likely to Change Unhealthy Behaviors.

Men believe less strongly than women that they have control over their future health or that personal actions contribute to good health. Further, women are more likely than men to contemplate changing unhealthy habits or to maintain healthy habits. Men, however, are more likely than women not to consider changing unhealthy behaviors and to deny that these behaviors are problematic.

They Have Traditional Views of Masculinity that Are Often in Conflict with Health.

There is a high level of agreement among people in the United States regarding typical feminine and masculine characteristics. Men and boys, in particular, experience a great deal of social pressure to conform to these stereotypic characteristics. These dominant norms of masculinity dictate, for example, that men should be self-reliant, strong, robust, and tough; that men should welcome danger; and that men should never reveal vulnerability, back down, or do anything "feminine." These idealized norms of masculinity create a conflict with actions that we could do to take care of ourselves or to be taken care of by those who love us.

Commenting on the reason so many men become damaged physically and emotionally, psychologist Herb Goldberg says, "They have confused their social masks for their essence, and they are destroying themselves while fulfilling the traditional definitions of masculine-appropriate behavior. They set their life sails by these role definitions. They are the heroes, the studs, the providers, the warriors, the empire builders, and the fearless ones."[15]

They Don't Express Their Emotions or Acknowledge Distress.

In general, women are more emotionally expressive than men—except when it comes to expressing anger. Men also report less fear or emotional distress than women do, and they are less likely than women to cry. Men's inexpressiveness can have both direct and indirect effects on their health and well-being. Self-disclosure, for example, is associated with improvements in immune functioning and physical health. Men are also more likely than women to exhibit emotionally inexpressive Type A behavior and to experience or express hostility, both of which are strongly linked with increased health risks—particularly for cardiovascular disease. Men are also disinclined to discuss experiences of pain or physical distress.

Unemployment Hits Them Harder.

With our economic system going through major transformations, more people are unemployed. Unemployment is consistently linked with a variety of negative health effects, and there is evidence that these negative effects are greater for men than for women. Unemployed men are more likely to commit suicide than unemployed women. One study among youth found that unemployment is also a risk factor for increased alcohol consumption, increased tobacco use, illicit drug use, suicide, and unintentional injuries, particularly for males.

An editorial in the March 2011 issue of the *British Journal of Psychiatry* indicates that depression rates in men are likely to increase due to increasing job loss for men. The study's lead author, Boadie Dunlop, MD, from Emory University School of Medicine in Atlanta writes, **"Compared to women, many men attach a great importance to their roles as providers and protectors of their families. Failure to fulfill the role of breadwinner is associated with greater depression and marital conflict."**[16] Dunlop goes on to say, "The recent recession afflicting Western economies serves as a harbinger of the economic future for men, especially for those with lower levels of education. Dubbed by some the 'Mancession,' the economic downturn has hit men, and their families, particularly hard."[17]

They Have Fewer Social Supports.

Men have much smaller social networks than women do. Men and boys also have fewer, less intimate friendships, and they are less likely to have a close confidant, particularly someone other than a spouse. Men's restricted social networks limit their levels of social support. In times of stress, for example, men mobilize less varied social supports than women. There is consistent evidence that the lack of social support is a risk factor for premature death—especially for men. Men with the lowest levels of social support are two to three times more likely to die than men with the highest levels of social support. Men's social isolation significantly decreases their chance of survival of heart disease, cancer, and stroke.

Each of these ten factors contributes to men's increased risk for premature death or disability. The good news is that all of these factors can be modified once a man becomes aware of their importance. We shouldn't be victims of our old belief systems. We can change them. But to change these old beliefs, we have to recognize the times in our lives when we tend to isolate ourselves.

Overcoming Our Isolation

Disconnection from ourselves and others can contribute to our health problems. "All the usual risk factors for heart disease—smoking, obesity, a sedentary lifestyle, and a high-fat diet—account for only half of all cases of heart disease," says heart expert Dr. Dean Ornish. "**Every so-called lifestyle risk factor laid at the door of cardiovascular illness by the medical community has less to do with someone having a heart attack than does simple isolation—from other people, from our own feelings and from a higher power.**"[18]

Our lack of connection is a problem at all stages of our lives, but it becomes increasingly evident as we age. In my book, *The Irritable Male Syndrome: Understanding and Managing the 4 Key Causes of Depression and Aggression,* I describe my research findings indicating that many men become more irritable, angry, and depressed as they move into middle-age. One spouse I interviewed said her fifty-three-year-old husband "used to be the nicest man you'd ever want to meet. Now he seems to dislike everyone: me, the children, even himself."[19]

Dr. Thomas Joiner counters a number of myths about why so many midlife men become angry and irritable and offers a surprising analysis. "Men's main problem is not self-loathing, stupidity, greed, or any of the legions of other things they're accused of," says Joiner. **"The problem, instead, is loneliness; as they age, they gradually lose contacts with friends and family, and here's the important part, they don't replenish them."**[20]

Midlife can be the beginning of the end for many men as they find themselves losing connection with friends and family. "As they age, men tend to drift off and wither, and as they do, they avoid healthy fixes," says Joiner. "A 2008 study found that men, far more so than women, had trouble trusting and reaching out for help from others, including from health care professionals."[21]

A huge jump in the suicide rate begins as men reach what is traditionally retirement age. Between sixty-five and seventy-four years of age, the suicide rate is more than six times greater for men than for women in the same age range. Between seventy-five and eight-five, the rate jumps to seven times greater. And for those over eighty-five, the rate of death by suicide is an astounding 17.5 times higher for men than for women.[22]

As the suicide statistics verify, men often feel increasingly alone as they get older, even when they are surrounded by those who care about them. "A postmortem report on a suicide decedent," says Joiner, "a man in his sixties read, **'He did not have friends...he did not feel comfortable with other men...he did not trust doctors and would not seek help even**

though he was aware that he needed help.'"[23] Does this sound familiar?

Many men over forty see themselves in opposition to those around them. "I feel like it's me against the world," one man in his fifties told me. According to Lynne McTaggart, award-winning journalist and author of the bestselling books *The Field* and *The Bond,* **"An enormous body of research reveals that the root of stress and ultimately illness is a sense of isolation, and most toxic of all appears to be our current tendency to pit ourselves against each other."**[24]

Many of us grew up believing that being a man meant competing for sex and power, and the best men were the ones who came out on top. Whether or not we played sports in school, we were influenced by Green Bay Packer's Vince Lombardi's admonition to his players, **"Winning isn't everything....It's the only thing."** We also heard sports journalist Grantland Rice when he said, "It's not that you won or lost but how you played the game." Even so, it was drummed into us that if we wanted to consider ourselves "real men," we'd better be winners, not losers, and how well we played made no difference. When winning becomes the only thing that is important, we become more and more competitive with others, which isolates us from those who could be our allies.

The Blessings of Being a Man

There is good news here. Despite the documented dangers of isolation, men are breaking free and reaching out for greater connection with others. All over the world, men are committing to healing themselves and their relationships. We seek new ways to boost energy, reduce stress, effectively handle physical and emotional pain, sleep better, develop skills for managing anger, lift depression, heal addictions, solve conflicts at work, have a more satisfying sex and love life, and play more crucial and positive roles within our family and community.

There is a catch, though. We can't heal alone. We can only heal ourselves as we heal others. In many of the workshops I attended with poet Robert Bly, mythologist Michael Meade, and psychologist James Hillman, they talked about the importance of "blessing." Too many of us were raised with curses rather than blessings. We were told there was something wrong with us, that we were bad and unworthy. At its core, the men's movement has been about telling our stories to each other and being seen, acknowledged, and held. It's about seeing ourselves and each other clearly, with all our imperfections and wounds, and loving all of what we see.

While the men's movement doesn't make the headlines, its reach is clearly revealed by the following facts:
- More than thirty thousand men have joined groups through the Sterling Institute[25]
- Forty-three thousand men have participated in the Mankind Project[26] and joined groups.
- More than fifty thousand men and women have learned about male/female brain differences at the Gurian Institute.[27]
- Five and a half million men have joined Promise Keepers[28] and are involved in church groups.

- Men's Health Magazine[29] is the world's largest men's magazine brand, with a monthly circulation of 1.85 million and twelve million monthly readers in thirty-nine countries. It is the top-selling magazine in the U.S.
- Wired Magazine[30] has 2.8 million readers a month who enjoy research-driven articles on brain science, along with articles on the latest tech tools and gadgets. Seventy-six percent of the readers are male.
- The Shift Network[31] is empowering a global movement of people who are creating an evolutionary shift of consciousness. In June 2011, I participated in The Men's Ultimate Summit,[32] a teleconference that brought together men's leaders from all over the world. This was followed up with The Shift Men's Initiation,[33] a five-day in-person program for men who want to help initiate thousands of men in 2012.
- The Young Men's Ultimate Weekend[34] was founded by Dr. Mark Schillinger in 2000 to mentor young men to live life with integrity, to give and get respect, to master their energy, and to interact with their families and communities by modeling honorable, confident behaviors so they can become responsible and moral adults.

The men's movement isn't only about large groups of men coming together; it is also about individual men stepping up to make a difference in the world. I recently met Peter Hymans, a man who has an ambitious plan to save humanity. "As a man, I observe our world teetering between hope and despair," Hymans told me. "Aware of my capability to bear arms and to break things and kill people in the same old bloody dance we have seen for so many centuries, I refuse to repeat that behavior." His plan is to convert a decommissioned missile silo and military facility, which once had megatons of killing power, into "a palace of human achievement—an academic wellspring and performing arts center aimed at joyful sustainability."

Bill Kauth, cofounder of the Mankind Project, and his wife Zoe Alowan founded Sacred Lifeboats[35] to bring about new Gift Communities[36] to prepare for the coming transformation of our world.

Howard LaGarde is training men and women to become Alpha Leaders.[37] LaGarde says, "We want to invigorate the community, families, and humanity to discover the core principles and practices of leadership that will improve the knowledge and future accomplishments of our species." Alpha Leaders hold great vision, forge responsibility, assure quality, and cause results. Alpha Leaders move others to higher levels of accomplishment.

One of the most recent expressions of a positive focus on men and masculinity is The Good Men Project.[38] The Project was founded by Tom Matlack[39] in 2009 as an anthology and documentary film featuring men's stories about the defining moments in their lives. Since then, it has expanded to focus on a wide range of men's health issues. Matlack says, "We explore the world of men and manhood in a way that no media company ever has, tackling the issues and questions that are most relevant to men's lives. We write about fatherhood, family, sex, ethics, war, gender, politics, sports, pornography, and aging. We shy away from nothing."[40]

The Good Men Project and other programs that focus on what is best in men bestow blessings on us all. We do this by telling the truth about what it means to be a man today. Through our stories, we seek to connect our hearts and souls to other men and women seeking to make the world a better place for us all.

My Father, Myself: The Rest of the Story

Following my father's suicide attempt when I was five years old, he was hospitalized at the State Mental Hospital in Camarillo, California. My uncle Harry and I visited him every Sunday. I still remember the two-hour drive from Los Angeles and my increasing apprehension as we approached the hospital. We would sit in a large room with other families. Mostly, my uncle would ask questions, but my father seemed very far away. When he would turn his attention to me, he didn't seem to know who I was. After six months of weekly visits, I finally begged my mother not to make me go. It was just too painful. Whatever "treatment" my father was getting didn't seem to be helping.

My uncle continued going to see him and would report back with hopeful statements that "he seems a little better this week." The doctors told my mother a different story when she pressed them for the truth. "He needs ongoing treatment," they told her, "and he may need it for the rest of his life." Six years after he was admitted to the hospital, my mother filed for divorce. When other kids asked about my father, I told them he had died. It seemed so much less shameful than trying to explain that he was in "the nut-house."

But my father wasn't dead, and he wasn't willing to spend the rest of his life locked up. When I was twelve years old, we got a call from my uncle saying that my father had escaped. "I had taken him out to lunch, and he said he needed to get some stamps at the post office," my uncle said. "When he didn't come back, I looked for him, but he was gone." My mother was terrified that my father would return and steal me away. I shared her fears, but I also longed to have my father come back for me, to tell me he missed me and that wanted to be my father once again.

But he never came back, and we never heard from him. I got used to being an only child raised by a single mother. However, I never got used to my mother's fear that I would grow up to be like my father. She never said anything, but I knew she watched me for signs of emotional swings. I learned to keep a tight lid on my feelings and feed my intellect instead. I went off to college at UC Santa Barbara and graduated magna cum laude. As I walked off the stage, diploma in hand, I blanched as I looked into the audience and saw my father. He disappeared as soon as I saw him, and I wondered if I was imagining his presence.

A few days later, I received a letter before my graduation from my uncle saying that he had seen my father in Los Angeles, talked with him briefly, and given him the information about my college graduation. He also gave me my father's address as well as the name he was using, Tom Roberts. My uncle encouraged me to see my father and try to help him. I called, and we set up a meeting.

I still remember the mixture of excitement and pure terror that I felt as I prepared to see him after all those years of absence. I didn't know whether I would find the depressed and suicidal man that I remembered as a five-year-old, the hospitalized patient who didn't know me, or the loving father I still saw in my dreams. I wasn't prepared for the man I actually met. He not only knew me, but he seemed overjoyed to see me. He was effusive in his praise at my graduating from college, and he was sure I would do great things in life. He seemed buoyant and in love with life.

But then his mood shifted, as though a cloud crossed in front of the sun, and he turned mean and angry. He blamed my mother and his family for sending him to "that concentration camp" and went on and on about how they had ruined his life. I still remember his eyes. They were wild and crazy and frightening. They wanted to hurt the people he felt had abandoned him. Later in life, I would remember those eyes when I was going through my own midlife angst, and my wife, Carlin, told me that my "beady eyes" chilled her.

I spent a lot of time with my father that summer of 1965 just after I graduated from college. Until then, I had only seen my father through the eyes of my mother, but now I was seeing him myself. I saw his loving and gentle side when he gave puppet shows for the children in his neighborhood. I also saw his dark sides when the demons emerged.

At the end of that summer, I began medical school at UC San Francisco, but I planned to spend a month in Mexico, traveling and seeing friends. My father invited me to spend a weekend with him in San Diego before I left for my vacation. The weekend started out fine. He took me to places he loved.

We went to the local bookstore, and he bought me books that meant something to him, including a book of letters from Vincent Van Gogh to his brother, Theo.

My last night there, we went to a restaurant for dinner. He seemed to be in an expansive mood. He began telling the people at the next table how he had found his long-lost son. Then he began talking more loudly and telling people at adjoining tables. Clearly, people were becoming uncomfortable, but he didn't seem to notice. Finally, he stood up on his chair and began telling everyone in the restaurant the good news of reuniting with his son.

Embarrassed and a bit frightened, I hustled him out of the restaurant and back to our hotel room. His expansive mood changed to hostility, and now his anger was directed at me. "You can't go on vacation," he yelled at me. "You have to come home and take care of me." I was shocked. I told him that I had worked hard and needed a vacation and he seemed quite able to take care of himself. "Then get the hell out of here," he screamed. "You'll never become a doctor if you can't even take care of your own father. You're no son of mine. Get out of here."

I left the hotel in tears and got on a bus to Mexico City. I tried to blot out his words, though I would never be able to forget the look in his eyes. I started medical school in the fall as planned, but I dropped out after three weeks and enrolled in the school of social welfare at UC Berkeley. It never occurred to me at the time that my father's words had influenced my decision to leave medical school.

I saw my father three more times after our trip to San Diego. Each time, he was happy to see me, and I felt joy at our reunion. Then his anger would seep through, followed by rage when I wouldn't agree to his demands. Finally, he'd walk out, telling me I was hopeless and that he didn't want to see me ever again. It took me a long time to work out my feelings about myself and my father and to overcome the curses he visited on me.

When he was seventy years old and I was thirty-three, we met again. My first book, *Inside Out: Becoming My Own Man*, had recently been published, and I had written about my father. I hadn't seen him for many years when I received a letter from a reader. "I love your book and was moved by the story of you and your father. He's in Laguna Honda Hospital in San Francisco, and I'm sure he'd like to see you." I wasn't so sure he wanted to see me, but I knew I had some things I needed to say to him.

I wrote him a letter and told him my truth: "I'm finished feeling guilty for not being the son you wanted. It's not my fault you became ill, and it's not my job to fix you. I still love you. You're the only father I'll ever have. You've punished everyone that ever loved you, and I'm the only one who still reaches out. But this is the last time for me. If you push me away again, you're going to end up a lonely old man. I'll feel sad for you, but I can no longer live with your pain and anger."

I figured I'd never hear from him, but I was wrong. When the letter arrived, I was afraid to open it, but I had to know what he had to say. "Dear Jed, all I can say is, 'You're right.' I've spent my whole life blaming other people for my problems. I don't want to do that anymore. I want to see you. Your father."

It was a short letter, but it touched me deeply. I couldn't quite believe that he had really changed, but I was willing to give him a chance. I did go see him. We met and began a new relationship, man to man. He met my wife and my children, and we went together to a family reunion where everyone had a chance to reconnect with the "black sheep" of the family. He lived until he was ninety, and for the most part, he was able to keep his anger and blame under control, though I know he struggled with his emotional demons all his life.

I've often wondered what our lives would have been like if my father had been offered a different kind of treatment when he became depressed. Certainly my choice to go into the mental health field was strongly influenced by my desire to help men like my father. What I learned in school, and later as a health care practitioner, convinced me that things had improved a great deal since my father was first hospitalized in 1948.

But treatment approaches still didn't seem to get at the core of what was really troubling people. I wanted to know how our present health system had developed and how it could be improved. This book is part of my quest to find a better way to help men and encourage a broader perspective on healing.

The Evolution of Our Profit-Based Health Care System

To better understand the benefits of new energy healing practices, we need to look at the evolution of our present health care system. At the turn of the twentieth century, a number of promising approaches to healing the body, mind, and spirit were vying for prominence. These included *allopathic medicine* (AMA-type medicine), *homeopathic medicine, naturopathic medicine,* and various forms of *energy medicine.*[41] In 1904, the American Medical Association (AMA) created the Council on Medical Education (CME) whose objective was to restructure the system. The ostensible goal was to standardize medical education and give it a more scientific foundation. The unstated goal was to consolidate power and eliminate the competition.

A professional educator, Abraham Flexner, was hired by the CME to evaluate the current system and issue a report, which he did in June 1910. The Flexner Report recommended standards for medical education. The positive consequence was that medical education gained a more scientific foundation. But there was a negative consequence as well: institutions and individuals who didn't go along with the AMA-approved approach to education were driven out of business. Flexner clearly doubted the scientific validity of all forms of medicine other than biomedicine. He deemed any approach to medicine that did not advocate the use of treatments such as vaccines or surgery as tantamount to quackery and charlatanism.

Another consequence of Flexner's advocacy of university-based medical education was the ever-increasing expense of such an education, which put it out of reach of all but upper class, white males. The curriculum of the small "proprietary" schools Flexner had condemned was often based on generations-old folk traditions rather than relatively recent Western science. They admitted African-Americans, women, and students of limited financial means.

In a 1958 article titled "Price Discrimination in Medicine" published in the *Journal of Law and Economics,* University of Chicago professor Reuben Kessel argued that the Flexner Report effectively began the cartelization of the American medical profession, a cartelization enforced by the American Medical Association and backed by the police power of each American state. This de facto cartel restricted the supply of physicians and raised the incomes of the remaining practitioners.[42]

It also limited our perspective on what most people consider good medical practice. According to Stephen Larsen, PhD, author of *The Healing Power of Neurofeedback,* "The new medicine was based on modern chemistry. It dictated that all biologically active medicines should be prescribed by physicians, should be subjected to experimental trials on animals, and then on humans."[43] He says that all other modalities were to be shunned, especially the *vitalist* approaches that talked about working with the *energy* or *structure of the body,* rather than its chemistry. **"From the manipulations of chiropractors or osteopaths to the use of energy devices in connection with the body, any healing approaches based on *physics* were rejected. In the new medical realm, *chemistry* was king."**[44]

But the times, indeed, are changing. "The exiled healing modalities are now coming back, dancing and slinking like tai chi masters through the cracks in the cultural paradigm," says Larsen. "A new reincarnation called 'Energy Medicine' seeks to provide an umbrella of common legitimacy to them all."[45]

Welcome to a new era in healing. I wish my father was here to benefit from it all, but I feel blessed to be able to share what I've learned with you. I hope you will find information in this book that will enhance your own health and wellbeing.

CHAPTER 2:
HOW PERPETUAL STRESS CAN KILL YOU

The stress response was our secret weapon for success through most of human history. It saved our lives, making us run from predators and enabling us to take down prey. The problem is that we are no longer responding to a wild animal attack that might occur once every six months, but instead we are dealing with hundreds of stresses every day. Human beings are turning on the same life-saving physical reaction to cope with aging parents, unhappy teenagers, costly gasoline, increasing food prices, traffic jams, and job insecurity. As a result, our stress response never turns off, and we're constantly marinated in corrosive hormones that used to prepare us for fight or flight, but now they just make us sick.

Robert Sapolsky is a Stanford University neurobiologist, MacArthur Genius grant recipient, and renowned expert on animal behavior. But being a genius hasn't protected Sapolsky from stress. In fact, he's stressed out of his mind. "The reality is I am unbelievably stressed and Type A and poorly coping," says Sapolsky. "I'm not good at dealing with stress." Fortunately for *him*, he has a good job. "But one thing that works to my advantage is I love my work. I love every aspect of it."[46] Fortunately for *us,* his work for the last thirty years has been studying the stress response in animals and humans and figuring out how to help us all learn how best to cope.

His books have included, *Monkeyluv, A Primate's Memoir* and *The Trouble with Testosterone.* In his widely acclaimed book *Why Zebra's Don't Get Ulcers: A Guide to Stress, Stress-Related Diseases, and Coping* he says, "A large body of convergent evidence suggests that stress-related disease emerges, predominantly, out of the fact that we so often activate a physiological system that has evolved for responding to acute physical emergencies, but we turn it on for months on end, worrying about mortgages, relationships, and promotions."[47]

Sapolsky's work is the subject of the National Geographic documentary *Killer Stress.*[48] The film focuses on groundbreaking research that reveals surprising facts about the impact of stress on our bodies. It shows how it can shrink our brains, add fat to our bellies, and even unravel our chromosomes. Understanding how stress works can help us figure out ways to combat it and mitigate negative impacts on our health.

Take a picture of this tag with your smartphone to read about and see a clip of the National Geographic special on stress featuring Robert Sapolsky.

Health Risks in a World of Perpetual Stress

Richard O'Connor, PhD, is an expert on treating stress and believes that our modern medical approach misses the mark. "Current practice overemphasizes control of symptoms: take an antidepressant; learn self-hypnosis for anxiety; take a pill to overcome your addiction to alcohol; find a doctor to give you drugs to make you feel less pain or discomfort. *By focusing on symptoms like this, we play into the vicious circle of disease.*"[49]

O'Connor says we are living at a time of "perpetual stress." He describes the dilemma we all face:

- Because there is constant stress, largely unrecognized, we're caught in fight-or-flight mode, unable to turn it off. This has nasty effects on various body and brain systems.
- Our minds try to deny both the reality and the effects of perpetual stress. But the effects keep building up until they become impossible to ignore.

- We blame ourselves and get sick. Or we blame others and get in trouble. Either way, we only add to our stress load.[50]

In my experience as a psychotherapist, I have found that stress underlies most of the psychological, social, and medical problems people face in contemporary society. **If we can get a handle on stress, we can take care of most of the problems we face in our lives.** I conducted a survey with more than six thousand men between the ages of sixteen and seventy-five. Ninety-one percent said they felt some degree of stress, and 70 percent felt their stress level was increasing and they often felt overwhelmed. It is not an exaggeration to say that stress is the most contagious plague of modern society. Even our pets are stressed. Veterinarian schools now teach future vets how to prescribe Valium, Prozac, and the latest antianxiety pills to soothe your dog and cat.

Here's how J. Douglas Bremner, MD, one of the world's experts on stress, describes what happens:

"Our bodies have biological systems that respond to life-threatening danger, acting like fear alarm systems that are critical for survival. When faced with a threatening situation, such as being attacked by a tiger, a flood of hormones and chemical messengers is released into our brains and bloodstream almost instantly.

"These hormones rapidly shift our energy resources away from noncritical tasks and toward more critical tasks that are required for survival. Energy is shunted to the brain and the muscles to help us think fast and run quick, and away from the stomach and digestive track as well as the reproductive system."[51]

The system works well when the stress is short-lived, and we can either fight or flee. The problems arise when we are under continual stress and we aren't able to engage the source of danger in a direct, physical way. Much of our present-day stress involves our minds going around and around worrying about what *could* happen. "Stress—or as I like to think of it, the mind that's running on overdrive—is now considered to be a leading factor in numerous illnesses," says Woodson Merrell, MD, chairman of the Department of Integrative Medicine at Beth Israel Medical Center and author of *The Source.* **"By some estimates, up to 80 percent of all illnesses are stress induced."**[52]

The Stress-Illness Connection

The American Institute of Stress is a nonprofit organization established in 1978 at the request of stress researcher Hans Selye. It serves as a clearinghouse for information on all stress-related subjects. According to the Institute, stress contributes to the following problems:

- **Cardiovascular Disease**: Coronary heart disease, sudden death, congestive failure, hypertension, stroke, and accelerated atherosclerosis
- **Malignancies**: Prostate, lung, and breast cancer
- **Gastrointestinal Tract Problems**: Esophageal reflux, peptic ulcer, irritable bowel syndrome, ulcerative colitis, regional ileitis, and hemorrhoids

- **Neurologic Disorders**: Alzheimer's, Parkinson's, multiple sclerosis, memory loss, migraine, and tension headache
- **Psychiatric Problems**: Depression, anxiety and panic disorders, post-traumatic stress disorder, mass hysteria, phobias, obsessive compulsive disorder, and alcoholism
- **Specific disorders**: Diabetes, arthritis, infertility, periodontal disease, immune system disturbances, and obesity[53]

Which problems do you have? Which ones are you worried you might get if your stress continues? **"By shifting from being at the mercy of your stress to being in control of your stress," says Dr. Woodson Merrell, "you can affect a dramatic increase in energy, and as a result you will be less likely to get sick."**[54]

Stress saps our energy and weighs us down in the same way as out-of-control personal debt. "Think of this in terms of living on an 'energy budget,' with which you pay out energy allotments," says Caroline Myss, world-famous medical intuitive and author of *Defy Gravity: Healing Beyond the Bounds of Reason*. "Like bad debts that keep accruing interest as we fail to pay them off, at some point the buildup of your negative patterns from the past will begin to consume the majority of your daily energy allotment, leaving you less and less power with which to manage the demands of your daily life: your health, your creativity, your relationships....Simply put, your negative history creates psychic weight, and the more psychic 'weight' you carry around with you, the longer you have to 'wait' for anything to heal, or for anything to change in your life, for that matter."[55]

Stress and Work: Job Loss and Overwork Are Increasing

Not too long ago, I lost my job as a counselor at a local health clinic. I was only there part time, yet I was devastated and rapidly slipped into a deep depression. Though it was clear I was being let go because of economic issues that had nothing to do with my competence, I felt like a failure. I would go from uncontrollable tears and feelings of sadness to uncontrollable rage with thoughts of revenge.

I kept expecting I would snap out of it any day, but the feelings went on for many months. I eventually saw a psychiatrist and was put on medication. It took me a full year to get back to my old self as I moved more fully into private practice. I thought, as a successful psychotherapist, I would be immune to the terrible dislocations men feel when they lose their jobs. I was wrong.

Job loss, and fears about losing our jobs, strikes at the very core of our male identity. The *Atlantic* magazine did a recent cover story with the provocative title "The End of Men." "Earlier this year, women became the majority of the workforce for the first time in U.S. history," the article reported. "Most managers are now women too. And for every two men who get a college degree this year, three women will do the same. For years, women's progress has been cast as a struggle for equality. But what if equality isn't the end point? **What if modern, postindustrial society is simply better suited to women?**"[56] This is a new reality that keeps men's stress levels going up and up.

If, as Freud said, love and work are the cornerstones of our humanness, men are in real danger. For many Americans, we first saw the future of men in the workplace through the eyes of filmmaker Michael Moore in his documentary film *Roger and Me*, which was completed in 1989. In the film, he chronicles the efforts of the world's largest corporation, General Motors, as it turns his hometown of Flint, Michigan, into a ghost town.[57] We saw a new image of the "out of work male" and the pain and suffering it caused both the man and his family.

In her book *Stiffed: The Betrayal of the American Man*,[58] Susan Faludi concludes **that male stress, shame, depression, and violence are not just a problem of individual men but a product of social betrayal of men that occurred after World War II. The biggest betrayal was the loss of a secure economic base for millions of Americans.** When we lose our jobs, or are in constant fear of losing our jobs, it can be destroy our self-esteem and undermine the foundations of our sense of manhood. Faludi interviewed men all over the country, and in industry after industry, from aerospace to technology, she found men often came undone when they lost their jobs.

One of the men Faludi talked to at length, Don Motta, could be speaking for millions of men in this country who have been laid off, downsized, or been part of a company that has gone under. "There is no way you can feel like a man. You can't. It's the fact that I'm not capable of supporting my family....When you've been very successful in buying a house, a car, and could pay for your daughter to go to college, though she didn't want to, you have a sense of success and people see it. I haven't been able to support my daughter. I haven't been able to support my wife. **'I'll be very frank with you,' he said slowly, placing every word down as if each were an increasingly heavy weight. 'I. Feel. I've. Been. Castrated.'"**[59]

But it isn't just men who have lost their jobs who are under stress. Men who have jobs are working more and more hours to keep those jobs. Social scientist Juliet Schor reported studies showing that 44 percent of us often feel overworked and overwhelmed. **"A third reported being chronically overworked. These overworked employees had much higher stress levels, worse physical health, higher rates of depression, and reduced ability to take care of themselves than their less stress-pressured colleagues."**[60]

Humpty Dumpty Men: The Stress of Job-Loss on the Family

We all remember the nursery rhyme featuring Humpty Dumpy, who typically is portrayed as an egg.

Humpty Dumpty sat on a wall,
Humpty Dumpty had a great fall.
All the king's horses and all the king's men
Couldn't put Humpty together again.

This perfectly illustrates the plight of many men I see today. Millions of us are vulnerable to changes that can undermine our wellbeing and shatter our lives, but most are unaware of what is coming our way. In her book *Stiffed*, Faludi interviewed Jerry Blair and his wife Barbara,[61] a couple who could represent many men and women today facing tough economic changes:

Jerry Blaire turned fifty a week before he lost his job, Faludi tells us. He had been a sales executive for a major computer company and had survived the cuts when technology stocks crashed. But now the company was "consolidating" and "streamlining" its sales force to be more "competitive" in the market of the twenty-first century. Jerry had been with the company for fifteen years and hoped to be with them until he retired, but suddenly he was no longer needed.

"When I was told, I couldn't believe it at first," Jerry says. "I knew it had been happening to others, but I didn't really think it would ever happen to me. I felt like I was too valuable to the company, that I had given too much for them to cut me out. **Being out of a job has put tremendous strain on our family,**" Jerry continues. **"Barbara was understanding at first, but clearly resented having to work longer hours in order to support us.** More than that, she was hurt by my constant angry outbursts or sullen silences. I knew I was pushing her away. Maybe, unconsciously, that's what I wanted. I felt ashamed that I couldn't be the kind of man I wanted to be. Even though we have always been a 'modern' family where we both had interests outside the home and both worked, I always felt it was really my responsibility to carry the work load."

A year after her last interview with Jerry and Barbara, Faludi called to see how they were doing. Barbara answered the phone, and after some minor pleasantries she told Faludi that she and Jerry had separated. **"He just became impossible to live with. He was angry and upset with everything I did.** He seemed to resent the fact that I was bringing in more money than he was. He had finally found a job in his field that paid considerably less, but it had opportunities for advancement. I kept telling him it didn't matter who made what, we were a family and we supported each other.

"He began to drink more, and one night he didn't come home at all. He missed work and looked awful when he dragged in the next morning. He said he had slept on the couch at his friend's house and had 'passed out and wasn't able to call.' One day, he told me he needed to move out. 'Things aren't right between us, and I have to find myself if I'm going to be able to get back on track.'"

Barbara began to cry softly. "I don't know what's happened to Jerry. He used to be so upbeat and positive. It seemed like we could weather any adversity. We talked about cutting back from work when the kids were grown and having more time for each other. Now we're alone, and he seems to have totally broken apart."

Jerry is the symbol of the modern man, the new Humpty Dumpty man. He's a guy who has done well in life, who is blindsided by forces that he has no control over. Barbara is a casualty of a war she didn't even know was going on. Mary Furlong, EdD, is a leading authority on technology and aging and an expert on the impact of the baby boom on society. According to Furlong, **"Job loss will have a more devastating impact on society than the war."**[62]

Why Stress Is Deadly: The Seven Secrets You Must Know to Protect Yourself

If stress is the cause of most of our problems, both physical and emotional, why haven't we devised methods to eliminate stress from our lives? Because there are things about stress that make it difficult to treat. In order to learn how energy healing treats stress at its core, we must first look at the hidden truths about stress:

1. Our stress response protects us in the short term, but harms us over time.

2. We are not built to live with the perpetual stresses of modern life.

3. Stress registers as an energy disruption in the body.

4. The underlying cause of all stress is trauma and the resulting misinformation that is stored as *cellular memory*.

5. Traumatic memories are stored as images, and 90 percent are unconscious.

6. Our antivirus program may be making us sick.

7. Our beliefs determine whether we stay well or become sick.

Short-Term Protection Interferes with Long-Term Health

According to biologist Bruce Lipton, PhD, author of *The Biology of Belief,* "Evolution has provided us with a lot of survival mechanisms that can roughly be divided into two functional categories: *growth* and *protection*."[63] The body is built to put energy into one of these two functions at a time. "Humans unavoidably restrict their growth behaviors when they shift into a protective mode," Lipton says. "If you're running from a mountain lion, it's not a good idea to expend energy on growth. In order to survive—that is, escape the lion—you summon all your energy for your fight-or-flight response. Redistributing energy reserves to fuel the protection response inevitably results in a curtailment of growth."[64]

Within each of our cells are incredible energy-producing bodies called *mitochondria*. Woodson Merrell , MD, says, "Mitochondria are like tiny factories—thousands of them are within each and every cell (with DNA as the plant supervisor)—and they work ceaselessly to transfer the potential energy from food, air, and water into active human energy."[65] But even these hard-working little factories produce a finite amount of energy, and that energy must be used for either protection or growth. **The more energy we spend on protection, the less is available for growth.**

Alex Loyd, in his book *The Healing Code,* offers a naval analogy to help us understand what's happening on a cellular level.[66] In the navy, when a ship is attacked, all maintenance, repair, and other normal activities cease. Even crew members who are sleeping or eating have to "man the battle stations." When the alarm goes off, our cells cease their normal growth, healing, and maintenance. Why? The alarm is supposed to indicate an immediate but temporary emergency, and all of those activities can wait a few minutes while we run or fight to save our lives.

The cells literally close up, like a ship battening down the hatches in a time of attack. Nothing goes in or out. A tender ship doesn't approach a battleship to give it food or to unload the garbage during a battle. In the same way, our cells don't receive nutrition, oxygen, and minerals, nor do they get rid of waste products and toxins while under stress. Everything stops except what is necessary to survive. This results in an environment inside the cell that is toxic and doesn't allow for growth and repair. This is why stress is the ultimate cause of so much ill health. **When most of our energy is going for protection, there isn't much left to keep us alive and healthy.**

In this short video, Dr. Loyd explains the nature of stress.[67] Take a picture of this tag with your smartphone to see a clip of Dr. Alex Loyd on how stress harms and what can heal us.

We're Stuck in a World of Perpetual Stress

We are not designed to deal with the many stress-inducing situations of the twenty-first century. For most of human history, the stressors we faced were mainly physical, like running away from wild animals. Now, they are almost entirely psychological. When was the last time you were frightened by a lion? The things that cause us stress in our modern world are the ones that go on inside our heads.

Here's how Richard O'Connor, PhD, describes our modern stress response in his book *Undoing Perpetual Stress: The Missing Connection Between Depression, Anxiety, and 21st Century Illness*: "We have to live with the fact that our nervous systems have not changed much for 160,000 years, since the first modern human appeared. We're not wired for the kinds of stress we face today. There is an essential conflict between what our bodies and brains were naturally designed for and what life makes us put up with now."

O'Connor recognizes that we face new challenges that our ancestors never had to deal with including, the breakdown of the family and community, lack of meaningful work, loss of contact with nature, and the intrusion of ambiguous dangers like traffic jams.

We can't run fast to escape these problems or call on friends and pick up big sticks to beat them to death—but that's what our bodies were designed for. "Under chronic stress, our neurotransmitters, hormones, and other 'information substances'—basic constituents of our animal selves—go haywire, affecting our immune, nervous, and endocrine systems and causing emotional distress and physical illness," says O'Connor. "We develop the Perpetual Stress Response."[68]

Stress Registers as an Energy Disruption in the Body

We often think of stress as being caused by external circumstances, some physical event that throws us off: someone cuts in front of us on the freeway; we have more expenses than money to cover them; we watch TV and see catastrophe's happening around the world and worry they could happen here.

But science tells us that regardless of the external circumstances, if there is a problem, it registers in the energy field of the body. These ideas from quantum physics were first discovered by people like Albert Einstein, who said, "All matter is energy." We might think of energy this way: One hundred years ago, before we had the electrical grid, if we wanted electricity, we needed to generate it ourselves. Where we live in the hills outside Willits, California, we are on solar power but still need a back-up generator in the winter. We put gas in the tank to fuel the generator. The generator requires a source of oxygen (air intake) and expels fumes as a byproduct. As long as the fuel lasts, we have the power to run our household appliances.

It's the same way in our cells. A cell has to have oxygen and glucose (fuel), and it has to be able to expel its waste products. When you stop that process, you get a "brown- out" where the cell doesn't function properly, and eventually you get a "blackout" just like the generator when it runs out of fuel. If the process goes too far, the cell will literally die. This is how stress sends the cells into a state of alarm and causes an energy shortage, leading to cellular damage and what we would eventually label a disease.

Trauma and Cellular Memories Are at the Core of Perpetual Stress

Dealing with continual stress makes us sick. But what makes the problem even worse is that these every day, small assaults on our body, mind, and spirit trigger memories of trauma from our past. As a result, the normal stresses of everyday life become magnified as they trigger traumatic memories from the past. What's more, the trauma does not have to be severe to cause disease. Most of us are actually suffering from post-traumatic stress disorder (PTSD).

We normally think of PTSD as associated with the trauma of war or other forms of extreme stress, but PTSD can happen to any of us and is much more common than most people know. The Adverse Childhood Experiences (ACE) Study has demonstrated that childhood experiences affect adult health decades after they first occur.[69]

The ACE Study is a collaboration between the Centers for Disease Control and Prevention (CDC) and Kaiser Permanente's Health Appraisal Clinic in San Diego. The lead researchers are Robert Anda, MD, at the CDC and Vincent J. Felitti, MD, at Kaiser. Over seventeen thousand adults participated in the research, making it one of the largest studies of its kind in the world. Their conclusions are startling:

- Childhood abuse, neglect, and exposure to other adverse experiences are common. **Almost two-thirds of study participants reported at least one ACE, and more than one in five reported three or more.**[70]
- Childhood experiences are related. If you experienced one, the chances of experiencing a second are 87 percent.
- Compared to people with an ACE score of 0, those with an ACE score of 4 or more were twice as likely to be smokers, 7 times more likely to be alcoholic, 10 times more likely to have injected street drugs, and 12 times more likely to have attempted suicide.
- The ACE Study also showed that as the ACE score increased, the number of risk factors for the leading causes of death increased.

The Adverse Childhood Experiences (ACE) Questionnaire

Dr. Anda has developed a mini-version of the ACE Study Questionnaire to help people calculate their own ACE Scores. The ACE Score is the basis for rating the extent of trauma a person experienced during childhood, and it can predict the likelihood that a person will experience one or more health, behavioral, and/or social problems.

Simply answer yes if you experienced any of the following during your first eighteen years of life:

1. Did a parent or other adult in the household **often or very often**: swear at you, insult you, put you down, or humiliate you? **Or** act in a way that made you afraid that you might be physically hurt?

2. Did a parent or other adult in the household **often or very often**: push, grab, slap, or throw something at you? **Or ever** hit you so hard that you had marks or were injured?

3. Did an adult or person at least five years older than you **ever**: touch or fondle you or have you touch their body in a sexual way? **Or** attempt or actually have oral or anal intercourse with you?

4. Did you **often or very often** feel that no one in your family loved you or thought you were important or special? **Or** that your family didn't look out for each other, feel close to each other, or support each other?

5. Did you **often or very often** feel that you didn't have enough to eat, had to wear dirty clothes, and had no one to protect you? **Or** that your parents were too

drunk or high to take care of you or take you to the doctor if you needed it?

6. Were your parents **ever** separated or divorced?

7. Was your mother or stepmother **often or very often** pushed, grabbed, slapped, or had something thrown at her? **Or sometimes, often, or very often** kicked, bitten, hit with a fist, or hit with something hard? **Or ever** repeatedly hit at least a few minutes or threatened with a gun or knife?

8. Did you live with anyone who was a problem drinker or alcoholic or who used street drugs?

9. Was a household member depressed or mentally ill, or did a household member attempt suicide?

10. Did a household member go to prison?

Now add up your yes answers: _____

This is your ACE Score.

Most of us have experienced a number of these childhood traumas, which makes us more susceptible to other traumatic experiences in our adult lives. However, most of us don't believe these experiences can do us any real harm. Have you ever heard someone (including yourself) say something like: "Hey, everyone I knew got hit when we were kids, and most of us had fathers who drank a lot. That stuff never hurt me." The ACE study shows that these experiences, though common, do cause us harm. The higher our ACE Score, the more likely we are to engage in behaviors that make us sick. These memories don't fade. They are stored in our cells. **These cellular memories are like little radio beacons continuously** sending out stress signals that can sap our energy and make us sick.

John Sarno, MD, professor at New York University medical school, stated, "Our best hope for healing incurable illness and disease in the future might very well lie in finding a way to heal destructive cellular memories. **If you can heal that cellular memory, then the illness or disease or chronic pain is very likely to heal.**"[71]

Throughout the natural world, scientists are finding that cells and organisms record their experiences even without the benefit of a brain. Scientists believe these cellular memories might mean the difference between a healthy life and an untimely death. Cancer can be a result of bad cellular memories replacing good ones. Psychological trauma, addiction, and depression may all be furthered by abnormal memories inside cells. Scientists suspect that diseases which turn up later in life may be due to errant memories programmed into our cells.

Now scientists are striving to understand how cells acquire these memories so they might treat disease at its root by adjusting how we hold these memories in our minds. "This may provide one of the most powerful ways of curing illness," says Eric Nestler, MD, PhD, Director of the Friedman Brain Institute at Mount Sinai Medical Center in New York. He says **for many diseases, conventional treatments today aren't much better than Band-Aids. They address a disease's symptoms, but not its cause.** "Harnessing this knowledge," Nestler says, "**offers the potential of really correcting the abnormality. The potential is there for a much more permanent fix.**"[72]

Traumatic Memories Are Stored as Images, and Most Are Unconscious

Think of your computer hard drive and all that is stored there. I know I've got stuff in there that I've totally forgotten about, but it's recorded and could be retrieved with the proper tools. Like files on our hard drive, our own memories are stored, but most are unconscious or subconscious.

Alex Loyd says, "The latest research seems to indicate that these memories are stored in our cells, literally all over our bodies. These memories are not flesh and blood; they are stored in our cells as an energy pattern."[73] He goes on to say that all data, everything that happens to us, is encoded in the form of cellular memories. Some of them contain destructive or inaccurate beliefs that cause the body's stress response to be activated when it shouldn't, which turns off the immune system and causes so many of our health problems. "The substance of these cellular memories is a destructive energy pattern in the body," says Loyd."[74]

The energy patterns of our experience are stored in our cells as picture memories, similar to the way our home computer stores information. "The fact that the cell membrane and a computer chip are homologues," says biologist Bruce Lipton, "means that it is both appropriate and instructive to better fathom the workings of the cell by comparing it to a personal computer....Computers and cells are *programmable*."[75] Antonio Damasio, MD, PhD, is one of the world's experts on brain science. He's a professor of neuroscience in the Department of Psychology and director of the Brain and Creativity Institute at the University of Southern California and has been doing research on the way the brain functions for more than three decades. He says that **memories are stored in the form of emotionally charged images or pictures, but most of these are unconscious.**

To understand how emotion works on the body, we must differentiate emotion from feeling. When we experience any of the primary emotions—sadness, happiness, anger, fear, surprise, disgust—they are expressed physically in ways that can be observed by another person. Feelings, by contrast, are our own conscious perception of all those changes caused by the emotion, and of very subtle changes that are happening in the way our cognitive apparatus functions.

"When we generate states of fear or anger or disgust or happiness, we produce withdrawal behaviors or approach behaviors that have been preserved through evolution because they have proved advantageous to survival," says Damasio. "We have inherited this system for sorting out what is good and what is bad, automatically, in order to preserve ourselves."[76]

That's why positive thinking and traditional psychotherapy have limited effectiveness in dealing with stress and traumatic memories. These techniques are limited to healing conscious memories. But as Dr. Damasio has demonstrated, since most of these memories are unconscious, we need a different set of techniques to deal with them. As we'll see, this is precisely what the energy healing techniques are able to accomplish.

Our Antivirus Program May Be Making Us Sick

Most of us have antivirus software on our computers to protect us from unwanted intrusions. The human hard drive, our brain, also has a kind of antivirus software. In the human hard drive, it is our memory of pleasurable or painful experiences that protects us from danger. This stimulus/response mechanism generally works pretty well.

This mechanism is particularly sensitive to traumatic memories. When something happens that causes us pain, we want to be sure we don't repeat that experience. Alex Loyd, in *The Healing Code,* recalls a client who had all the ingredients for success: a 180 IQ, graduation from an Ivy League school with honors, and being tabbed for greatness on Wall Street. But things never worked out right. "I keep sabotaging myself in my career," his client recalls. "Everybody says I should be a mover and a shaker on Wall Street, but every time I'm getting close to something like that, I find a way to mess myself up."[77]

Looking back to find early traumatic memories that may have contributed to the problem, the client found one, but it seemed too insignificant to matter. It was a *Popsicle memory* that turned out to be the key to the problem. It went back to a memory when his client was five or six. It was a summer day, and Mom had given the sister a Popsicle but would not give the client one until he finished his dinner. No big deal, right? That couldn't cause a huge block to success, could it?

It isn't what happens to us that is the problem, but how we interpret what happens. In this case, the client interpreted the Popsicle memory to mean that he wasn't loved as much as his sister, that he was somehow inadequate, defective, not good enough. And these cellular memories got triggered in later life and sabotaged his success.

The problem with these memories and the way we interpret them is that they are so common and seemingly innocuous that we don't recognize them as traumatic. "These prelanguage and prelogical-thinking memories can really become a bugaboo to us throughout our lives," says Loyd. "And we have thousands of these." When we go through a trauma, even a small one, our higher rational thinking is disconnected to some degree. We go into shock.

When a later experience triggers a similar feeling, when we feel unloved or "less than," unsupported, or vulnerable, our protective mechanism kicks into gear to prevent us from being hurt again. Our adult brain sees it as self-sabotage, but our cellular memory sees it as self-protection. We've all got these Popsicle memories that can seem too small to matter, but can undermine our health and wellbeing.

I had one of these childhood traumas when I was six or seven years old. A friend of my mother's was watching me while my mother was at work. When my mother returned, I was left to take care of myself for the short time it took for my mother to drive her to her house and return. It got dark, and I became terrified my mother had abandoned me or imagined something had happened to her. I quickly went into total panic.

I walked out to the curb and looked for her car. When I didn't see it, I started to sob uncontrollably. Shortly thereafter, my mother returned, and she seemed upset with me for crying and being outside where neighbors might see me. She probably had only been gone twenty or thirty minutes, but in my mind it felt like forever.

Years later, as an adult, any time my wife came home later than expected, I would begin to feel the same panic. One night, my wife was particularly late (she had met some friends and lost track of the time). As the hour got later, I went from worry to panic to total meltdown with fantasies that she had been killed in an accident. When she arrived home happy to see me, I was sobbing and angry. She couldn't understand why I was so upset, and I couldn't either. I dismissed my feelings as being "childish."

No matter how many times I tried to talk myself out of feeling frightened when my wife was a little late, I couldn't do it. When we keep having these unwanted feelings and experiences, Loyd says, "Your protective programming system is making a determination that somehow the circumstance you are in is related to a trauma. These memories and this memory belief system become programmed into the hard drive in our human computer. Pain memories are prioritized over any other kind of memory in order to allow us to survive and grow up."[78]

These deeply programmed pain memories originally had a survival value, but now they cause us stress that leads to illness. But since the memories are mostly unconscious, we have a difficult time healing them. Even when we can remember the original trauma, we can't seem to calm our troubled hearts. **But fortunately, the tools of energy healing were made to get through to the where the trauma is stored in our cells and to heal us completely.**

Our Beliefs Determine Health or Disease

Dr. Loyd shares the story of meeting and falling in love with his wife. They had many, many things in common and shared their beliefs about themselves, love, and marriage. "On the day that Tracey and I got married," he says, "I can honestly say that I thought we were about as ready as anyone could ever be. We had been through premarital counseling, taken personality assessments and compared them, written down what we wanted in life and what we didn't want, and how we would handle certain situations. Boy, were we ready![79]

"So we got married, and less than a year later, both of us wanted a divorce. What in the world happened? I now know that when Tracey and I said, 'I believe,' we were talking only about what we consciously believed."[80] But the problem, as it is with so many of us, is that 90 percent of our beliefs are unconscious. "After we got married, circumstances happened for both of us that reactivated pain memories which bypassed the conscious beliefs that Tracey and I had agreed on. I would blame Tracey, and she would blame me. We would get upset, we would pout, we would do all kinds of things thinking that it was the circumstance happening right then that was the issue."[81] Fortunately they were able to work things out and are happily married.

My wife, Carlin, and I had similar experiences, and I know many other couples have as well. Our beliefs can either help us heal or create problems in our relationships and in our lives. Twelve-Step recovery programs such as AA call unhelpful beliefs "stinkin' thinkin'." But that only refers to the conscious thoughts. It's usually the unconscious ones that do us in.

New research shows that our beliefs trigger for illness and disease in the body. Often these beliefs were formed when we were children, but they are no longer helpful as adults. Our unconscious thoughts can harm us, or our thoughts can set us free. "Every cell in your body has a mindful intelligence that receives input, analyzes it, and sends out messenger molecules through the nervous system and the bloodstream to communicate with the rest of the complex, web-like matrix of your body," says Dr. Woodson Merrell. **"In this way, thoughts effect physical changes, and physical changes cause a reciprocal change in thought."**[82]

I'll conclude with this little story that illustrates how stress can build up slowly until it overwhelms us. We need regular health practices to keep us on track:

A young lady confidently walked around the room while explaining stress management to an audience. With a raised glass of water (everyone knew that she was going to ask the ultimate question, "half empty or half full?"), she fooled them all. "How heavy is this glass of water?" she inquired with a smile. Answers called out ranged from 8 oz. to 20 oz.

She replied, "The absolute weight doesn't matter. It depends on how long I hold it. If I hold it for a minute, that's not a problem. If I hold it for an hour, I'll have an ache in my right arm. If I hold it for a day, you'll have to call an ambulance. In every case, it's the same weight, but the longer I hold it, the heavier it becomes." She continued, "And that's the way it is with stress. If we carry our burdens all the time, sooner or later, as the burden becomes increasingly heavy, we won't be able to carry on.

"As with a glass of water, you have to put it down for awhile and rest before holding it again. When we're refreshed, we can carry on with the burden. So, as early in the evening as you can, put all your burdens down. Don't carry them through the evening and into the night. Pick them up tomorrow. Whatever burdens you are carrying now, let them down for a moment. Relax; pick them up later after you've rested. Life is short. There may not be so many then and they won't be so heavy." [83]

Now that we've looked at the way stress works in our lives and how it can weigh us down if we don't deal with it, let's move on to take a look at how "energy" can work to heal the stresses in our lives. I'll also give you a quick course on "everything you always wanted to know about quantum physics, but were afraid to ask."

CHAPTER 3:
THE SCIENCE BEHIND ENERGY HEALING

Two worlds came together on July 26, 1971, when James "Scotty" Reston, a *New York Times* reporter, wrote an article entitled, "Now, About My Operation in Peking," describing his firsthand experiences with acupuncture and Traditional Chinese Medicine (TCM). Reston had been accompanying President Richard Nixon on his trip to China when he developed a case of appendicitis and had to undergo an emergency appendectomy.

While in the hospital, he experienced the five-thousand-year-old traditions of Chinese medicine still unknown in the West. The article ignited sparks throughout the United States. It was at that moment that "acupuncture" entered our vocabulary, and Eastern and Western medical practices began coming together in a big way. This interest in acupuncture continues to this day, with more and more physicians and non-physician health practitioners involved in its use.

With increasing acceptance of complementary and alternative medicine, acupuncture will likely be used more commonly. It will also serve to broaden the traditional concepts of health and illness. Likewise, the techniques of energy healing, though still viewed by many establishment practitioners as "alternative," will likely become more popular and accepted as time goes on.

The Day the Mind/Body Split Occurred

In order to understand how energy healing works to heal the separation between body, mind, and spirit, we have to go back to the day the split occurred. Well, we don't actually know the day, but we do know the year. It was 1641, the year *Meditations on First Philosophy,* by Rene Descartes ("I think, therefore, I am") was published. Descartes was one of the key figures in the scientific revolution that began in Europe in the 1600s and continues today. He created analytic geometry and his theories provided the basis for the calculus of Sir Isaac Newton.

Descartes was incredibly smart, but he didn't have an easy life. His mother died when René was a year old. Around the age of eleven, Descartes entered a Jesuit College. Following his graduation, he went to law school in accordance with his father's wishes, but found his passions lay elsewhere. Like many young people, he "tuned in and dropped out."

"I entirely abandoned the study of letters," he said. "Resolving to seek no knowledge other than that of which could be found in myself or else in the great book of the world, I spent the rest of my youth traveling, visiting courts and armies, mixing with people of diverse temperaments and ranks, gathering various experiences, testing myself in the situations which fortune offered me, and at all times reflecting upon whatever came my way so as to derive some profit from it."[84]

Although the mid-1600s were a time of great scientific fervor and discovery, it was also a time when science and religion clashed. In 1633, Descartes had completed work on his major project, *Le Monde,* which included a section known as *Le Traité de l'Homme* (*Treatise on Man*) that explained the workings of the human body in strictly physical and mechanical terms.

He had admired the work of the Italian physicist, mathematician, and astronomer Galileo Galilei. But when he tried to buy Galileo's latest book, *Dialogue Concerning the Two Chief World Systems* (1632), he learned that all copies had been burned and that Galileo had been sentenced to house arrest by the Inquisition in Rome.

"I was so astonished that I almost decided to burn all of my papers or at least to let no one see them," Descartes wrote to a friend. "For I could not imagine that he—an Italian and, as I understand, in the good graces of the Pope—could have been made a criminal for any other reason than that he tried, as he no doubt did, to establish that the earth moves."[85]

Descartes, being a good Catholic as well as a lover of wisdom, but concerned that he not run afoul of the Inquisition, came up with an ingenious way to advance science and to keep peace with the Church. To show how science and religion could be compatible, he split the world up into two different types of substances: mind and body. Science would learn everything about the body—what Descartes called "extended matter"—while religion would deal with the soul or mind.

When Sir Isaac Newton published his major scientific work the *Principia* in 1687, Cartesianism remained the reigning view in natural philosophy and served as the backdrop for much ongoing research. Newton expanded on the work of Galileo to better define the relationship between energy and motion. He developed the idea of a "clockwork universe," a kind of intricate, but orderly clock that was originally wound up by God, but now ticked along as a perfect machine with all the gears governed by natural laws.

This is view most of us learned in science class in school, where we were taught that the building blocks of the universe were solid little atoms of matter with electrons whirling around the periphery in their own orbits, much as the planets orbited around the sun. We could look at models, and though we didn't totally understand the physical universe, it seemed to make sense and gave us the feeling that things were pretty simple and straightforward, if not to us, at least to the physicists and other scientists who studied the nature of reality. The universe, in the classical physics developed by Newton, had a single, well-defined history, and scientists were well on the way to understanding how the universe came into being and where it was headed.

Matter Matters, But Energy Is King

It turns out the universe isn't as simple and well-organized as a clock. In the early 1900s, Albert Einstein and other scientists such as Heisenberg, Dirac, Bohr, and Planck discovered that the universe is not made of discrete, solid particles, but is made of energy. We all know Einstein's famous equation

$E=mc^2$. It says that mass (m) can be converted to energy (e) and vice versa. The conversion factor is the speed of light (c) squared, an enormous number when you consider that the speed of light is a whopping 186,000 miles per second. **This means a small amount of matter can be transformed into a huge amount of energy. And it is energy, not matter, that turns out to be the key ingredient in understanding how things work in the world.**

To understand what energy is and what it has to do with healing, it will help if we know something about the science of quantum physics. But don't freak out. Trust me, you don't have to *learn* quantum physics, you just have to learn a little bit about what it has to teach us about understanding energy.

The first thing I learned when I began to delve into quantum physics was that I had to leave the world of "common sense," the world I could see, touch, and manipulate. I called this world "the tubular structures" world. I had to leave the world of "things" and enter the world of "energy" and "spirit." I also had to try to imagine a world that was much smaller than anything in my experience. As physicist and author Ransom Stephens says, "Quantum physics phenomena are at a scale over thirty-four orders of magnitude smaller than the world we live in. We just don't experience it, except on our electrical gadgets through things like transistors and diodes."[86]

I had to let go of what I knew about reality from science based on Newton and enter the world of Einstein. Here's how world-renowned mathematician Stephen Hawking and physicist Leonard Mlodinow describe these two worlds: "Classical theories such as Newton's are built upon a framework reflecting everyday experience, in which material objects have an individual existence, can be located at definite locations, and follow definite paths." On the other hand, theories based on quantum physics offer a different picture of reality. "It is a picture in which many concepts fundamental to our intuitive understanding of reality no longer have meaning."[87]

"The picture most people call 'scientific' is obsolete," says Ervin Lazlo, arguably the world's greatest systems theorist and interdisciplinary scientist and philosopher. He tells us that science is in the midst of "a shift from matter to energy as the primary reality" and that, **In the emerging concept of the new science, there is no categorical divide between the physical world, the living world, and the world of mind and consciousness."**[88] That is a very radical and transformative statement from a scientist with solid credentials. I don't completely understand it, but I trust that it's true.

There Is a Field. I'll Meet You There

Albert Einstein was born in Germany in 1879. He enjoyed classical music and played the violin. One story Einstein liked to tell about his childhood was of a wonder he saw when he was four or five years old: a magnetic compass. The needle's invariable northward swing, guided by an invisible force, profoundly impressed Albert. The compass convinced him that there had to be "something behind things, something deeply hidden."

The thirteenth century poet Rumi may have had a glimpse into the ultimate nature of the universe and its hidden world when he wrote these words:

Out beyond ideas of wrongdoing
and rightdoing there is a field.
I'll meet you there.[89]

In the world of Newton, the basic building blocks of the universe are atoms, which were seen as solid little balls with discrete numbers representing their mass. Einstein showed that atoms are actually not made out of matter at all, but consist of non-material energy. As scientist Bruce Lipton, PhD, and cultural commentator Steve Bhaerman say in their book *Spontaneous Evolution,* "Today, it is fully established that physical atoms are comprised of a menagerie of subatomic units such as *quarks, bosons,* and *fermions.* Interestingly, particle physicists perceive these fundamental atomic units as vortices of energy resembling nano-tornados."[90] That's a powerful image and a shift of how we see the world. Instead of solid objects that we can see, touch, or measure, scientists now understand that the world is made up of energy. We have to let go of our image of solid little balls with electrons whirling around in fixed orbits and replace it with "nano-tornados" of energy make that make up the universe.

Quantum physics does more than demonstrate that our emphasis on the material world to the exclusion of the energetic world is wrong. It also shows that the world is interconnected in surprising ways, and we are all part of a larger whole. Einstein says it simply: "The field is the sole governing agency of the particle." It is the field that is the universe's energy matrix, that governs all matter. "There is no place in this new kind of physics both for the field and matter, for the field is the only reality," Einstein concludes.[91] **Change** the energy field and we change the material world. Heal our energy imbalances, and we can heal ourselves.

Welcome to a World of Paradox

A paradox is a statement or proposition that seems self-contradictory or absurd but in reality expresses a possible truth. In the world according to Newton, things are what they seem. There is a sense of simplicity and security in our ability to understand how things work. In the world of Einstein, everything gets a little weird and we have to be able to accept the paradoxical nature of reality.

One of the earliest paradoxes in Einsteinian physics is that light behaves both as a particle and as a wave. **"The idea that something can be both a wave and a particle defies imagination," says physicist Paul Davies, "but the existence of this wave-particle 'duality' is not in doubt."**[92]

Our new understanding of energy, and hence energy healing, is full of ideas that seem strange and contradictory. The ability to understand that two competing concepts can exist at the same time is the key to being able to derive benefits from the new understanding of energy and the new science of energy healing. In the Newtonian world, matter and energy are separate and therefore don't influence each other. In the world of Einstein, they are intertwined and offer wonderful new possibilities that can benefit us all. But it is a world that many people have a hard time accepting.

"A century after Einstein presented his mass-energy equation $E=mc^2$ and the belief that matter and energy are inherently interrelated and entangled," say Lipton and Bhaerman, "many people tenaciously hang onto the illusion of a material-based reality. The insanity we see around us, provided we're not so caught up in it ourselves that we don't notice it, is a byproduct of trying to live a Newtonian existence in an Einsteinian world. **Interestingly, the invisible energy field that shapes matter, as defined by quantum physicists, has the same characteristics as the invisible shaping fields that metaphysicians define as 'spirit.'"**[93]

So, why is all that important to know? For one thing, it offers a more accurate understanding of our world. Quantum physics was developed in the first few decades of the twentieth century, after Newtonian theory was found to be inadequate for describing nature at the molecular and atomic levels. Quantum physics doesn't replace Newtonian physics; it expands upon it and offers us a more complete view of the world. Secondly, it helps us understand real-life phenomena that would otherwise make little sense.

It turns out that what is going on in our atoms and molecules has a great deal to do with our health and wellbeing. "The manifestation of a disease, such as cancer, may show up at a macro level when you see and feel a tumor," says biologist Bruce Lipton, PhD, in his book *The Biology of Belief*. "However, the processes that instigated the cancer were initiated at the molecular level within the affected progenitor cells. In fact, most biological dysfunctions (except injuries due to trauma) start at the level of a cell's molecules and ions. Hence, we need a biology that integrates both quantum and Newtonian mechanics."[94]

In other words, quantum mechanics can help us change things inside the cell to heal illness *and* prevent diseases before they occur.

The mind/body split allowed science and religion to coexist, but it has created problems we have had to live with for more than 350 years. In an article in the prestigious *British Medical Journal*, researchers say, "Descartes' ideas of splitting mind and body have become dominant in medical circles and, in some form or other, have become articles of faith for most doctors, psychiatrists, and psychologists."[95] The mind/body split developed in mainstream medicine as separate disciplines, each robustly defending the boundaries of its own defined job description. Physicians treat the body, while psychiatrists treat the mind and "ne'er the twain shall meet." Separating mind, body, and spirit may simplify things, but it doesn't allow real people like you and me to live an integrated and satisfying life.

What Doctors Can Learn From Physicists

Andrew Weil, MD, is a Harvard University–trained physician and one of the most well-respected medical authorities alive today. In his 1983 book, *Health and Healing,* he introduced us to the emerging fields of "holistic health" and "integrative medicine." He made the startling declaration: "All illness is psychosomatic."

"This proposition," he says, "will be a hard one, but the difficulty is semantic only. *Psychosomatic* is a dirty word, its meaning muddied by years of wrong usage. All it means is 'mind-body,' nothing more. It does not mean 'unreal or 'not serious' or 'not physical' or 'fake,' just 'mind-body.' **To say all illness is psychosomatic is to say only that all illness has both physical and mental components."**[96]

In the chapter titled, "What Doctors Can Learn from Physicists," he explains that conventional medicine is based on the old Newtonian physics, while holistic and integrative approaches are based on the newer, more complete science of quantum physics. "Regular medicine of the current century," he says, "views the human organism as a complicated mechanism. It minimizes or ignores consciousness and mind as important determinants of health, illness, and responses to treatments."[97]

I wish Dr. Weil had been a teacher when I started medical school in 1965. At that time, most doctors viewed psychological aspects of health with suspicion. When I told one of my professors that I was thinking of becoming a psychiatrist, he laughed derisively and said, "Do you know what psychiatry is?" When I looked confused, he went on to say, "Psychiatry is the a-hole of medicine."

Andrew Weil felt things hadn't changed much over the twenty ensuing years. "Medical doctors often dismiss psychology as pseudoscience and refer to their own colleagues in psychiatry as 'witch-doctors.'"[98]

Weil understood that holistic health and integrative medicine need to be grounded in science, but they also need to be connected to our current understanding of the world based on the new information developed in the field of quantum mechanics over nearly a hundred years. "Sooner or later," says Weil, "the theoretical revolution in physics will catch up with medical science. I hope the change will come sooner, because the exaggerated scientism of regular medicine is leading us in dangerous directions."[99]

Amit Goswami, PhD, is a retired professor from the theoretical physics department of the University of Oregon in Eugene, where he had served since 1968. He is a pioneer of the new paradigm of science called "science within consciousness." Deepak Chopra, MD, says Goswami has "one of the most brilliant minds in the world of science." In his book *The Quantum Doctor: A Quantum Physicist Explains the Healing Power of Integral Medicine*, he says, "A quantum doctor is a practitioner of medicine who knows the fallacies of the Newtonian classical physics-based deterministic worldview that was discarded in physics many years ago. A quantum doctor is grounded in the worldview of the new physics, also called quantum physics."[100] Quantum science is influencing all fields from physics and medicine to psychology and biology.

The New Biology: The Crash and Rebirth of Bruce Lipton[101]

Bruce Lipton had wanted to be a biologist since he was seven years old. "I stepped up onto a small box in Mrs. Novak's second grade classroom, high enough to plop my eye right onto the lens and eyepiece of a microscope," he remembers. "A paramecium swam into the field. I was mesmerized. My whole being was transfixed by the alien world of this cell that, for me, was more exciting than today's computer-animated special-effects movies."

He is internationally recognized for his research on cloned stem cells and is a tenured faculty member at the prestigious University of Wisconsin School of Medicine. When James Watson and Francis Crick described the structure and function of the DNA double helix, it seemed that science had discovered the secret of life and the way genes control our destiny. "In the long-running debate over nature vs. nurture, the pendulum swung decidedly to nature," Lipton says. "So if you are born with a defective happiness gene, you can expect to have an unhappy life."

Like many men, Lipton became very successful at work while things in his personal life were falling apart. He felt he had inherited the "bad genes" and his life was destined to crash. His father died after a prolonged, pain-fraught battle with cancer, and Lipton felt distraught and overwhelmed. He tried to keep his research programs going despite the considerable stresses building up in his life, and things began deteriorating at home.

"I was in the midst of an emotionally draining and economically devastating divorce," he recalls. "My financial resources were rapidly depleted as I tried to feed and clothe my new dependents, the judicial system. Economically challenged and homeless, I found myself living pretty much out of a suitcase in a most abysmal 'garden' apartment complex. Most of my neighbors were hoping to 'upgrade' their living standards by seeking accommodations in a trailer park."

This story may seem familiar to you. I know it did to me. I remember working long hours at a job I no longer liked, my wife and I were fighting constantly, and the kids were afraid of our anger. I knew something had to change. I remembered my father's despair and was afraid I might follow his path and attempt suicide. I didn't want to put my children through that, so I knew I had to make a major life change. Lipton also made a decision to break out of his old life.

Lipton remembers the day he hit bottom and things began to change. "I threw the phone through the glass door of my office, shattering the 'Bruce H. Lipton, PhD, Associate Professor of Anatomy, U.W. School of Medicine' sign, all the while screaming, '*Get me out of here!*'"[102] Lipton not only left the university, he left the country and took a job at lower paying job at a medical school in the Caribbean. When he returned, he had a new lease on life and a new view of biology. Like Lipton, many other scientists have now done extensive studies, and the "new biology" offers a much more hopeful and helpful understanding of how the environment influences our genes.

It's the Environment, Stupid: Epigenetics and the New Science of Self-Empowerment

In the years after Watson and Crick discovered the molecular structure of DNA and its double helix, the scientists viewed genes as the main influence on our lives. Lipton calls this view "the primacy of DNA," with the flow of information a one-way street from DNA to RNA to proteins. "Proteins are the molecular building blocks that provide for the cell's structure and behavior," says Lipton. "DNA is implicated as the 'source' that controls the character of the cell's proteins."[103]

But more recent research has overturned this view. "While the Human Genome Project was making headlines," says

Lipton, "a group of scientists were inaugurating a new, revolutionary field in biology called *epigenetics*. **The science of epigenetics, which literally means 'control above genetics,' profoundly changes our understanding of how life is controlled.**"[104]

The new, more sophisticated understanding of the flow of information in biology "starts with an environmental signal," says Lipton, "then goes to a regulatory protein, and only then goes to DNA, RNA, and the end result, a protein." Political consultant James Carville helped Bill Clinton win the presidency by reminding everyone, "It's the economy, stupid." Lipton says, "It's the environment, stupid," to bring our attention back to what is really important in human biology.[105]

See and hear Dr. Lipton[106] talk about the myth that our genes control our behavior. Take a picture of this tag with your smartphone to see a clip of Dr. Bruce Lipton on the new biology.

The Healing Code and Energy Healing

Alex Loyd, the best-selling author of *The Healing Code*, says his book resulted from his desire to help his wife overcome a life-long depression so serious that it was destroying their relationship and endangering her life. "We were desperate for help," he says. "We tried everything: counseling, therapy, vitamins, minerals, herbs, prayer, alternative emotional release techniques…everything!"[107] Nothing worked for them until they found an energy healing approach to address her problems. Loyd points out that there are many helpful practices under the umbrella of energy healing. The one that was most helpful to his wife Tracey (now called Hope) he named the Healing Codes.[108]

The "One Thing" Behind the Healing Codes

Loyd recounts a scene from the original *City Slickers* movie with Billy Crystal where Crystal's character is talking with Curly, the rough and tumble old cowboy (played by Jack Palance). Although Curley is a man of few words, Crystal comes to recognize that he is quite wise. Curly tells him that the secret of life is one thing. Crystal hangs on the next words as he asks Curly to elaborate. But Curly tells him he must find the "one thing" for himself.

We've all had the experience of finding the one special thing that opens our eyes to the world. I recognized the power of love when I met my wife, Carlin, and again when our children and grandchildren were born. In *The Healing Code,* Loyd offers the "one thing" he believes will help us heal our ills and create wellbeing and joy in our lives. He also offers two corollaries. "We believe that as far as your life, your health, and your prosperity are concerned, these three things make all the difference."[109]

One Thing and Two Corollaries

One Thing #1: There is one thing on planet Earth that can heal just about any problem in your life.

Corollary #1: There is one thing on planet Earth that will turn off One Thing #1.

Corollary #2: There is one thing on planet Earth that will turn One Thing #1 back on.

One Thing #1:

The one thing on planet Earth that can heal most any problem in our lives is the immune and healing systems of the body. Most of us are not aware of the millions of healing events going on in our body every second. Our immune system goes after invading organisms. Our kidneys filter our blood. Our body temperature is kept within a healthy range. We shed millions of old cells while new ones are created. Our nervous system alerts us to external threats and keeps us connected to others. Everything is kept in balance, and we rarely have to think about it.

Corollary #1:

The one thing that can turn *off* the natural healing system of the body is stress. Remember in the last chapter we talked about a ship under the stresses of battle? When that is occurring, there is no time to take on supplies or get rid of waste. Similarly, when our cells are under stress they can't take in critical nutrients or get rid of toxins. Most of us know that stress can cause all kinds of physical, emotional, and spiritual problems in our lives, but we don't really understand how it works.

Biologist Bruce Lipton, PhD, offers a simple vision of how stress can harm us. Evolution has provided us with a lot of survival mechanisms that can roughly be divided into two functional categories: *growth* and *protection*. The body is built to put energy into only one of these two functions at a time. "Humans unavoidably restrict their growth behaviors when they shift into a protective mode," Lipton says. [110]

Our protective stress response works fine when the threat is short-lived. We can afford to turn off our growth functions long enough to escape from a short-lived threat.   But in our modern world of perpetual stress, we have problems. There is only so much energy to go around. If we dedicate it to protection, even unconsciously, there isn't enough for all the healthy growth functions. "In fact," says Lipton, "you can shut down growth processes so completely that it becomes a truism that you can be 'scared to death.'" [111]

Corollary #2:

The one thing on planet Earth that can turn One Thing #1 back on is the energy healing of our hearts and spirits. Issues of the heart and spirit are encoded in the cells of our body based on beliefs that offered survival value when we were growing up and evolving. When we experience early trauma, even from seemingly minor events, we create blocks to the flow of healing energy through us. We also create false beliefs such as:

- "If I let you know my true feelings, you'll abandon me."
- "I always have to act strong. If I show weakness, I'm not a real man."
- "I have to push through the pain. Never complain. Winning is everything."

Removing these false beliefs and energy blocks through energy healing allows the unnecessary chronic stress responses to be turned off. It also allows for the growth processes of the body to once again function normally.

Why Does the Mainstream Health Community Continue to Oppose Energy Healing?

Energy healing is still viewed by the mainstream health community as "alternative," "complementary," "fringe," or even "quackery." This shouldn't surprise us because medicine is a conservative practice and change occurs slowly. **"All truth passes through three stages," said eighteenth century German philosopher Arthur Schopenhauer. "First, it is ridiculed; second, it is violently opposed; third, it is accepted as self-evident."**

Not all purported health practices turn out to be helpful. For instance, heroin first came into widespread use as a treatment for morphine addiction. It didn't turn out to be very helpful as an addiction treatment. But as Schopenhauer points out, many valuable scientific discoveries are ridiculed at first and later found to be of great value. Here are a few of the scientists who were reviled for their quackery, only to be later proven correct:

- John L. Baird (television camera). When the first television system was demonstrated to the Royal Society, scientists scoffed and ridiculed it.
- C.J. Doppler (Doppler Effect). He proposed a theory of the optical Doppler Effect in 1842, but was bitterly opposed for two decades because it did not fit with the accepted physics of the time.
- William Harvey (circulation of blood). His discovery of blood circulation caused the scientific community of the time to ostracize him.
- Wilbur and Orville Wright (flying machines). Even after their Kitty Hawk success, American authorities refused to come to their demonstrations and *Scientific American* magazine wrote articles about "The Lying Brothers."
- Ignaz Semmelweis (washing hands saves lives). He tried to convince his medical colleagues that their refusal to wash their hands was killing pregnant women. He was ridiculed and driven out of the profession.

The Fight to Convince the Establishment That A Simple Solution Could Save Lives

The experiences of Ignaz Philipp Semmelweis illustrate the difficulty health care innovators have getting their ideas accepted by the mainstream medical community. Ignaz's family wanted him to go into the military or become a lawyer, but Semmelweis wanted to help people. He graduated from the Vienna Medical School in 1844 with high honors. He continued his studies with some of the most respected practitioners in Europe at the time and applied for the position of assistant in the First Obstetrical Clinic of the university's teaching institution, the Vienna General Hospital, where he would learn about birth and death and make discoveries that would forever change the course of medical practice.

Semmelweis soon concerned himself with the problem of *puerperal fever*, the scourge of nineteenth century European birth clinics. Most women at the time delivered at home, but those who were forced to use hospitals—due to poverty, illegitimacy, or birth complications—suffered a mortality of 25–30 percent. The disease was considered an inevitable aspect of contemporary hospital-based obstetrics, a product of unknown agents operating in conjunction with elusive atmospheric conditions.

Despite strong resistance from his superior, who had the accepted the disease as unpreventable, Semmelweis vowed to find the cause of so much misery and death. He observed closely and collected data. **He came up with the simple idea that "washing hands saved lives."** When he forced everyone on his unit to wash their hands and their instruments before delivering babies, the mortality rate dropped from 30 percent to 2 percent.

One would think with these kinds of results, there would be an immediate change in procedures and Semmelweis would become respected, rich, and famous. But that did not happen. Although his younger colleagues applauded his findings, many of the older, established physicians didn't believe the results.

The larger political environment also had an impact on Semmelweis. In 1848, a liberal revolution swept Europe, and Semmelweis took part in the events in Vienna. After the revolution had been defeated, Semmelweis found that his political activities had created further obstacles for his professional work. Not only was Semmelweis opposing the medical orthodoxy of the time, he was on the wrong side of those in political power. His superior at the hospital, Johan Klein, refused to reappoint Semmelweis in March 1849. Things went downhill emotionally for Semmelweis after that.

He left the hospital, developed a successful private practice, and continued to publish the results of his studies in books and articles. He became increasingly depressed, knowing that so many lives were being lost because the mainstream establishment refused to institute his simple practices. In 1861, Semmelweis's increasing bitterness and frustration at the lack of acceptance of his method finally broke his hitherto indomitable spirit. He became alternately apathetic and pathologically enraged that he could not do more to save mothers and children from dying.

In July 1865, Semmelweis was committed to a private asylum in Vienna for "treatment." His emotional pain from the many years of rejection erupted and he became violent. He was beaten by the staff and died from his injuries two weeks later. He was forty-seven years old. **Only later did his observational evidence gain wide acceptance. More than twenty years after his death, Louis Pasteur's work offered a *theoretical* explanation for Semmelweis's observations—the germ**

theory of disease. Most of us know the name Louis Pasteur. Few remember Ignaz Philipp Semmelweis, who gave so much to women, children, and the world of medicine.

Lessons for Energy Healers from Ignaz Semmelweis

For me, the story of Ignaz Semmelweis is testimony to the courage of a man who did everything he could to help save the lives of those less fortunate. It demonstrates the power of old paradigms and how difficult it is to get the establishment to change its practices, even in the face of overwhelming evidence. It reminds us of the difficulty practitioners of energy healing are having getting their treatment approaches accepted by the mainstream health community. If Ignaz Semmelweis were here to guide us, I imagine he might offer the following advice:

1. Remember the words of the Jonathan Swift: "When a true genius appears in this world, you may know him by this sign, that the dunces are all in confederacy against him."
2. Stand up for the less powerful, whether they are poor women, wounded veterans, or depressed men. Give them the best treatment available, even if the medical establishment seeks to discredit you.
3. Health care and politics can never be separated. Good health and good government go together.

4. Surround yourself with colleagues, friends, and family who will support you when you are down and cheer you up when things seem hopeless.

5. Remember that many in the establishment will feel threatened and lash out when you offer a different approach to healing. Understand their fear and be kind to them.

6. Offering evidence that something works is important, but showing *how* and *why* it works brings lasting support.

7. The truth will set you free. Stand up for the truth, even when it hurts to do so.

8. Follow the Dalai Lama, who said, **"Never give up. No matter what is going on, never give up."**

Dawson Church, PhD, author of *The Genie in Your Genes: Epigenetic Medicine and the New Biology of Intension*, says, **"I believe that Energy Psychology has a potential for the alleviation of human suffering that rivals any advance in psychology or medicine in the last five centuries. That's a huge claim, but it's not hyperbole. Try it for yourself: you'll be a convert within an hour—and it will change your life thereafter!"**[112]

CHAPTER 4:
THE ULTIMATE "POWER TOOL" FOR GUYS WHO WANT THEIR LIVES TO WORK

The TV sitcom *Home Improvement* starring comedian Tim Allen was one of the most popular TV shows during the 1990s. Tim's character was a stereotypical American male, who loved power tools, cars, and sports. He was a former salesman for the fictional Binford Tool Company and was a loveable, cocky know-it-all. The series centered on the Taylor family: father Tim, wife Jill, and their three sons. Tim loved his family and was forever trying to win their favor and prove himself, but he constantly screwed things up.

Each episode included Tim's own home improvement show, called *Tool Time*, a "meta-program," or show within a show. Tim was a spectacularly accident-prone handyman, often causing massive disasters on and off the set, much to the consternation of his coworkers and family (and the audience's amusement). In the real world, Tim would have lost his job early on. Many of Tim's accidents were caused by his devices being used in an unauthorized manner as he recited his mantra: "More power!" He once tried to power up his

Christmas lights so they could be seen from outer space. You can imagine the disaster.

Tim and his next-door neighbor, Wilson, were best friends. Every time Tim screwed up in his everyday life, he went to Wilson for advice. As always, Wilson had the answer, often using a philosophical or historical quotation to make his point. Although they were friends, Wilson had no first name and his face was always half-hidden. He and Tim talked over the fence, but never touched or connected more fully. They were stereotypical male friends who kept each other at a distance and never let themselves be vulnerable or truly seen.

I believe the show was so popular because it spoke to a deep truth about men in our culture today. We long to have more power in our lives, but we don't know how to find it and use it effectively. We hunger for the love and respect of our families, but too often feel unneeded and ineffectual. We crave companionship, but have few male friends with whom we can be truly intimate. We make jokes and act like we know what we're doing, but we often feel ashamed of who we really are.

Men's Shame

"Shame is a deflating feeling of personal worthlessness," say Roy Schenk and John Everingham, coeditors of the anthology, *Men Healing Shame*. "Like when you're suddenly laid off without explanation even though the company is doing well. You're hurting and feel there's nobody to blame but yourself. Yet *you can't for the life of you figure out what you did wrong.* **'There must be something *wrong* with me, but what?' This is** *shame.* **Not *guilt*, but shame. You just want to disappear, or lie in bed, hoping to wake up and find out that it was only a dream."**[113]

I had just such an experience when I was fired from a job not too long ago. I knew the reason had to do with budget constraints and virtually nothing to do with my competence and skills, but I immediately felt ashamed. When I was first told to leave, I didn't know what to say. Even though I could see it coming for many months and had grown tired of the job and looked forward to leaving, I was absolutely stunned. "Shame is a wordless emotion," says Gershen Kaufman, author of *Men's Shame*. "Only much later do we attach meanings to it. In the midst of shame, we feel an urge to hide. We want to cover ourselves, retreat, disappear, turn off all those watching eyes—most of all, our own."[114]

Although shame is a part of most people's lives, as men we are particularly vulnerable. "There are cultural injunctions in our society to compete, be successful, achieve, and perform," says Kaufman. "That's especially true for men: we are supposed to be successful, and failure for men is shameful."[115]

I still have a vivid memory from when I was about four years old and hearing my mother talk with her friends about the men they knew who were out of work. My father was one of them. I don't remember their words exactly, but I immediately felt ashamed. I made a vow that I would never allow women to talk about me like that. My fear of experiencing that shame pushed me to succeed in my career at any cost.

I would literally rather die than risk losing my job. When I finally did lose a job, I became seriously depressed and angry.

James Gilligan, MD, has spent a lifetime studying the causes of male violence and concludes that shame is at the core. Starting at a very young age, most guys learn how to protect themselves against feelings of humiliation and shame. We often use anger, and sometimes violence, to keep shame from overwhelming us. **"I have yet to see a serious act of violence that was not provoked by the experience of feeling shamed and humiliated, disrespected and ridiculed,"** says Gilligan, "and that did not represent the attempt to prevent or undo this 'loss of face'—no matter how severe the punishment, even if it includes death."[116]

Gilligan found that we could learn a lot about the shame that most men fear by studying the most violent men he encountered in prison. "The prison inmates I work with have told me repeatedly," says Gilligan, "when I asked them why they had assaulted someone, that it was because 'he disrespected me' or 'he disrespected my visit' (meaning 'visitor'). The word 'disrespect' is so central in the vocabulary, moral value system, and psychodynamic of these chronically violent men that they have abbreviated it into the slang term, 'he diss'ed me.'"[117]

In working through my own shame over the years, I've found that taking my health into my own hands was particularly empowering. The more I learned and practiced energy healing, the better I felt about myself and my ability to deal with the inevitable stresses of life. **I've found that the simple tools of energy healing are the real "power tools" men seek.**

They not only help remove unwanted emotions like shame, but they can help heal physical problems as well.

The Six Pillars of Energy Medicine

Energy medicine is based on the supposition that illness results from disturbances in the body's energies and energy fields and can be addressed via interventions into those energies and energy fields.[118] It is one of five domains of "complementary and alternative medicine" identified by the National Institutes of Health (NIH):

- Energy medicine (such as healing touch, Reiki, and qi gong).
- Biologically based practices (such as the ingestion of herbs, vitamins, minerals, and amino acids).
- Manipulative and body-based practices (such as chiropractic, osteopathy, massage, Rolfing, and reflexology).
- Mind/body medicine (such as hypnosis, visual imagery, meditation, and biofeedback).
- Whole medical systems, which may incorporate elements of the above, such as Traditional Chinese Medicine, Ayurvedic medicine, naturopathy, homeopathy, and various indigenous healing traditions.[119]

David Feinstein, PhD, and Donna Eden have written numerous articles and award-winning books, including *Energy Medicine*[120] and *The Promise of Energy Psychology: Revolutionary Tools for Dramatic Personal Change*.[121] They say that conventional medicine, at its foundation, focuses on the biochemistry of cells, tissue, and organs. Energy medicine, at its foundation, focuses on the fields that *organize* and *control* the growth and repair of cells, tissues, and organs, and on ways of influencing those fields.[122]

"This affords energy medicine several strengths in comparison with the conventional medical model," they say. "Six of these strengths can, in fact, be thought of as the pillars that establish energy medicine as a significant development in health care." These six pillars are summarized below:[123]

Pillar 1: Reach—energy medicine can address biological processes at their energetic foundations so is able to impact the full spectrum of physical conditions.

Not just the sum of its mechanical parts, the human body is a system of living energy. The skin discharges about thirty photons per square centimeter per second. Each cell emits electromagnetic radiation. Electrical signals govern every physiological process. Yet Western medicine continues to focus on the chemistry of the body with little concern for its energies or organizing fields, and it offers primarily pharmaceutical and surgical interventions rather than energy treatments. Leading-edge science does not, however, support this unilateral approach. The influence of energy fields on gene expression may, in fact, prove to be at the core of energy medicine's substantial reach in healing and preventing even elusive health conditions. According to cell biologist Bruce Lipton, hundreds upon hundreds of scientific studies over the past fifty years have revealed that **"every facet of biological regulation"** is profoundly impacted by the **"invisible forces"** of the electromagnetic spectrum.

Pillar 2: Efficiency—energy interventions can regulate biological processes with precision, speed, and flexibility.

Electromagnetic frequencies are a hundred times more efficient than chemical signals such as hormones and neurotransmitters in relaying information within biological systems, yet conventional medicine still does not take advantage of the potent ways energy can transmit information. There *are* some notable exceptions, such as the use of heart pacemakers, harmonic frequencies that dissolve kidney stones, pulsed magnetic stimulation machines, and the use of magnets for alleviating tendonitis, facial paralysis, and optic nerve atrophy.

Energy medicine practitioners are able to identify imbalances in the body's energies. They can then directly intervene so the waveform patterns emitted by diseased tissue or other malfunctioning systems are modified. To the extent that such procedures can be refined and taught, **energy medicine will offer interventions that are substantially more precise than medication and more flexible and noninvasive than surgery, significantly reducing the time involved in the healing process without producing unwanted side effects.**

Pillar 3: Practicality—energy medicine fosters healing and prevents illness with interventions that can be readily, economically, and noninvasively applied.

As the Nobel Prize–winning biochemist Albert Szent-Györgyi observed, "In every culture and in every medical tradition before ours, healing was accomplished by moving energy." While a range of interventions using electrical devices, magnets, crystals, needles, aromas, and ingested substances are all used in energy medicine, the tool used by the largest number of practitioners for intentionally moving and harmonizing the body's energies and fields is the human hand.

A practitioner can tap, massage, pinch, twist, or connect specific energy points on the skin. Because everyone's hands carry a measurable electromagnetic charge, specific areas of the body can be surrounded with the hands to produce a field effect, or the hands can be used to move and align the body's energies by tracing specific energy pathways along the skin.

Other noninvasive and readily accessible interventions include the use of specific postures and movements that have beneficial effects on the body's energy system. Such noninvasive treatments might routinely be considered in health care settings, in accord with the principle that the least invasive measure likely to impact an illness should be the first applied. These low-tech procedures are not only readily available and easily added to the practitioner's treatment repertoire with a modicum of continuing education, their purported preventive and noninvasive qualities make them highly cost-effective in contrast to the rapidly rising costs of conventional medicine.

Pillar 4: Patient Empowerment—energy medicine includes methods that can be utilized on an at-home, self-help basis, fostering a stronger patient and practitioner partnership in the healing process.

Energy medicine uses the term "energy" in two senses. Energy is the *medicine*, and energy is also the *patient*. You heal the body by activating its natural healing energies (energy as the "medicine"), and you also heal the body by restoring energies that have become weak, disturbed, or out of balance (energy as the "patient"). People can be shown a variety of exercises or postures that are designed for specific energy effects in both senses. They can self-administer techniques that activate their own inner healers in a generic manner and that also bring balance to specific energy systems that need attention.

While conventional medicine may recommend exercise, a healthy diet, stress reduction, and other common sense steps for better health, its core procedures are medication, radiation, and surgery, and these must be administered by the health care professional. Energy medicine, on the other hand, recognizes energy as a vital, living, moving force in each individual and lends itself to being self-administered. It is inherently democratic. The body's healing energies are free, everyone's birthright. Energy medicine teaches people to marshal these energies to counter illness and enhance health.

Pillar 5: Quantum Compatibility—energy medicine adopts nonlinear concepts consistent with distant healing, the healing impact of prayer, and the role of intention in healing.

A great incongruity in Western medicine is that its core paradigm is a century behind the paradigm used by modern physics. Einstein's formula showing that energy and matter are interchangeable was published in 1905. As scientists are able to peer more deeply into the unimaginably miniscule building blocks of nature, such as quarks, leptons, and bosons, some are speculating that at its base, matter may not be made of particles at all—it may be more like strings of vibrating energy.

The physical body itself is continually vibrating and resonating with other energies in the environment. While Western medicine has developed few interventions that are based in the recognition that energy is at the foundation of, or at least intimately intertwined with, physical matter, scientists from many other disciplines are working within this perspective. They are, for example, recognizing the potential explanatory power of fields that are "totally unlike any of those presently known" in the ways they hold and transmit information, display quantum properties such as nonlocal influence, and interact with consciousness.

Such fields might explain, for instance, the beneficial effects of prayer and distant healing that have been widely observed and amply documented, as well as the role of intention, placebo effect, and other psychological factors in health and healing. **The impact of human intention on physical systems within as well as outside the body has been scientifically demonstrated and reveals a shortcoming of the conventional medical paradigm and highlights a strength of the energy medicine paradigm.**

Experiments demonstrating the role of intention on physical and social processes range from focused thoughts affecting seed germination to highly significant reductions in crime rates after groups of people used meditation to focus on sending love and healing to troubled areas of the world.

Pillar 6: Holistic Orientation—energy medicine strengthens the integration of body, mind, and spirit, leading not only to a focus on healing but to achieving greater wellbeing, peace, and passion for life.

An essential difference between energy medicine and conventional medicine involves the concepts of diagnosis and treatment. Energy medicine is concerned with the person as an integrated energetic system, impacting body, mind, and spirit. "Diagnosis" focuses on disruptions and imbalances in the body's energy system. "Treatment" is not of the disease or its symptoms per se. It is rather designed to correct such energetic imbalances.

Energy medicine, in fact, offers many methods that instantaneously impact the entire body. The mechanism by which it is possible for energy interventions to have this "holistic" influence is the body's connective tissue, which is, for many healers, thought of as a communication medium.

According to Dawson Church, PhD, author of *The Genie in Your Genes: Epigenetic Medicine and the New Biology of Intention*, "Every organ of your body is encased within the body's largest organ, which functions as a liquid crystal semiconductor" that processes information by being able "to store energy, amplify signals, filter information, and…move information in one direction but not in another."[124] With the connective tissue acting as a giant liquid crystal electrical semiconductor, energy interventions can simultaneously be brought to every cell of the body.

This whole-body effect carries significant advantages. For instance, as discussed earlier, when medications meant to correct chemical imbalances in a specific area of the body move through the bloodstream, they often inadvertently upset chemical balances in untargeted organs and systems. When energy interventions are applied, on the other hand, they are conducted through the connective tissue, so the information is simultaneously received throughout the body. This allows the energies to be coordinated with the body's entire energy system, resulting in harmonious self-regulation.

Energy Medicine, Energy Psychology, and Energy Healing

For most of human history, healing practices were integrated, and there was no separation between mental and physical healing. In modern times, we have separated problems that have an emotional basis from those that are thought to originate in the body. Contemporary medicine applies health science, biomedical research, and medical technology to diagnose and treat injury and disease, typically through medication or surgery.[125] Psychology is the science of behavior and mental processes.[126] But there is a broader definition of medicine that combines body, mind, and spirit. It is derived from the Latin phrase *ars medicina*, meaning *the art of healing.*

Cyndi Dale, a recognized expert in the field of energy healing and best-selling author of the award-winning *The Subtle Body: An Encyclopedia of Your Energy Anatomy*, says, "The term *energy healing* refers to a variety of philosophies and methodologies that recognize a balanced flow of energy in the body as the primary source of health and wellness. **When your energy is in harmony, you are in a natural state of physical and emotional wellbeing. When your energy is out of balance, various symptoms of disease, discomfort, and disorder can arise."**[127]

Although some practitioners view energy medicine, energy psychology, and energy healing as separate fields of study, I feel they overlap and are deeply connected. That's why I'm using the term 'energy healing' in this book to refer to the full range of these practices.

Energy Healing: The Swiss Army Knife for the Body, Mind, and Spirit

Tool Time Tim probably didn't own a Swiss Army knife. He would have considered it a "wimpy" tool. Like our modern civilization, he was addicted to machines that cost a lot of money, made a lot of noise, and polluted the environment. Our world is drowning in power tools. But are they really what we need? Our medical system boasts the highest tech surgical techniques available and the latest, fastest-acting drugs. But are they really the best resources for treating what ails us?

What would you give to have a tool that can fix most of the things that really need fixing, is easy to use, can be taken wherever you go, never needs to be plugged in, and costs nearly nothing? Think of it as a super-charged Swiss Army knife with everything you need to address any emergency and heal any wound. It may not blow your socks off or reach to the moon. It is simple, yet powerful—kind of like the Swiss Army and their famous knife.

The Swiss Army is one of the strongest in Europe. It is a tough, well-trained professional fighting force so formidable that it has kept the country from being invaded through two world wars. Every able-bodied Swiss male is required to serve and remains in the army as a reservist until age fifty. As a condition of preparedness, each soldier is provided with the most advanced technology and the simplest: a folding pocketknife.

This tool dates back to 1886 when the Swiss Army decided to equip every soldier with a regulation, single-blade folding knife. In 1889, a new rifle was introduced. To disassemble the rifle, a screwdriver was needed. So a decision was made to create a multipurpose tool incorporating four elements: a knife, screwdriver, reamer, and can-opener.

The tool I'll be giving you in this book also has four elements, which you'll appreciate and use even more than your Swiss Army knife. I call this Swiss Army knife for the mind, body, and spirit your *energy healing power tool.* This tool will give you what you need to create the kind of life you want. It can shift your brain's electrochemistry to:

- Immediately reduce the stress you are feeling in your life
- Help overcome unwanted emotions such as anger, jealousy, fear, guilt, and shame
- Help you deal effectively with the changes of life after age forty
- Alleviate physical and emotional pain
- Enhance your abilities to love, succeed, and enjoy life

The energy healing power tool is ancient in origin, but in its modern form it draws from wisdom garnered from both the East and the West.

Your Energy Healing Power Tool: Four Tools in One

Although there are many techniques and practices that might fall under the umbrella of "energy healing" (*The Encyclopedia of Energy Medicine*[128] compiled by Linnie Thomas lists sixty-six different approaches), **I've chosen to focus on the four that I've found to be most effective, easiest to learn, and are scientifically sound. I've ordered them, intuitively, following my father's love of baseball.**

Earthing is a natural lead-off hitter that will get you to first base fast. Heart coherence is a great contact hitter and almost never strikes out. Third-place hitters are best known for "keeping the inning alive," and attachment love does that better than anyone. Emotional freedom techniques (EFT) may be the most powerful hitter on the team. All have their part to play in stopping killer stress. You'll likely use them all, but you may find that certain ones work best for you in different circumstances.

The four tools are:

1. Earthing
2. Heart coherence
3. Attachment love
4. Emotional freedom techniques (EFT)

Let's take a quick look at each of these elements. We'll also examine them in more detail in upcoming chapters.

Tool #1: Earthing[129]

For millions of years, our ancestors moved across the landscape either barefoot or in moccasins made from the hides of animals. The women walked to gather food. The men walked to find animals for food. We slept connected to the Earth. But in modern times we've begun wearing rubber-soled shoes that keep us insulated from the healing energies of the Earth.

According to cardiologist Stephen Sinatra, MD, coauthor of the book *Earthing: The Most Important Health Discovery Ever?* "Earthing involves coupling your body to the Earth's eternal and gentle surface energies. It means walking barefoot outside and/or sitting, working, or sleeping inside while connected to a conductive device that delivers the natural healing energy of the Earth into your body."[130]

In some ways, all the major problems we face today—from global warming to peak oil, from obesity to depression, from joblessness to the increase of divorce—could be helped if we were able to reestablish our connection to the Earth. Social psychologist Sam Keen put it simply: "The radical vision of the future rests on the belief that the logic that determines either our survival or our destruction is simple:

1. The new human vocation is to heal the Earth.
2. We can only heal what we love.
3. We can only love what we know.
4. We can only know what we touch."[131]

For those who learn to use the Earthing tool, getting in touch with the Earth is more than a metaphor, it is a physiological reality. In Chapter Five, you'll learn more about how to use this valuable tool and why so many world-class athletes have come to depend upon it.

Tool #2: Heart Coherence[132]

Heart disease is still the major killer of men. According to the National Centers of Disease Control (CDC):

- Heart disease is the leading cause of death for men in the United States.
- Half of the men who die suddenly of coronary heart disease have no previous symptoms.
- Between 70 percent and 89 percent of sudden cardiac events occur in men.[133]

Millions of men are taking medications to treat or prevent heart disease. And once again, there is another choice to consider. According to David Servan-Schreiber, MD, PhD, author of *The Instinct to Heal: Curing Stress, Anxiety, and Depression Without Drugs and Without Talk Therapy,* there is an intimate connection between the heart and the emotion centers in the brain, and by learning methods that produce heart coherence, we can not only protect our hearts but the rest of the human body as well. [134]

The Institute of HeartMath, founded in 1991 by stress researcher Doc Childre, has been doing cutting-edge research on heart coherence under the leadership of research director Rollin McCraty, PhD. Researchers found that people could maintain extended periods of physiological coherence by actively generating positive emotions. In Chapter Six, I'll share the techniques of heart coherence so you can learn to reduce stress and increase health and wellbeing.

Tool #3: Attachment Love[135]

Attachment love is the energy essence of a successful relationship. Attachment love is based on the latest scientific findings that show we are emotionally attached to and dependent on our partner in much the same way that a child is on a parent for nurturing, soothing, and protection. Most of us understand that children need a secure attachment to their parents in order to grow up be healthy and happy. But many of us believe that we outgrow these dependency needs when we become adults. Men, in particular, are taught that maturity means "standing on our own two feet" and not needing others in order to fulfill our needs.

As we've learned from previous chapters, males are more vulnerable than females at every stage of life, and we become more isolated as we age. Learning how to develop and maintain a deep attachment to a spouse or partner allows us to overcome our isolation, reduce our levels of stress, and keep our love lives growing more fully as we age.

Even practitioners who are familiar with the field of energy healing may be surprised that I view "attachment love" as an essential tool for keeping stress from killing us. But I've found it to be essential. Without love, we are lost, and without being securely attached to our mate, love can easily die. You'll learn more about the importance of "attachment love" in Chapter Seven.

Tool #4: Emotional Freedom Techniques (EFT)[136]

EFT is a powerful new discovery that combines two well-established sciences so you can benefit from both at the same time:

Mind/body medicine

Acupuncture (without needles)

I learned about emotional freedom techniques (EFT) when an acupuncturist I had gone to for shoulder pain told me about EFT. I wanted help in the worst way, but I couldn't tolerate the needles. She assured me they wouldn't hurt (and in fact, they didn't hurt), but I still got light-headed and nearly passed out. I faint at the sight of blood *and* needles. You can fully understand why I dropped out of medical school.

I was immediately drawn to EFT because the founder, Gary Craig, was a hands-on kind of guy. He says, "I am neither a psychologist nor a licensed therapist. Rather, I am a Stanford engineering graduate." You'll learn more about EFT and how to use it in Chapter Eight.

Energy Healing: An Idea Whose Time Has Come

I first heard about Dr. Mehmet Oz in 2000 when I was writing my book *The Whole Man Program: Reinvigorating Your Body, Mind, and Spirit After 40.* Dr. Oz was one of the top heart surgeons in the world at New York Presbyterian Hospital/ Columbia Medical Center. I wanted to find someone with the best scientific credentials to help me better understand heart disease so I could help other men. Dr. Oz was a wonderful resource. He is still one of the best surgeons in the world, but he has since expanded his view of what constitutes good medicine.

Dr. Oz is now advocating a kind of medicine that does not require a scalpel. In 2007, Dr. Oz rocked the health world by proclaiming to a worldwide television audience on the largest stage in the world, *The Oprah Show*, that we are entering a new era of medicine.

"We're beginning now to understand things that we know in our hearts were true but could not measure. As we get better at understanding how little we know about the body, we begin to realize that **the next big frontier in medicine is energy medicine.** It's not the mechanistic parts of the joints moving. It's not the chemistry of our bodies. It's understanding, for the first time, how energy influences how we feel."

Dr. Mehmet Oz, November 20, 2007, *The Oprah Show*

Dr. Oz has a list of awards, accomplishments, and appointments as long as your arm (just Google him and see for yourself). He is routinely called "America's doctor" and has his own television show. He has authored multiple *New York Times* best-selling books on health. He has also been a regular on *The Oprah Show.* So why would someone of Dr. Oz's stature march out onto the world's stage and make an announcement like that, knowing that many of his mainstream medicine colleagues would cringe or attack him for it?

The last thing in the world many mainstream medical doctors and pharmaceutical companies want is to point their customers to a highly specialized segment of natural medicine called *energy medicine.* But Dr. Oz is an unusual man who truly believes in finding the best medicine for his patients and for all of us. Dr. Oz believes we are only beginning to understand what contributes to healing and wants all of us to expand our definition of health care. "You have to take Eastern approaches and bring them to the West, and share West with the East."[137]

Dr. Oz is the perfect person to unite Eastern and Western health practices. He spent most of his childhood in Turkey. "It's a unique country, because it truly bridges the East and the West," Oz said. "People who believe in integrated medicine and people who believe in high-tech conventional medicine all work here together."[138]

Another world-renowned health expert, who recognizes we are entering the Age of Energy, is Carolyn Myss. Since 1982, she has worked as medical intuitive providing individuals with an evaluation of the health of their energetic anatomy system. "We now think of ourselves not simply as physical bodies," she says, "but also as 'energy systems' that require various kinds of treatment. Our energy system is the harbor of our psyche, emotions, mental capacities, unconscious or subconscious mind, and spirit. All these aspects of ourselves require forms of treatment and care based on sophisticated philosophies of psychological integration."[139]

James L. Oschman, PhD, is a world authority on energy and complementary medicine. A biophysicist and cell biologist, Oschman is one of the few academic scientists who has focused on the scientific basis for various complementary or alternative medicines. He has published twenty-six full-length scientific articles in academic scientific journals and forty articles in alternative and complementary therapy journals. In his books, *Energy Medicine: The Scientific Basis* and *Energy Medicine in Therapeutics and Human Performance*, he documents the existence of a high-speed communication system that extends throughout the human body and that responds to the energetic environment.[140]

This system provides the regulatory circuitry that maintains a high level of functioning for healing or obtaining optimal performance. Diseases and injuries compromise the regulatory circuitry. This communication system is the substrate for *systemic cooperation.* An understanding of energy field interactions between organisms accounts for the beneficial effects of a variety of hands-on and hands-off therapies.

The Promise and Power of Energy Healing

In their book *New Psychotherapy for Men,* William S. Pollack and Ronald F. Levant say, "Men suffer under a code of masculinity that requires them to be: aggressive, dominant, achievement-oriented, competitive, rigidly self-sufficient, adventure-seeking, willing to take risks, emotionally restricted, and constituted to avoid all things, actions, and reactions that are potentially 'feminine.' Such a code is bound to take a toll on men's longevity."[141] They conclude, "Men are in dire need of psychological treatment and psychotherapy."[142]

The problem is that men, on the whole, are suspicious of psychotherapy. We often resist efforts to get us involved. Clearly, the same kinds of social pressures that cause the problems in the first place make it difficult for men to reach out for help. I've spent a good deal of my career trying to help other men get past their resistance to counseling and good medical care.

Until I learned about energy healing, I assumed that I just needed to try harder to overcome men's resistance to getting help. I'm beginning to recognize that men may be smarter about treatment than we had once thought. Could it be that men have resisted traditional medical and psychiatric treatment because deep down inside they knew there was something better for them? Could energy healing be what men have been waiting for? I've found energy work very helpful in my own life and in the lives of many men I counsel. Of course, it's great for women as well, but I've found that men in particular find the techniques useful.

Here are some of the key aspects of energy healing that make it particularly attractive to men:

- There is no long, drawn-out "tell me your life story" feature to these energy techniques, as is often the case in conventional psychotherapy.
- You don't have to take time off work to sit in a doctor's office to get help.
- There are no pills or medications (with their side effects) to take.
- There is no painful reliving of past traumatic events.
- The techniques are active. They are things we can actually do.
- Using energy healing, we can fix the problems, not just understand them or medicate them.
- It takes a fraction of the time required for conventional medical or psychological treatments.
- Anyone can learn how to use it effectively.
- It doesn't cost an arm and a leg. In fact, you can learn these techniques for free.
- It draws on the best of what works from Eastern and Western medicine.
- It offers solutions for problems that often cannot be solved by conventional approaches.
- It draws on the solid scientific findings.

In Part II, you will learn more about these helpful energy healing tools and how you can use them in your own life.

PART II:
USING YOUR ENERGY HEALING TOOLS

CHAPTER 5
EARTHING

I had finished writing my last two books, a process that kept me at the computer the better part of four years. I was feeling stiff and old and felt like I needed some kind of physical challenge to balance all the mind work I had been doing. When talking to my son Evan in one of our regular phone conversations, he immediately had an idea of something we could do together. "Let's run a marathon," he suggested excitedly. "You want something that will engage you physically? I could use some exercise myself. Let's run together!" I immediately filed his response in the category of "Be careful what you ask for, you just might get it."

When I thought of a physical challenge, I was thinking of something more like a long walk or a short run. I wasn't thinking about a *twenty-six-mile-long run*. But I didn't want to dampen his excitement, so I gave a tempered response. "Well, that would certainly be a challenge," I told him, "but I'm not sure I could run a marathon at my age, even if I trained for it." I had done a number of "fun runs" in my thirties and forties. But even the *Bay to Breakers* run in San Francisco, which I had enjoyed running a number of times, was only 7.5 miles and wasn't an easy run, though it was a great deal of fun.

Evan's enthusiasm was not diminished. "That's fine, we'll find a race where there's a 10K, half marathon, and full marathon. We'll train for six months, and I'll run the marathon. You can run whichever race you feel you're ready to do.

"Okay," I agreed. "I'm in."

We soon found a race that met our requirements, the Humboldt Redwoods run, just thirty miles north of where I live in Willits, California. Evan lives in Bend, Oregon, and the plan was for him to train there and me to train in Willits. He would drive down before the race and we would run it together.

We started our training in mid-April, and I hoped I would be able to get in some kind of shape by October. The workout routine was demanding. We ran short distances three days a week, worked out at the gym two days a week, and did one long run of increasing distance once a week. One day a week, we rested. We talked with each other on the phone regularly to offer support and compare how we were doing.

As things turned out, my son stopped training after two months. "I keep injuring myself," he said. "I'll have to try again next year."

I kept training, increasing my long run gradually until I was running twenty-one miles by the end of September. I couldn't believe I might actually run twenty-six miles. Come race day, I signed up for the marathon. My wife, Carlin, was there to cheer me on, and Evan kept in touch by cell phone.

It was, without a doubt, one of the greatest experiences of my life. I ran through one of the most incredible redwood forests remaining on the planet. Trees more than three hundred feet tall and over twelve hundred years old surrounded the route.   It was about as close as I could ever imagine to running in heaven. Although I finished dead last (well, not dead—I was alive and kicking in the last 385 yards with my wife and son cheering me on), I felt I had accomplished something special. After the race, I learned I was second in my age division. My sixty-six-year-old body was definitely tired at the end, but I felt exhilarated. I didn't collapse with exhaustion after the race, didn't sustain any injuries, and walked hand-in-hand with my wife back to our hotel room. Let's just say we had another kind of celebration later that night.

The Secret to My Marathon Success: Earthing

When I started my training in April, I was reading up on the latest information on energy healing. I visited the website of James Oschman, PhD, one of the leading researchers in the field and author of *Energy Medicine: The Scientific Basis.* I learned about a new book called *Earthing: The Most Important Health Discovery Ever?* by Clint Ober, Stephen Sinatra, and Martin Zucker. Oschman wrote the foreword to the book and said, "Among the many surprising revelations this book holds is an obvious, fundamental, and yet overlooked answer to the question of inflammation—recognized as the central health issue of our time."[143]

The world "inflammation" caught my attention. Over the years playing sports, I'd had all the common injuries, including sprains, strains, shin splints, and Achilles tendonitis and the attendant inflammation. I had memorized RICE (rest, ice, compression, and elevation) to alleviate the inflammation, but I also knew that as I aged, injuries would become more common and take longer to heal. I needed another edge if I was going to run a marathon, and I sensed that Earthing might be the answer.

I ordered the book and began reading. I was immediately drawn to the chapter on sports. I learned that Earthing had been used with athletes competing in the Tour de France cycling competition. I've never cycled, but I know the Tour de France is one of the most brutal athletic events in the world—comparable to running three marathons a day for twenty-one straight days. If Earthing could help these guys, I knew it could help me.

Earthing helped me reduce inflammation and injury and helped me recover quickly after my training runs. I'm convinced it was the key ingredient allowing an "old man" to engage in activities that are generally reserved for the young. Whether I run another marathon or not, I want to stay in good shape. Earthing is a simple, effective way to do that. We are all born to be athletes, whether as long-distance runners or just walkers who enjoy getting out in nature. And we are meant to be athletes all our lives, not having to "retire" when we're young, or live with chronic injury and pain, as so many people do as they get older.

Earthing at a Glance[144]

What Is Earthing?

Earthing involves coupling your body to the Earth's eternal and gentle surface energies. It means walking barefoot outside and/or sitting, working, or sleeping inside while connected to a conductive device that delivers the natural healing energy of the Earth into your body. Earthing also goes by the name *grounding*.

What Earthing Is Not.

You are not in any sense being electrocuted. In fact, when you "plug in" the Earthing devices into the electrical outlet, you're only using the ground plug (for those of us not electrically inclined, that's the fatter prong at the bottom). So there's no electricity at all, just the connection through the ground plug to the Earth. Earthing is among the most natural and safest things you can do.

What Happens?

Your body becomes suffused with the negative-charged free electrons abundantly present on the surface of the Earth. Your body immediately equalizes to the same electric energy level, or potential, as the Earth.

What Do You Feel?

Sometimes you feel a warm, tingling sensation and often feelings of ease and wellbeing.

Will You Feel Better?

Usually, yes, and often rapidly. The degree of improvement varies from person to person. The important thing is to make Earthing a long-term addition to your daily routine and to do it as much as possible so as to gain maximum benefit. When Earthing is stopped, symptoms tend to slowly return.

What Does Earthing Do?

Observations and research indicate the following benefits from Earthing. We expect many more to emerge with ongoing studies. Earthing:

- Defuses the cause of inflammation, and improves or eliminates the symptoms of many inflammation-related disorders
- Reduces or eliminates chronic pain
- Improves sleep in most cases
- Increases energy
- Lowers stress and promotes calmness in the body by cooling down the nervous system and stress hormones
- Normalizes the body's biological rhythms.
- Thins blood and improves blood pressure and flow
- Relieves muscle tension and headaches
- Reduces or eliminates jet lag
- Protects the body against potentially health-disturbing environmental electromagnetic fields (EMFs)
- Accelerates recovery from intense athletic activity

Look over the list. Which benefits would you like to have in your life? If this were a new wonder drug, you'd probably be willing to pay a lot of money to get these benefits. But as you'll see, you can have all of this without the cost or side effects of "miracle drugs." You can learn more about Earthing at http://earthinginstitute.net/.[145]

Earthing, Inflammation, and the Holy Grail of Medicine

Like meridian tapping, the basic idea of Earthing has been with us for a long time. Throughout history, humans have strolled, sat, stood, and slept on the ground—the skin of our bodies touching the skin of the Earth—oblivious to the fact that such physical contact transfers natural electrical energy to the body. The modern lifestyle has disconnected us from the Earth's energy, making us more vulnerable to stress and illness.

Many health-enhancing discoveries are made by regular people who put two and two together and come up with an insight that is obvious and simple but that no one had thought of before. Clint Ober, who "discovered" Earthing, is one of those guys. He grew up on a farm in Montana. As he remembers his early years, he chased cows, baled hay, and spent long summer days walking barefoot up and down long rows of beets and beans pulling weeds. As a young man, he entered the fledgling cable television industry and became one of the leading cable entrepreneurs in the country.

Like many discoveries that revolutionize how we see ourselves and the world, this one was sparked by one of those "aha" experiences that seem to grab our hearts. "My 'light-bulb' went off one day in 1998," Ober recalls. "I was sitting on a park bench and watching the passing parade of tourists from all over the world. At some point, and I don't know why, my awareness zeroed in on what all these different people were wearing on their feet. I saw a lot of those running shoes with thick rubber or plastic soles. I was wearing them as well. It occurred to me rather innocently that all these people— me included—were insulated from the ground, the electrical surface charge of the Earth beneath our feet. I started to think about static electricity and wondered if being insulated like that could have some effect on health." [146]

He reflected on his years in television and cable, and some thoughts began to come together. "Before there was cable, you commonly had lots of flecks ('noise,' we call it) in the TV picture. Or you had 'snow' or lines of all kinds of electromagnetic interference. In the cable industry, you have to ground and shield the entire cable system in every home to prevent extraneous electromagnetic signals and fields from interfering with the transmission carried through the cable. That's how you provide the viewer with a perfect signal and a crisp picture."[147]

After years of research, he teamed up with cardiologist Stephen T. Sinatra, MD, and health writer Martin Zucker to write the book, *Earthing: The Most Important Health Discovery Ever?* James L. Oschman says, **"Earthing seems to do away with or dramatically improve so many health challenges common in this day and age: insomnia, the chronic pain of multiple diseases and injuries, exhaustion, stress, anxiety, and premature aging."** [148]

How can Earthing help with so many chronic illnesses? One answer seems to be that it helps reduce inflammation in our bodies. Inflammation is now believed to be the underlying cause of more than eighty chronic illnesses, and more than half of Americans suffer currently from one or more of them. **"Inflammation may turn out to be the elusive Holy Grail of medicine—the simple phenomenon that holds the key to sickness and health,"** says William Meggs, MD, PhD, of East Carolina University in his book *The Inflammation Cure: How to Combat the Hidden Factor Behind Heart Disease, Arthritis, Asthma, Diabetes & Other Diseases.*[149]

Earthing for the Athlete in Every Man

In an age of rampant chronic disease, reconnecting with the Earth's energy beneath our very feet may provide a way back to better health and keeping our bodies in top condition throughout our lives. This is what first attracted Dr. Jeff Spencer. Spencer, a former Olympic cyclist, works with elite athletes and applies cutting-edge methods to support optimum health and enhance recovery from exertion and injury. This was his assignment during five Tour de France competitions. During four of them—2003, 2004, 2005, and 2007—he utilized Earthing.

But before he was willing to try it on his athletes, he had to see if it worked. "I was not willing to use anything for my patients that I didn't know worked from my own firsthand experience," he said. "For about five years, I had been suffering with the consequences of mercury poisoning. At one point, my health was quite debilitated. I had been receiving treatment for it and was improving gradually. I was getting better. But after grounding myself one night, I felt significant improvement. When I awoke the next morning, I felt much better. I had more energy. I had had difficulty concentrating before, but now I had greater clarity of thinking. I had less pain. Less irritability. My body felt like it had been washed from inside out. After three or four nights of sleeping better and feeling better, I knew that this was something for real. I recognized that this is something that could have tremendous value not just for me, but also for my patients and the cyclists at the Tour de France."[150]

Spencer talked Clint Ober into creating a prototype sleep system that his athletes could use in the 2003 race. "The challenge is that the Tour is so difficult mentally and physically that the riders have a hard time sleeping. And if you don't sleep, you don't recover. If you don't recover, the body breaks down, the mind goes down, and you can unnecessarily get injured or sick, which is catastrophic for a top Tour effort."[151]

Ober was able to develop a system and teach Spencer how to use it. It was really quite simple. The athletes slept on a special sheet that was grounded to the Earth (more on how it works and how to use it later). Spencer and his athletes were amazed at the results. The usual fatigue and tendon inflammation that accompanies these kinds of endurance races didn't happen with the athletes who were using Ober's grounded sheets.

Clearly, Earthing was beneficial for world-class cyclists. But it also has been shown to be beneficial for other athletes. If something works to give an athlete an added advantage in competition, the word spreads fast. Chike Okeafor, the former linebacker for the National Football League's Arizona Cardinals, says he suffered a lot of injuries and missed many games—until he discovered Earthing. "I've been sleeping grounded regularly for more than five years after experiencing the effect of grounding on a leg injury. It was a hamstring injury in the back of my knee, plus some deep bruising of the thigh, incurred during a practice session."[152]

Okeafor goes on to share his astonishment at the healing effects of Earthing. "As I lay on a grounded sheet, I watched a computer monitor connected to a real-time thermal imaging camera. I was amazed to see the colors depicting the intensity of the inflammation from the injury cool down quickly, like within fifteen minutes. The intensity was dramatically different within an hour so. I felt the difference physically, but to see the changes like that so rapidly was mind-blowing."[153]

Positive results have been shown for other sports. Clearly, Earthing can help whether you are a runner, weight lifter, golfer, basketball player, or just a regular guy who wants to stay in shape. As I watched the NBA basketball tournament playoffs in 2011, I was aware that a lot of the players were dealing with injuries. A common problem for those involved with sports, as well as the rest of us just trying to do our jobs, is back pain.

Here's how a nurse came to rely on Earthing to help her and her patients: "I suffered with back pain for twenty-five years. It was something I had to live with because you can't take narcotic painkillers and work with patients. You have to be very clear-headed. So Tylenol was my drug of choice. That was it.

"As a nurse, I was skeptical about this Earthing idea when I first heard about it. But I decided to give it a try, and I'm sure glad I did. I've been sleeping grounded for four years and wouldn't think of sleeping any other way. Within two or three days, I noticed a difference. I remember calling my daughter at the end of the first week and telling her that my back wasn't hurting anymore."[154]

Earthing May Be the Original Energy Healing Power Tool

We live on a planet alive with energy. Ober, Sinatra, and Zucker describe it as a "six sextillion (that's a six followed by twenty-one zeroes) metric ton battery that is continually being renewed by solar radiation, lightning, and heat from the molten core at the center." Just like the Earth, your body is mostly water and minerals, and both are excellent conductors of electrons. As we move upon the Earth, our bodies are able to transfer these electrons from the Earth to our bodies.

Our ancient ancestors knew nothing about the science of how this works, but they had a firm understanding of the importance of being in connection with the Earth. For them, the Earth was sacred. It was the Mother that brought life to all. Throughout human history, we have tuned into the cycles of Nature for survival and health. Qi (pronounced *chee*) is a central principle in the long history of Chinese wisdom and is seen as the energy or natural force that fills the universe. From India's Vedic tradition, the equivalent concept is *prana*, or "vital force."

All natural things—plants, animals, and humans—grow and are influenced by the natural cycles of energy coming from the Earth. Native Americans honored and recognized the importance of being connected to the Earth. The late Ota Kte (Luther Standing Bear), a writer, educator, and tribal leader from the Lakota Sioux tradition, described our relationship to the Earth this way: "The old people came literally to love the soil. They sat on the ground with the feeling of being close to a mothering power. It was good for the skin to touch the Earth, and the old people liked to remove their moccasins and walk with their bare feet on the sacred Earth. The soil was soothing, strengthening, cleansing, and healing."[155]

It is time we reconnected to the power of Earth.

Remember When We Naturally Spent Time Connected to the Earth?

When I was a kid, I remember most vividly the last days of the school year before summer vacation. My friends and I would become antsy for the previous month or so, waiting, waiting, waiting for school to end and summer to begin. On the last day of school, we would run home and take our shoes off. It took a few days before our feet toughened up enough to walk around without having to take each step carefully, but it was the first rite of summer and we knew we had to feel the pain temporarily until we were able to run around the neighborhood barefoot.

Summers were carefree times when I was growing up. We played sports, dipped our feet in the stream that ran by our house, and felt the joy of being outdoors. It never occurred to me that one of the reasons summers were so joyful was that we spent so much time connected to the earth.

What the Science Is Saying About Earthing: Report from Cardiologist Stephen Sinatra, MD

Stephen Sinatra, MD, is a board-certified cardiologist and certified psychotherapist with more than thirty years of experience in helping patients prevent and reverse heart disease.

"In 2001," Sinatra says, "I was invited to speak at an electromedicine conference in San Diego. That's where I met Clint Ober. He had just completed his second study—how grounding affected cortisol and stress—and he was interested in discussing his research with a cardiologist who had an interest in electromedicine."[156] Sinatra began working with Ober and together with other researchers found important *health benefits* from connecting to the Earth, as well as *physical and emotional problems* when we are disconnected.

For Sinatra, this was medicine at its best. "This was literally electromedicine from the ground up. A secret of the ages right under my feet. **For me, the original anti-inflammatory and the ultimate antioxidant had been found.**"[157]

It isn't surprising that Sinatra teamed up with Ober and Martin Zucker to write the book, *Earthing*. "I envision Earthing becoming a major practical tool against cardiovascular disease. In fact, it looks like a big winner in the practice of medicine in general."[158] In the book, they present research and observations collected during more than twelve years that strongly suggest the biggest anti-inflammatory on the planet is—get this!—the planet itself. Basically, they say that we live on top of a global treatment table!

Ready to Start Earthing? Here's What You Do.

This may be the simplest energy healing tool you can use. But remember, I warned you that even knowing the scientific basis for Earthing, you may fall into the trap of thinking, "This is too easy. It can't really help with pain or inflammation." But hang in there. Once you've tried it and see the results produced, you'll be glad you stayed with it. You may not be a world-class professional athlete who will do anything to stay in shape, but you already know how good it feels to have all your parts working and how miserable you feel when your body is out of whack.

1. **Take your shoes off**.

We intuitively knew what was right when we were young. As soon as we were out of school, we took off our shoes and spent the summer barefoot. Now science validates our youthful wisdom. The late William Rossi, DPM, a Massachusetts podiatrist, footwear industry historian, scientist, and author, said in a 1999 article in *Podiatry Management*, "A natural gait is biomechanically impossible for any shoe-wearing person. It took four million years to develop our unique human foot and our consequent distinctive gait, a remarkable feat of bioengineering. Yet in only a few thousand years, and with one carelessly designed instrument, our shoes, we have warped the pure anatomical form of human gait, obstructing its engineering efficiency, afflicting it with strains and stresses and denying it its natural grace of form and ease of movement head to foot."[159] So, when you can take off your shoes, you'll walk better and feel better.

But shoes aren't only bad for our mechanics. More importantly, our modern rubber-soled shoes, made from petrochemicals, prevent us from receiving the healing energies from the Earth. "The sole (or plantar surface) of the foot is richly covered with some 1,300 nerve endings per square inch," Dr. Rossi wrote in a 1997 article in *Footwear News*. "That's more than found on any other part of the body of comparable size."[160]

Getting our feet back in touch with the Earth may be the simplest and best medicine we can take.

2. When you wear shoes, wear leather-soled shoes.

"Why are so many nerve endings concentrated there?" asks Dr. Rossi. "To keep us 'in touch' with the Earth. The foot is the vital link between the person and the Earth. The paws of all animals are equally rich in nerve endings. The Earth is covered with an electromagnetic layer. It's this that creates the sensory response in our feet and in the paws of animals."[161]

Even if we decide to walk barefoot more, there are times we need to wear shoes to prevent injury and keep our feet warm. What can we do? Get back to wearing leather-soled shoes. Dr. Rossi bemoaned the fact that modern shoe soles have separated us from the energy of the Earth and feeling of the ground, which is so important to our health and wellbeing. He wrote, "The bottoms of our footwear are virtually 'deadened.' A cross section of a shoe reveals several layers: outsole, midsole, insole filler material, footbed, cushioning, and sock liner. An almost total block out of sensory response."[162]

We forget that prior to World War II, most everyone wore shoes with leather soles. But as cheap oil became available, even shoes were made of oil-based products. Dr. Sinatra notes that even makers of fancy men's dress shoes are increasingly switching to rubber, plastic, and other nonconductive material, just as casual and work shoes before them.

I still remember wearing moccasins when I was a kid. I loved playing cowboys and Indians and much preferred to be the Indian. I recently bought a pair of sturdy moccasins. It turns out that I stumbled on to the original "earth shoe." As Ober, Sinatra, and Zucker say in their book, *Earthing*, "Leather (processed from hides), a conductive material when moist, has been the traditional source of shoes and sandals. The original lightweight, soft sole, heal-less and simple moccasin—a piece of crudely tanned leather that envelops the foot and is fastened on with rawhide thongs—is possibly the closest we have ever come to an 'ideal' shoe. It dates back more than 14,000 years."[163]

3. **When you're at home and work, get "barefoot substitutes."**[164]

Another way we can get the health benefits of grounding is by using simple devices that were originally used for research studies on Earthing but are now available to the public. They provide inside connectivity to the Earth outside. They are connected by a wire to a ground rod placed directly in the Earth or plugged into the ground port of a grounded electrical outlet. They can be utilized during sleep, work, and even while watching TV.

There are universal chair/desk/mouse/bed/floor mats and pads that can be used interchangeably to fit any setting. A pad placed on a desktop conducts through your forearms or wrists, on the floor through your feet, and on your chair through your butt. They can be placed on the bed to conduct through any part of your body that makes contact with it. Normal perspiration through clothes, such as a dresses, pants, socks, or long sleeves, permits varying degrees of conductivity. The pad utilizes a metallic fiber mesh and conductors coupled to a wire connected to a grounded outlet in the wall or an outside rod.

I tried it out, and it's pretty nifty. They include a little test device that ensures the outlets in the house have a proper ground. Then you plug into the ground slot. There's no connection to the electricity so it's totally safe. **To learn more about these simple, easy to use, devices for connecting to the earth go to www.Earthing.com. Check out the store and if you find something you'd like to try, founder Clint Ober is offering a special discount for the readers of this book. At the end of your order, simply type in the special coupon code "menalive" and receive a 5% discount.**

Connecting to the Earth: Simple, Fun, and Effective

A few years ago, my wife and I went to Australia. I have always been intrigued with the country "down under," particularly the Aboriginal culture with its practice of the walkabout. A walkabout refers to a rite of passage during which male Australian Aborigines undergo a journey during adolescence and live in the wilderness for a period as long as six months. In this practice, they trace the paths, or "song-lines," their people's ancestors took that celebrate their lives and their heroic deeds.

In modern times, Aboriginal peoples take off for a walk when the spirit moves them. I found it to be a very enlightening process. I've always enjoyed walking, but when I returned, it seemed to have engaged me in a deeper way. One of the men in my men's group commented that I seemed much more relaxed and stress-free, even a year after I had returned. "You always seemed busy and 'on the go,'" he told me. "But now you seem like you 'mosey' along."

I understood what he meant. Before going to Australia, I often felt rushed, going from one appointment to another.

Afterward, I didn't schedule myself so fully and had time to walk around town between appointments. I would often run into just the people I wanted to talk with, or I didn't know I wanted to talk to them until our paths crossed.

Walking has transformed my life. It has even changed my "professional life." I rarely sit through meetings any more. I like to take a break and go out for a walk. When I'm in charge of a meeting, I often suggest that we walk together and walk while we talk. People have reported that they enjoy the meetings much more and actually get a lot more done this way.

Simple Walking Can Prevent and Treat Depression and Other Ills

Engineers who study the human body marvel at how exquisitely well designed it is for walking. It's an activity that comes to people so naturally, so effortlessly, that even babies who receive no prompting will eventually start to walk on their own, as if propelled by instinct. According to Stephen S. Ilardi, PhD, author of *The Depression Cure: The 6-Step Program to Beat Depression without Drugs*, "For the vast majority of human history—until the advent of the automobile a few generations ago—people walked a lot.

"Our remote ancestors walked an estimated ten miles a day. For them, 'a day at the office' often meant a day spent tracking down dinner. Even as recently as the nineteenth century, when most Americans still made their living on the farm, people spent the better part of each day working and traveling on foot. Before car ownership became the norm in the 1940s, most people continued to walk several miles a day. But things are different now. **Each day, the average American travels over forty miles in a car, and less than one mile on foot.**"[165]

We all know exercise is good for us, and walking is the simplest form of exercise we can do. But did you know that walking can heal depression and other emotional ills? Studies conducted by Dr. Jim Blumenthal at Duke University in the early 1990s showed that simple walking was as effective for treating depression as the popular antidepressant Zoloft. And you didn't need a "heavy dose" of exercise to get good results. Blumenthal simply had his patients take *a brisk half-hour walk three times a week.* That's it.…just a good old-fashioned walk. The two treatments worked about equally well for the first few months, but by ten months into the study, the exercisers were much more likely than those taking Zoloft to remain depression-free.

Subsequent trials have repeated these results, showing again and again that patients who follow aerobic exercise regimens see improvement in their depression comparable to that of those treated with medication, and that both groups do better than patients given only a placebo. So how does it work?

Molecular biologists and neurologists have begun to show that exercise may alter brain chemistry in much the same way that antidepressant drugs do, by regulating the key neurotransmitters serotonin and norepinephrine. At the University of Georgia, neuroscience professor Philip Holmes and his colleagues have shown that, over the course of several weeks, exercise can switch on certain genes that increase the brain's level of galanin, a peptide neurotransmitter that appears to tone down the body's stress response by regulating another brain chemical, norepinephrine.

So if you want to activate this powerful energy healing tool, get moving. Take your shoes off and get connected to the Earth again. Get some good walking shoes or moccasins with leather soles. When you're inside, consider getting the barefoot substitutes that ground you while sleeping in bed or working at your computer. Let's move on now to the next powerful tool you can use for health and wellbeing: heart coherence.

CHAPTER 6
HEART COHERENCE

I've always prided myself on having a healthy heart. When I'd have my yearly health checkups, the doctor always commented that I had the low blood pressure of an athlete. I do keep in good shape, but I haven't considered myself an athlete since high school when I played basketball and wrestled.

At age sixty-six, I decided I wanted to do some kind of physical challenge to recapture some of the feeling I used to get when I really stretched myself physically. As I detailed in Chapter Five, my son suggested we both train and run a marathon. A week before the race, I ran into an unexpected problem. At odd times, my heart would begin speeding up and beating hard. I'd get light-headed and short of breath. I'd never had anything like that happen before so I went to see my doctor. She didn't think it was anything serious, but she sent me to a cardiologist to get a thorough checkup. I have to admit, I was more worried that the doctor wouldn't let me run the marathon than that there might be something wrong with my heart.

After extensive testing, the heart specialist concluded that my heart was having some kind of electrical malfunction. He also concluded it wasn't serious and described some things that could be done if it got worse. "There are medications we have that can get your heart back in rhythm, and if that doesn't work there are some simple surgical procedures we can try." I didn't even want to think about any of those. But my next concern was about the marathon. I had trained for six months and very much wanted to run, but knew I'd have to follow doctor's orders on this one.

I was surprised when he said, "I don't see any reason you shouldn't run. If you have one of those episodes when you're running, you'll want to stop. But if not, you should be fine." I asked him what had caused the speeding up of my heart and if there was anything I could do to prevent it from happening. "We don't really know what causes these things," he told me, "and there's nothing I would recommend now." That's all I needed to hear. I was good to go. But still, I didn't want my heart acting up during the race. I strongly suspected that stress was causing my heart problems, and I looked for something I could do to calm my heart and reduce my worry.

Living with Heart Coherence

My experience has been that when *conventional* medical practitioners say, "There's nothing you can do," or, "There are some excellent new medications we can try, and if that fails there is always surgery," there is often an *alternative* medical option that may be more helpful. I thought I had read something interesting about heart health in a book by David Servan-Schreiber, MD, PhD. I checked my bookshelves and found the book: *The Instinct to Heal: Curing Stress, Anxiety, and Depression without Drugs and Without Talk Therapy.*[166]

There were two chapters on the heart. I realized I had skipped them the first time around, going right to the chapters on anxiety and depression—issues I knew I needed help with at the time. Now, reading these chapters, I was amazed at the new understanding scientists have of the heart. Servan-Schreiber is cofounder of the Center for Complementary Medicine at the University of Pittsburgh Medical Center. He has conducted his own research and reported on some of the latest research being done throughout the world. Here are some of the findings he reports in the book:

- **Stress is possibly an even greater risk factor for heart disease than smoking.**
- An episode of depression coming within six months of a heart attack is a more accurate predictor of death than most measurements of heart function.
- When the emotional brain is out of order, the heart suffers and wears out.
- The heart/brain relationship works both ways. Proper functioning of the heart turns out to influence the brain.
- If there were a medication capable of harmonizing this intimate interplay between the heart and the brain, it would have beneficial effects on the whole body.
- This "miracle drug" would reduce stress and fatigue, overcome anxiety, and shield us from depression. At night, it would help us sleep better, and in the daytime, it would help us function more effectively, enhancing our capacities for concentration and performance.

I learned from Servan-Schreiber that this "miracle drug" was called "heart coherence." It was first described in 1991 by Rollin McCraty, PhD, a fellow of the American Institute of Stress and the research director at the Institute of HeartMath in Boulder Creek, California. "We introduced the term heart coherence to describe the degree of order, harmony, and stability in the various rhythmic activities within living systems over any given time period," says McCraty. "By contrast, an erratic, discordant pattern of activity denotes an incoherent system whose function reflects stress."[167]

I looked into the HeartMath techniques and found them interesting, easy to learn, and more importantly, they helped me stop my heart from speeding up unexpectedly. I ran my marathon, finished the same day I started, and have been using the HeartMath techniques to deal with many issues in my life. Before I tell you how you can learn and use these simple techniques, let me tell you about the science behind heart coherence and how Dr. Servan-Schreiber came to use the HeartMath techniques.

Doctor, Heal Thyself

Dr. Servan-Schreiber remembers being on top of the world when he was in his early thirties. "I was doing cutting-edge research on brain function, had my own research lab, and the world at my feet." He was also a founding member of

Doctors Without Borders/Médecins Sans Frontières (MSF), an international medical humanitarian organization working in nearly seventy countries to assist people whose survival is threatened by violence, neglect, or catastrophe. He had dedicated his life to helping others.

He and his staff were conducting brain scan studies, and when one subject scheduled for a scan didn't arrive, he decided to be scanned himself rather than waste the time. When he was drawn into the circular tube that would measure his brain functions, he was excited to see pictures of his own brain. Moments later, his elation turned to terror. His colleague came in and helped him out of the scanning machine. "David, there's something wrong with the pictures," he said. "The scan shows you have brain cancer."

After dealing with the initial shock and a tearful exchange with his father in France, he underwent the traditional treatments of having the tumor surgically removed and the follow-up radiation and chemotherapy. When he asked his own doctors if there was anything else he could do to help himself heal, they told him "No, we don't know why some people get cancer and others don't. Just live your life as before and pray that the treatments work."

Like so many successful men, Servan-Schreiber returned to his high-paced lifestyle, drinking lots of soft drinks and eating high-fat fast foods. He did get better, for a time, but the tumor returned, and he once again had surgery, radiation, and chemo. Even doctors who are trained to look at all the options available tend to trust what is known and familiar and go along with their own doctor's recommendations.

But this time he decided to take his medical care into his own hands and learn all he could about alternative ways of treating cancer. He found out there was a great deal he could do to change his lifestyle, including the elimination of sugar from his diet, reducing fats, exercising, and reducing stress. The stress-reducing techniques he found most helpful involved learning to develop heart coherence. He wrote about his journey and what he'd learned in a new book, *Anti-Cancer: A New Way of Life,*[168] and shares his experience in a moving video clip[169] on YouTube.

Take a picture of this tag with your smartphone to see Dr. Servan-Schreiber's story about how he found alternative ways to deal with his brain cancer.

The Heart Has a Mind of Its Own: The Science Behind HeartMath

For centuries, the heart has been considered the source of emotion, courage, and wisdom. At the Institute of HeartMath (IHM) Research Center,[170] they are exploring the physiological mechanisms by which the heart communicates with the brain, thereby influencing information processing, perceptions, emotions, and health. They are asking questions such as:

- Why do people experience the feeling or sensation of love and other positive emotional states in the area of the heart, and what are the physiological ramifications of these emotions?

- How do stress and different emotional states affect the autonomic nervous system, the hormonal and immune systems, and the heart and brain?

Over the years, Dr. Rollin McCraty and the researchers at the Institute of HeartMath have experimented with different psychological and physiological measures, but it was consistently heart rate variability, or heart rhythms, that stood out as the most dynamic and reflective of inner emotional states and stress. It became clear that negative emotions led to increased disorder in the heart's rhythms and in the autonomic nervous system, thereby adversely affecting the rest of the body. In contrast, positive emotions created increased harmony and coherence in heart rhythms and improved balance in the nervous system. The health implications are easy to understand: disharmony in the nervous system leads to inefficiency and increased stress on the heart and other organs, while harmonious rhythms are more efficient and less stressful to the body's systems.

Our heart beats in a rhythm. Research at the Institute of HeartMath[171] found that when we are overstimulated, overloaded, stressed, frustrated, worried, or anxious the rhythm becomes jagged and irregular. The more stressed we are, the more chaotic and incoherent the heart rhythm becomes (see left half of graph below). When our hearts are "incoherent," everything gets out of whack, from our sleep patterns to our ability to function well at work.

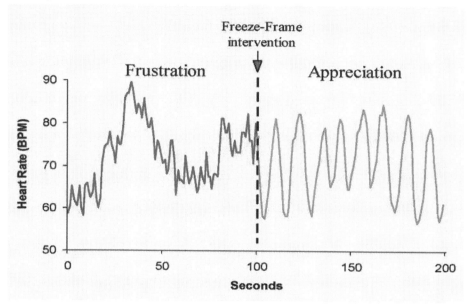

So what can make our heart rhythm smooth out fast? **Research shows that sincere positive feelings—like love, care, gratitude, appreciation, compassion, or joy—smooth out our heart rhythm into a harmonious coherent pattern.** (See right half of graph above). These nurturing feelings also reduce the stress hormone cortisol and increase DHEA (the vitality hormone) to help us sleep more soundly and wake up feeling more refreshed.

What's interesting here is that both of the above graphs are of the same person feeling one way and then another within a period of a few minutes. This smooth, coherent heart rhythm is the pattern that naturally occurs during deep, restful sleep. And what's exciting for those of us who are sleep deprived is that we can learn to move intentionally into this smooth pattern.

But heart coherence can do more than help us sleep well. Positive emotions create increased harmony and coherence in heart rhythms and improve balance in the nervous system. The health implications are easy to understand: disharmony in the nervous system leads to inefficiency and increased stress on the heart and other organs.

Research by Dr. Robert Emmons demonstrates that *gratitude* is a particularly positive emotion. "Gratitude is a key to happiness," he says. In his book *Thanks: How Practicing Gratitude Can Make You Happier,* he describes findings from a study of people who kept a simple journal of things they were grateful for each day for three weeks. He found that those who practiced gratitude slept better, had more energy, reported fewer symptoms of illness, felt better about their lives as a whole, and were more optimistic about the future.[172]

The word "emotion" (E-motion) literally means "energy in motion." It's derived from the Latin verb meaning "to move." While a "feeling"—a closely related concept—is any conscious experience of sensation, an emotion is a *strong* feeling. A feeling such as *love, joy, sorrow,* or *anger* literally moves us. Big changes occur in our bodies when we are experiencing strong emotions, and they move us to interact with others.

In their book *The HeartMath Solution,* authors Doc Childre and Howard Martin say, "Emotions serve as carrier waves for the entire spectrum of feelings. **When our hearts are in a state of coherence, we more easily experience feelings such as love, care, appreciation, and kindness. On the other hand, feelings such as irritation, anger, hurt, and envy are more likely to occur when the head and heart are out of alignment.**

Our emotional experiences become imprinted in our brain cells and memory, where they form patterns that influence our behavior." [173]

Emotions are such an intrinsic part of our lives that we tend to take them for granted. Think what life would be like if we held a child or grandchild in our arms, but couldn't feel the emotions of joy, awe, and wonder. The world would be a cold and dismal place if we couldn't feel passion and desire when we fall in love. We also know the pain and suffering we feel when we are consumed by anger, grief, or jealousy. And we've all had the experience of feeling closed down emotionally, when we couldn't feel anything and just felt numb.

One of the most important findings from energy healing is that these tools can be used to free our emotions. Researchers at HeartMath observed the heart acting as though it had a mind of its own and was profoundly influencing the way we perceive and respond to the world. In essence, it appears the heart affects intelligence and awareness. **"The heart with a mind of its own"—what an interesting concept.**

The Heart's Electromagnetic Field

The heart is the most powerful generator of electromagnetic energy in the human body, producing the largest rhythmic electromagnetic field of any of the body's organs. **The heart's electrical field is about sixty times greater in amplitude than the electrical activity generated by the brain. Furthermore, the magnetic field produced by the heart is more**

than five thousand times greater in strength than the field generated by the brain.

This field, measured by an electrocardiogram (ECG), can be detected anywhere on the surface of the body. It can be detected a number of feet away from the body, in all directions, using SQUID-based magnetometers.[174]

The Heart's Electromagnetic Field

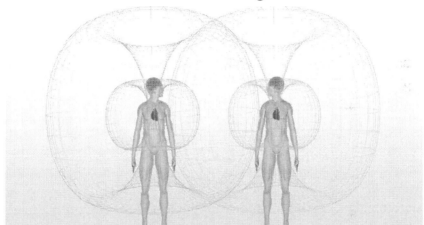

Research at the Institute demonstrates the intriguing finding that the electromagnetic signals generated by the heart have the capacity to affect others around us. Their data indicate that one person's heart signal can affect another's brainwaves, and that heart/brain synchronization can occur between two people when they interact. Finally, it appears that as individuals increase heart/brain coherence, they become more sensitive to the subtle electromagnetic signals communicated by those around them. Taken together, these results suggest that cardioelectromagnetic communication may be a little-known source of information exchange between people and that this exchange is influenced by our emotions.

So not only is heart/brain coherence good for your own health and wellbeing, it can be good for your spouse, children, and friends. The more we can find ways to keep our emotions positive, the better our own lives will be and the better those around us will feel. Of course, this is easier said than done. But there are simple techniques you can easily learn that can bring about miraculous results.

Heart/Brain Communication

Traditionally, the study of communication pathways between the "head" and heart has been rather one dimensional, with scientists focusing primarily on the heart's responses to the brain's commands. However, research now shows that communication between the heart and brain is actually a dynamic, ongoing, two-way dialogue, with each organ continuously influencing the other's function. Research shows the heart communicates to the brain in four major ways:

- Neurological communication (nervous system)
- Biophysical communication (pulse wave)
- Biochemical communication (hormones)
- Energetic communication (electromagnetic fields).

Taken together, the results of these studies demonstrate that intentionally altering one's emotional state through heart focus modifies neurological input from the heart to the brain.[175] The data suggest that as people experience sincere positive emotional states in which the heart's rhythms become more coherent, the changed information flow from the heart to the brain may modify brain function and influence performance. These findings may also help explain the significant shifts in perception, increased mental clarity, and heightened intuitive awareness many individuals report when practicing the HeartMath techniques.

Recent research indicates the heart is far more than a simple pump. The heart is, in fact, a highly complex, self-organized information processing center with its own functional "brain" that communicates with and influences the cranial brain via the nervous system, hormonal system, and other pathways. These influences profoundly affect brain function and most of the body's major organs, and they ultimately determine quality of life.

This was the beginning of the new discipline of "neurocardiology," which has since provided critically important insights into the nervous system within the heart and how the brain and heart communicate with each other via the nervous system. After extensive research, one of the early pioneers in neurocardiology, Dr. J. Andrew Armour, introduced the concept of a functional "heart brain" in 1991. His work revealed that the heart has a complex intrinsic nervous system that is sufficiently sophisticated to qualify as a "little brain" in its own right. The heart's brain is an intricate network of several types of neurons, neurotransmitters, proteins, and support cells like those found in the brain proper. Its elaborate circuitry enables it to act independently of the cranial brain, to learn, remember, and even feel and sense.

Numerous experiments have now demonstrated that the messages the heart sends the brain affect our perceptions, mental processes, feeling states, and performance in profound ways.

The Mental and Emotional Systems

Dating back to the ancient Greeks, human thinking and feeling have been considered separate functions. These contrasting aspects of the soul, as the Greeks called them, have often been portrayed as being engaged in a constant battle for control of the human psyche. In Plato's view, emotions were like wild horses that had to be reined in by the intellect. The seventeenth century philosopher René Descartes tried to make peace with the Catholic Church by splitting the world into two different types of substances: mind and body. Science would learn everything about the body, what Descartes called "extended matter," while religion would deal with the soul or mind.

But increasingly, we are learning that mind and body are intimately connected, and our mental and emotional lives are related. In his best-selling book *Emotional Intelligence,* Daniel Goleman argues that the pervading view of human intelligence as essentially mind intellect is far too narrow, for it ignores a range of human capacities that bear equal, if not greater, weight in determining our successes in life.

He builds a strong case for a largely overlooked domain of intelligence, called emotional intelligence, which is based on such qualities as self-awareness, motivation, altruism, and compassion. According to Goleman, it is a high EQ (emotional quotient) more than a high IQ that marks people who excel in the face of life's challenges.

Anyone who has ever been in the conventional nine-to-five working world knows that most problems have to do with people's emotions—their anger, resistance, suspiciousness, and so on—rather than problems with their intellectual knowledge. The latest research in neuroscience confirms that emotion and cognition can best be thought of as separate but interacting functions or systems, each with its unique intelligence.

Ongoing research at the Institute of HeartMath is showing that the key to the successful integration of the mind and emotions lies in increasing the coherence (ordered, harmonious function) in both systems and bringing them into phase with each other.

This helps explain the tremendous power of emotions, in contrast to thought alone. Our emotions are powerful motivators of future behaviors. For instance, when we feel irritable, we are on the lookout for things that our partners might do that we don't like. We may pick a fight, convinced that the other person provoked us, when it was our emotions that set us up for conflict.

Emotions can easily bump mundane events out of awareness, but non-emotional forms of mental activity (like thoughts) do not so readily displace emotions in the mental landscape. Likewise, experience reminds us that the most pervasive thoughts—those least easily dismissed—are typically those fueled by the greatest intensity of emotion.

Because emotions exert such a powerful influence on cognitive activity, research shows that intervening at the emotional level is often the most efficient way to initiate change in mental patterns and processes. Research at the Institute of HeartMath and other centers demonstrates that the application of tools and techniques designed to increase coherence in the emotional system can often bring the mind into greater coherence as well.

Emotional Wellbeing Can Have A Profound Impact on Your Health

A growing body of compelling scientific evidence is demonstrating the link between mental and emotional attitudes, physiological health and long-term wellbeing.

- A Harvard Medical School Study of 1,623 heart attack survivors found that when subjects became angry during emotional conflicts, their risk of subsequent heart attacks was more than double that of those who remained calm.[176]
- Men who complain of high anxiety are up to six times more likely than calmer men to suffer sudden cardiac death.[177]
- A twenty-year study of more than seventeen hundred older men conducted by the Harvard School of Public Health found that worry about social conditions, health, and personal finances all significantly increase the risk of coronary heart disease.[178]

- According to a Mayo Clinic study of individuals with heart disease, psychological stress is the strongest predictor of future cardiac events such as cardiac death, cardiac arrest, and heart attacks.[179]
- Three ten-year studies conclude that emotional stress is more predictive of death from cancer and cardiovascular disease than smoking. People who are unable to effectively manage their stress have a 40 percent higher death rate than non-stressed individuals.[180]
- An international study of 2,829 people between the ages of fifty-five and eighty-five found that individuals who reported the highest levels of personal "mastery"—feelings of control over life events—had a nearly 60 percent lower risk of death compared with those who felt relatively helpless in the face of life's challenges.[181]

How You Can Use the Simple Heart-Coherence Tool to Reduce Stress and Improve Health

Hewlett-Packard, Motorola, and all five branches of the U.S. military are now using HeartMath techniques to teach employees how to become more mentally and emotionally balanced and provide for individual and organizational transformation. In addition, educators have found that school children can better manage their behavior and improve their ability to absorb academic information by using the techniques pioneered by Doc Childre and Rollin McCraty at the Institute of HeartMath.

We've all heard about the many benefits of meditation. It can calm the mind and body, release tension, and reduce the negative effects of stress. Meditation also helps us gain more inner balance and peace. More medical professionals are recommending meditation as a way to decompress and relieve stress. A 2004 Centers for Disease Control and Prevention survey found that nineteen million people in the United States practice some form of meditation. Even though many of us know the benefits of meditation, we don't always take time to do it. I've found that I can use the quick heart-coherence tool to reduce stress even when I'm too busy to take time to relax.

You can use the Quick Coherence® Technique[182] to bring your heart rhythms into coherence and enable your brain to synchronize with your heart's coherent rhythm. You can start by learning how to shift into a heart-focused, positive emotional state with three simple steps. Create a coherent state in about a minute with the simple but powerful steps of the Quick Coherence® Technique. Using the power of your heart to balance thoughts and emotions, you can achieve energy, mental clarity, and feel better fast, no matter where you are. Use Quick Coherence® especially when you begin feeling a draining emotion such as frustration, irritation, anxiety, or anger. Quick Coherence® will allow you to find a feeling of ease and inner harmony that's reflected in more balanced heart rhythms, thus facilitating brain function and more access to higher intelligence.

The Quick Coherence® Technique helps create a coherent state, offering access to your heart's intelligence. It uses the power of your heart to balance thoughts and emotions, helping you achieve a neutral, poised state for clear thinking. It is a powerful technique that connects you with your energetic heart zone to help you release stress, balance your emotions, and feel better fast. I've found that the Quick Coherence® Technique is easy to learn, has solid science to back up its value, and is a very effective tool for reducing stress in your life.

There are three steps:

Step 1: Heart Focus. Focus your attention on the area around your heart, in the center of your chest. The first couple of times you try it, place your hand over the center of your chest to help keep your attention in the heart area.

Step 2: Heart Breathing. Breathe deeply but normally, and feel as if your breath is coming in and going out through your heart area. As you inhale, feel as if your breath is flowing in through your heart, and as you exhale, feel it leaving through this area. Breathe slowly and casually, a little deeper than normal. Continue breathing with ease until you find a natural inner rhythm that feels good to you.

Step 3: Heart Feeling. As you maintain your heart focus and heart breathing, activate a positive feeling. Recall a positive feeling, a time when you felt good inside, and try to re-experience the feeling. It may be a memory of your family or your children when they were young. One of the easiest ways to generate a positive, heart-based feeling is to remember a special place you've been or the love you feel for a close friend or family member or treasured pet. This is the most important step.

Quick Coherence® is especially useful when you start to feel a draining emotion such as frustration, irritation, anxiety, or stress. Using Quick Coherence at the onset of less intense negative emotions can keep them from escalating into something worse. It also works after you've had an emotional blow-up to bring yourself back into balance quickly.

You can do the Quick Coherence® Technique anytime, anywhere, and no one will know you're doing it. In less than a minute, it creates positive changes in your heart rhythms, sending powerful signals to the brain that can improve how you're feeling. Apply this one-minute technique first thing in the morning, before or during phone calls or meetings, in the middle of a difficult conversation, when you feel overwhelmed or pressed for time, or anytime you simply want to increase your coherence. You can also use Quick Coherence whenever you need more coordination, speed, and fluidity in your reactions.

I've found this is a deceptively simple technique. Like many of you will learn, it seems so easy that even a child could do it. It is very effective for children as well as adults. But don't be fooled by its simplicity. It produces amazing results. Try it on for size and see how it fits you. If you find you'd like to learn other, related techniques for reducing stress, you can visit the Institute of HeartMath website.[183]

Practice, Practice, Practice

Do you remember the joke about the guy in New York who was stopped on the street with the question, "How do I get to Carnegie Hall?" The answer, of course, is "Practice, practice, practice." Well, I don't think I'll ever become a great musician and open at Carnegie Hall to a packed house. But I can practice heart coherence. It has become a well-used energy healing tool.

When I'm having a bad day, things often start to escalate. I may have slept poorly the night before and woke up with a headache. My wife was harried, and I left home feeling slightly irritable. The client I had been hurrying to meet canceled on me. You know the kind of day I mean. Each little imbalance seems to contribute to the next. By the end of the day, I'm about ready to explode, and the next person I encounter gets the brunt of my frustration.

When I use the Quick Coherence® Technique, I'm able to head off these days from hell before they ever get started. When I first feel those "ticklings of tension," as I call them, I whip out my Quick Coherence tool, and I can feel my heart and soul relaxing. As we become more attuned to the rhythms, we begin to learn more about love and how to reduce stress in our relationships.

CHAPTER 7:
ATTACHMENT LOVE

I got married and started graduate school the same year, 1966. The world was simpler then. The world population was 3.4 billion, unemployment in the U.S. was 4.5 percent, and the cost of a first-class postage stamp was five cents. In my course work in psychology, we read Sigmund Freud, and I was glad to get some guidance from the father of modern psychology. He said, "Love and work are the cornerstones of our humanness."

"Well, I have the *love thing* down," I thought. I had married my college sweetheart. And I was sure with a master's degree in social welfare, the *work thing* wouldn't be a problem.

By 2009, things had changed. The world population had doubled to 6.8 billion, unemployment was 9.3 percent, and the cost of a first-class postage stamp was forty-four cents. I had lost my secure job with the state and later with the county and was in private practice as a psychotherapist. The love thing also turned out to be more complicated than I thought when I got married at age twenty-two. My wife and I had gotten a divorce in 1976, and our two children went back and forth between the two of us. I had a disastrous rebound marriage with a woman who slept with a gun under her pillow. Luckily,

I got out of that marriage with my life, though my emotions were shot. When I met and married Carlin, I knew I had finally matured enough to have a relationship that would last. But I found out there were still things I needed to learn about love.

That learning came in an unexpected way. I needed to have a bunch of continued education units to renew my therapy license, and time was running out. At the last minute, I found a seven-day conference called The Evolution of Psychotherapy that would give me all the units I needed. The names of the speakers read like a who's who of the most well-known experts in the field: Daniel Amen, Aaron Beck, Deepak Chopra, Andrew Weil, Martin Seligman, James Hillman, William Glasser, John Gottman, Jean Houston, Thomas Szasz, and Harville Hendrix. Among all these professionals, it turned out that the person who most affected the way I looked at men, women, sex, and love was a soft-spoken woman from Canada named Sue Johnson.

Attachment Love: The Energy Essence of Intimacy

"I have always been fascinated by relationships," Johnson told the conference attendees. "I grew up in Britain, where my dad ran a pub, and I spent a lot of time watching people meeting, talking, drinking, brawling, dancing, and flirting. But the focal point of my young life was my parent's' marriage. I watched helplessly as they destroyed their marriage and themselves."[184]

Johnson continued, "My response to my parent's' pain was to vow never to get married. Romantic love was, I decided, an illusion and a trap. I was better off on my own, free and unfettered. But then, of course, I fell in love and married. Love pulled me in even as I pushed it away."[185] Sound familiar?

Many of us have been burned by love and vowed to keep ourselves safe and not get pulled in again. But, inevitably, we do. Then we vow that this time, it's going to be different. This time, we're not going to make the same mistakes. And things seem wonderful—for a while. But more often than not, the same problems come up over and over. The fights start, along with the cold silences that are much worse than the fights. "Not again," we lament. "What the hell went wrong?"

Unlike most of us, Johnson vowed to find the answer to these perpetual questions. She wanted to know why couples start off fine then get off track. She watched couples interact and slowly began to figure out the rules of success and failure.

"Love, it seemed, was all about nonnegotiables," she said. "You can't bargain for compassion, for connection. These are not intellectual reactions; they are *emotional* responses. So I started to simply stay with the couples' experiences and let them teach me about the emotional rhythms and patterns in the dance of romantic love. I began to tape my couple sessions and replay them over and over again."[186]

One of the common complaints she heard from men was feeling unappreciated. **"I don't matter to her," she remembers a middle-aged man saying. "I am way down on her list. I come somewhere after the kids, the house, and her family. Hell, even the dog comes before me! I just bring home the money. So I end up feeling somehow empty. You never know if the love will be there or not."**[187]

Looking back over my own life with Carlin, I realize that the times I've become angry and abusive or withdrawn and silent most often happened when my emotional needs weren't being met. I would be overrun with fears of being neglected or abandoned. But I felt ashamed of my emotional neediness. And then I would feel ashamed of feeling ashamed. I became enveloped in confusion. I wanted more than anything to be understood and appreciated. But I knew my judgments, hurt, and anger were driving Carlin farther and farther away.

After years of study and experience with couples, Sue Johnson developed what she called emotionally focused therapy, or EFT for short. I found it interesting that this set of techniques had the same initials as emotional freedom techniques (EFT), which I'll discuss more fully in the next chapter. Although the kind of attachment love techniques Sue Johnson teaches may seem very different from the emotional freedom techniques and other energy healing tools, I feel they actually work very well together. Most people who work with attachment love *wouldn't* consider them a type of energy healing, but I believe they are. **Attachment love gets at the energy essence of our innate desire for sex, love, and intimacy.**

A New Scientific Theory of Love

When I first met Johnson, she had just completed a tremendous amount of research on attachment love and was releasing her new book, *Hold Me Tight: Seven Conversations for a Lifetime of Love.* The conference was held in Los Angeles and triggered old memories of growing up there. Like Johnson, my early experiences were colored by the pain and suffering I saw in my family. My parents rarely fought, but I can still picture my father's angry eyes and my mother's shaming whispers to her friends about my father's inability to make a good living. Many therapists go into the field to try to understand their own parents, what happened to them, and what is happening to so many families today.

As I developed my therapy skills, it became evident that a lot of the problems people come to therapy to address have to do with their relationships with loved ones: a spouse, a parent, a child. It is clear that couples work is helpful, but working with them had been difficult and not always successful. Dealing with two people, with two sets of hot emotions and escalating fights, is not for the faint of heart.

Sue Johnson had similar experience, but she found answers that are changing the way we see ourselves, our relationships, and how we can help ourselves and others. Couples therapy is in the midst of a revolution. The key element in this revolution is the development of a new science of love and love relationships. As baseball legend Yogi Berra told us, "If you don't know where you're going, you wind up somewhere else." Without a clear model of love and the process of connection and disconnection, it is difficult to know how we can heal our past and have the kinds of loving relationships we want in the present.

The most recent scientific studies on love offer surprising understandings. They tell us that the nature of our emotional attachment with our partner is the foundation for the kind of love we truly long to have—a love that is secure, intimate, and gets better as time goes on.

In their book *Attached: The New Science of Adult Attachment and How it Can Help you Find—and Keep—Love,* Dr. Amir Levine and Rachel Heller tell us that "*dependency* is not a bad word."[188] They go on to describe the key findings from the new science of love:

- Your attachment needs are legitimate.
- You shouldn't feel bad for depending on the person you are closest to—it is part of your genetic makeup.
- A relationship, from an attachment perspective, should make you feel more self-confident and give you peace of mind. If it doesn't, this is a wake-up call![189]

This certainly wasn't what I learned in graduate school when I was studying Freudian theory and being taught psychotherapy for individuals and couples. I was taught that maturity means being independent and self-sufficient. If I felt afraid or needed to be held and comforted, I felt that I was acting like a baby. I was sure that if I didn't "act like a man," I'd have no chance to find a woman who would want me or be able to hang onto one once I found her.

I now understand that my desire for nurturing and connection was based on science, not sentimentality. It was one of those life-changing "aha" moments. My whole life, I had been putting myself down whenever I felt I needed love, touch, and nurturing. I told myself, and others told me, that if I acted "needy," I wasn't a real man.

- "Quit acting like a child."
- "Don't look so defeated."
- "Man up!"

These were some of the words that cut me to the core and enveloped me in shame. I learned early on, as did most men, to keep my feelings locked inside and show the world that I could "take it" like a man without flinching or showing any weakness. It was truly an experience of emotional freedom to realize there wasn't something wrong with me. **The real problem isn't our desire for emotional nurturing and intimacy, it is a culture that denies our real needs and teaches people that to be "normal" is to be distant and independent.**

When Men Aren't Allowed to Be Attached, Their Grief Turns to Rage

In my therapy practice, I see men who are so hungry for love they become irritable and angry when they don't get it. When one member of a couple gets angry, the other usually withdraws or becomes angry herself. Either way, many men often end up feeling lonely, and women end up feeling hurt and confused. "I don't understand what's going on," one woman told me. "Sometimes he seems so needy, he's like a little kid. At other times, he totally rejects my love and almost seems to hate me."

Anthropologist David D. Gilmore finds this same dynamic with men throughout the world. In his book *Misogyny: The Male Malady,* he says, "Misogyny is not a single-sided hatred of women or a desire to dominate, but rather an affective ambivalence among men."[190] His research shows that most men love and hate women, simultaneously and in equal measure, that most men need women desperately, and that most men reject this driving need as both unworthy and dangerous.

Sam Keen also recognized this near-universal ambivalence men have toward women when their attachment needs are not allowed expression and given support. He posits an archetypal WOMAN that influences the way all men relate to a specific woman. "It was slow in dawning on me that WOMAN had an overwhelming influence on my life and the on the lives of all the men I knew," Keen says in his book, *Fire in the Belly: On Being a Man.*[191]

When our attachment needs aren't met, whether in childhood or adulthood, we approach our partners as men dying of thirst in the desert. We become desperate for the lifesaving love she can give, but we feel ashamed that we need it and angry at her for our dependence. "The secret men seldom tell, and often do not know (consciously), is the extent to which our lives circle around our relationships to WOMAN," says Keen. "She is the audience before whom the dramas of our lives are played out. She is the judge who pronounces us guilty or innocent. She is the Garden of Eden from which we are exiled and the paradise for which our bodies long. She is the goddess who can grant us salvation and the frigid mother who denies us."[192]

It's no wonder we feel that we can't live with them and can't live without them. This also offers an explanation about why so many midlife men withdraw from their wives just when the children are grown and they can finally have the time together they wanted. Men hunger for this intimacy, but they are afraid of it and often reject it when it is offered. Traditional male conditioning teaches us that we must be independent in order to maintain our freedom. Attachment love teaches us that real freedom is only possible when we accept that we are dependent on those we love.

Say Good-bye to James Bond and the Lone Ranger

"The attachment view of love was, and perhaps still is, radically out of line with our culture's established social and psychological ideas of adulthood," says Johnson.[193] She goes on to detail the kind of cultural norms both women and men have grown up believing:

- Maturity means being independent and self-sufficient.
- We value the notion of the invulnerable warrior who faces life and danger alone, with images like the Lone Ranger or James Bond.
- Even therapists have the view that mature adulthood is synonymous with being self-contained. Johnson says that many therapists use words like *undifferentiated, codependent, symbiotic,* or even *fused* to describe people who seem unable to be self-sufficient.
- Men who show their emotional, vulnerable sides are often viewed as *wimps, Momma's boys,* or *"weak."*
- Men and women are taught to deny important parts of themselves. What we demand of men, we deny to women and vice versa. For instance, men **must be** and women **cannot be**: logical, aggressive, active, outspoken, rugged, tough. Men **cannot be** and women **must**

be: emotional, nurturing, passive, tender, receptive, tender.

It's no wonder that most of us would rather die than allow ourselves, or those we love, to see how emotionally vulnerable we really are. From the cradle to the grave, we are conditioned to believe that it isn't manly to cry, to ask to be held when we are afraid, or to be talked to with quiet words of kindness and love. I remember a cartoon illustrating our view that "real men" need to be tough by H. Kliban, a cartoon which is a bit weird, but insightful. It shows a man and a woman sitting across from each other in a restaurant having a romantic dinner. The woman has just picked up a fork and stabbed the man in the bridge of his nose. The caption reads, "That's what I love about you, Louie…You're tough."

I still wince every time I think of the cartoon. I can still remember the pain of trying to force myself to be tough. I still hurt remembering all the times I tried to prove to women that I was worthy of their love by demonstrating that I could take whatever punishment life handed out to me. I can't tell you how many times I've heard a woman complain to me about her husband: "It's as though I've got another child in the home. He's so needy and demanding of my attention. I just wish he'd grow up." It's no wonder men choose to be "lone rangers" rather than admit how emotionally vulnerable we are.

So listen up, guys, we need to let go of our old beliefs of what it means to be a man. We need to say good-bye to the Lone Ranger and James Bond, the iconic impervious man still going strong after four decades. We need to stay away from therapists who use words like *undifferentiated, codepend-*

ent, needy, symbiotic, or *fused* to describe people who seem unable to be self-sufficient or aggressively assert themselves with others.

Emotional Isolation Is the Killer, and Attachment Love is the Life-Saver

The old messages that require us to be strong, silent, and independent are ingrained into our psyches. In my practice, I see too many men who feel the loss of connection with their partners, but rather than standing up for their needs, they bale out of the relationship. They are like confused homing pigeons that long for the comfort and security of their family, but fly 180 degrees in the wrong direction. Our social blinders keep us from seeing and appreciating the attachment needs we have.

Psychologist Jim Coan of the University of Virginia says, "The people we love are the *hidden regulators* of our bodily processes and our emotional lives. When love doesn't work, we hurt."[194]

In fact, "hurt feelings" is a precisely accurate phrase. Brain imaging studies by psychologist Naomi Eisenberger of the University of California show that rejection and exclusion trigger the same circuits in the same part of the brain, the anterior cingulate, as physical pain. In fact, this part of the brain turns on any time we are emotionally separated from those who are close to us.[195]

"Attachment theory teaches us that our loved one is our shelter in life," says Johnson. "When that person is emotionally unavailable or unresponsive, we face being out in the cold, alone and helpless. We are assailed by emotions: anger, sadness, hurt, and above all, fear."[196] Dr. Johnson concludes, **"Contact with a loving partner literally acts as a buffer against shock, stress, and pain."**[197]

The latest research demonstrates that being securely attached to our partner is not only essential to a loving relationship, it is essential to our health. James House of the University of Michigan declares, **"Emotional isolation is a more dangerous health risk than smoking or high blood pressure."**[198]

This need for emotional connection is not a sentimental notion, Johnson says. "Love is not the icing on the cake of life. It is a basic primary need, like oxygen or water," Johnson asserts. "Once we understand and accept this, we can more easily get to the heart of relationship problems."[199]

Research by men's health expert, Thomas Joiner, PhD, validates these findings. In his recent book *Lonely at the Top: The High Cost of Men's Success,* Joiner says the main problem men share is loneliness, and this problem is deadly.[200]

"A 2008 study found that men, far more than women, have trouble trusting and reaching out for help from others, including from health care professionals. A postmortem report on a suicide decedent, a man in his sixties, read, 'He did not have friends...He did not feel comfortable with other men...He did not trust doctors and would not seek help even though he was aware he needed help."[201] These words would fit many men I know, including myself, before I learned about the importance of attachment love.

Male loneliness, I have found, is often evident in our relationships with those we love. Our early training to become "lone rangers" often keeps us isolated and alone. But the new science of love tells us that we can break these old patterns. I still remember the lines from the Eagles song "Desperado": "You better let somebody love you. You better let somebody love you. You better let somebody love you, before it's too late."

The Real Reason Marriages Fail and How You Can Protect Your Own

According to a landmark study by Ted Huston of the University of Texas, when marriages fail, it's frequently not increasing conflict that is the cause. Rather, the cause is decreasing affection and emotional responsiveness. Indeed, lack of emotional responsiveness, rather than level of conflict, is the best predictor of how solid a marriage will be five years in. The demise of most marriages begins with a growing absence of responsive intimate interactions. The conflict comes later.[202]

This third energy healing tool allows us to bring the best of who we are into our relationships. With all the changes going on in the world, we need our intimate relationships more than ever. We can become healthy, wealthy in the things that money can never buy, and truly wise in the ways of intimacy and love. What more could a man want?

If the theories of Sigmund Freud were seminal in the twentieth century, those of John Bowlby will guide us in the twenty-first. Bowlby was a British psychiatrist, notable for his interest in child development and for his pioneering work in attachment theory. Born in 1907, Bowlby, like many upper-class children of the time, was primarily raised by nannies and governesses. His parents allowed him to join them at the dinner table after he turned twelve, and then only for dessert. He was then sent off to boarding school and later attended Trinity College, Cambridge.

Bowlby's life was changed forever when he volunteered to work in the innovative residential schools for emotionally disturbed children being started by visionary A. S. Neill. These schools focused on offering emotional support rather than the usual stern discipline. As he learned more, he came to believe that the quality of the connection to loved ones and early emotional deprivation is critical to the development of personality and to an individual's habitual way of connecting with others.[203] "As a psychologist and as a human being," says Johnson, "if I had to give an award for the single best set of ideas anyone had ever had, I'd give it to John Bowlby hands down over Freud or anyone else in the business of understanding people."[204]

Jaak Panksepp,[205] in his neurobiological studies, finds that loss of connection from attachment figures triggers "primal panic," a special set of fear responses. As Bowlby notes, the words "anxiety" and "anger" come from the same etymological root and both arise at moments of disconnection, when attachment figures are nonresponsive. **I firmly believe that a great deal of men's anger stems from feeling disconnected from those whose love and nurture we depend upon.**

Bowlby died in 1990. He didn't live to see the second revolution sparked by his work: the application of attachment theory to adult love. Research documenting adult attachment began just before Bowlby's death. Social psychologists Phil Shaver and Cindy Hazan, then at the University of Denver, asked men and women questions about their love relationships to see if they exhibited the same responses and patterns as mothers and children. They wrote a "love quiz" that examined the attachment style of men and women between the ages of fourteen and eighty-two. The men and women were clear about what they needed the most:

- Emotional closeness from their lover
- Assurance that their lover would respond when they were upset
- Support when they felt separate and distant from their loved one
- Knowledge that their lover "had their back"

They also learned that when people feel secure with their lovers, they can reach out and connect easily; when they feel insecure, they either become *anxious, angry, controlling,* or *distant* from their lover. Does this make sense to you? It really resonated with me. The times I got the angriest were those times when I felt disconnected from my wife. And of course, the angrier I became, the more she withdrew. Learning to break those cycles is one of the gifts of learning attachment love skills.

Many of us can identify with the title of a Notorious Cherry Bombs song, "It's Hard to Kiss the Lips at Night that Chew Your Ass Out All Day Long."[206]

The Pain and Suffering When We Don't Feel Secure With the One We Love

If you look through the attachment lens, the negative spirals that distressed couples create and are victimized by are all about separation distress—the deprivation and emotional starvation that comes from emotional disconnection. "When we cannot get an attachment figure to respond to us, we step into a wired-in sequence of protest, first hopeful and then angry, desperate and coercive," says Johnson.[207] We seek contact any way we can. One of Johnson's clients told her, "I poke him and poke him—anything to get a response from him, to know I matter to him." If we cannot get a response, despair and depression come to claim us.

If we cannot find a way to turn toward our partner and shape a safe connection, there are really only two other secondary strategies open to us, and they map onto two emotional realities with exquisite logic. **Strategy one is to become caught in** *fear of abandonment* **and demand responsiveness by** *blaming and shaming our partner.* Of course, this often threatens the other and pushes this person further away, especially if this strategy becomes habitual and automatic. **Strategy two is to** *numb out* **attachment needs and feelings and** *avoid engagement* **(and conflict). In this strategy, we shut down and withdraw.** Unfortunately, this shuts the other person out. Both these secondary strategies are ways of trying to hang onto an attachment relationship and deal with difficult feelings. But they aren't healthy and frequently create a result 180 degrees from what we want.

In my relationship with Carlin, I used to become blaming and shaming, although I didn't see it at the time. To me, I just wanted connection. I desperately wanted her love and respect, but the way I went about getting it created more distance. Carlin would numb out and withdraw. Gradually, I began to recognize that my anger was causing her to withdraw more, and she began to see that her shutting down and withdrawing was causing me to become more frightened and angry.

I recognized similar patterns with clients who came to me for therapy. I could often see it more clearly in them than in my own relationship. Once they learned to order and name their feelings, things began to change for the better. The *blamers* speak of feeling alone, unimportant, abandoned, and insignificant. Underneath their anger, they are extremely vulnerable. *Withdrawers* speak of feeling ashamed and afraid of hearing that they are failures. They believe they can never please their partners and so feel helpless and paralyzed.

The Emotionally Attached Couple

Like all of the tools described in this book, a trained therapist can be very helpful, but it is not necessary. With a commitment to the relationship and a willingness to be open to learning new skills, couples can do a lot of this work on their own. Here's what Johnson says in the introduction to her book, *Hold Me Right: Seven Conversations for a Lifetime of Love:*

"Forget about learning how to argue better, analyzing your early childhood, making grand romantic gestures, or experimenting with new sexual positions. Instead, recognize and admit that you are emotionally attached to and dependent on your partner in much the same way that a child is on a parent for nurturing, soothing, and protection. Adult attachment may be more reciprocal and less centered on physical contact, but the nature of the emotional bond is the same."[208]

She goes on to say that emotionally focused couple work creates and strengthens the emotional bond between partners by identifying and transforming the key moments that foster an adult loving relationship: being open, attuned, and responsive to each other.

I've found that both men and women find it easier to accept that women need this kind of emotional support. **However, we often resist the reality that men need it just as much, or even more than, women.** It took me and my wife a long time to accept that it was "manly" to ask for help, support, and nurturing, that I wasn't acting like a child if I cried or felt frightened and lost. It helped us both to remember that our boys needed just this kind of love when they were little. We never felt that our little girl needed more nurturing than our little boys. It stands to reason that when we grow to be adults, men need this just as much as women.

Activating Attachment Love In Your Own Life

In her book *Hold Me Tight: Seven Conversations for a Lifetime of Love,* she tells us how to understand the true nature of love and how we can all express it more fully in our relationships. In Dr. Johnson's program, the key to a lifetime of good sex and love is "emotional responsiveness." The basis of Dr. Johnson's approach is to teach people the secrets contained in the phrase "How *ARE* you really?"

A is for *Accessibility*: Can I Reach You?

This means staying open to your partner even when you have doubts and feel insecure. It often means being willing to struggle to make sense of your emotions so these emotions are not so overwhelming. You can then step back from disconnection and tune in to your lover's attachment cues.

R is for *Responsiveness*: Can I Rely On You to Respond to Me Emotionally?

This means tuning in to your partner and showing that his or her emotions, especially attachment needs and fears, have an impact on you. It means accepting and placing a priority on the emotional signals your partner conveys and sending clear signals of comfort and caring when your partner needs them. Sensitive responsiveness always touches us emotionally and calms us on a physical level.

E is for *Engagement*: Do I know you will value me and stay close?

The dictionary defines "engaged" as being absorbed, attracted, pulled, captivated, pledged, and involved. Emotional engagement here means the very special kind of attention that we give only to a loved one. We gaze at them longer and touch them more. Partners often talk of this as being emotionally present.

The ARE Questionnaire: How's Your Love Flowing?[209]

Johnson has developed a simple questionnaire that allows us to easily assess the strength of our emotional connection. Simply read each statement and circle T for true or F for false. To score the questionnaire, give one point for each true answer. You can complete the questionnaire and reflect on your relationship on your own. Or you and your partner can each complete it and then discuss your answers together as described just after the questionnaire. Remember, we don't have to have perfect scores to have a relationship that survives and thrives. This will help you recognize your relationship strengths and weaknesses. We all have some of both.

From your viewpoint, is your partner *accessible to you?*

1. I can get my partner's attention easily. **T F**
2. My partner is easy to connect with emotionally. **T F**
3. My partner shows me that I come first with him/her. **T F**
4. I am not feeling lonely or shut out in this relationship. **T F**
5. I can share my deepest feelings with my partner. He/she will listen. **T F**

From your viewpoint, is your partner responsive to you?

6. If I need connection and comfort, he/she will be there for me. **T F**
7. My partner responds to signals that I need him/her to come close. **T F**
8. I find I can lean on my partner when I am anxious or unsure. **T F**

9. Even when we fight or disagree, I know I am important to my partner and we will find a way to come together. **T F**

10. If I need reassurance about how important I am to my partner, I can get it. **T F**

Are you positively emotionally engaged with each other?

11. I feel very comfortable being close my partner. I trust him/her. **T F**

12. I can confide in my partner about almost anything. **T F**

13. I feel confident, even when we are apart, that we are connected to each other. **T F**

14. I know my partner cares about my joys, hurts, and fears. **T F**

15. I feel safe enough to take emotional risks with my partner. **T F**

Johnson says that a score of seven or above indicates that you are well on your way to a secure bond and can use the tools here to deepen what you already have. Don't worry if you scored below seven. It just means you haven't understood the importance of emotional bonding in a healthy relationship.

I realized that although I consciously believed each one of these statements was important in having a good relationship, unconsciously I had a lot of conflicts. I found that when Carlin felt insecure and wanted me to call home more often or asked for reassurance, I felt she was being "too needy." When I was hurting and wanting to be held, I often felt I was "acting like a child." It takes some work for most couples to overcome all the societal messages that tell us we shouldn't need each other in these deeply emotional ways.

Dr. Johnson shares her ideas on how we can tell if our marriage is in trouble and how to prevent a breakup in this video clip.[210] Take a picture of this tag with your smartphone to see and hear Dr. Johnson's important message of hope.

The Approach-Avoidance Dance: Men and Women Are Conditioned Differently

As a therapist, I often see couples locked into patterns that cause them both pain, but that are difficult to break. George gets angry at Patty and so she feels hurt and withdraws. The more Patty withdraws, the more it angers George. It's likely that George's anger comes because he doesn't feel Patty is there for him, but he isn't conscious of that fact or feels ashamed to admit it. The angrier George becomes, the more fearful Patty gets, which causes her to withdraw even more. These kinds of cycles can wear a couple down and cause them to feel hopeless.

If you were able to cut through the surface conflict to the core of what is really going on, George might say, "I get so mad with Patty. Whenever I try to tell her something important, she's always got better things to do. She doesn't listen. She withdraws. It drives me up the wall." Patty might say, "It scares me when George looks at me that way and has such anger in his voice. I feel like I've failed at something, but I don't know what it is. I just want to run away and lick my wounds." George believes he's just reacting to Patty, and she is convinced she is simply reacting to George. She withdraws. He gets angry. His anger triggers her withdrawal, and her withdrawal triggers his anger. Neither recognizes what is going on, and both end up feeling misunderstood and alone.

Of course, the roles can be reversed. Sometimes it's the woman who gets angry, and it is the man who withdraws. We often feel someone must be to blame. But the truth is that no one is to blame. We each need and depend on our partner, and if they seem unable or unwilling to meet our needs, we get scared. The destructive pattern, "the dance," is to blame. When couples recognize how things work, they can join together to change the nature of the dance.

Gender conditioning often plays a part as well. "In our society, women tend to be the caretakers of the relationship," says Johnson. "They usually pick up on distance sooner than their lovers and they are often more in touch with their attachment needs. So their role in the dance is most often the pursuing, more blaming spouse. Men, on the other hand, have been taught to suppress emotional responses and needs, and also to be problem solvers, which sets them up in the withdrawn role."[211]

Gender differences are also seen in the different ways men and women reach out to be touched. Tiffany Field, PhD, is director of the Touch Research Institute (TRI) at the University of Miami Medical School.[212] The TRI distinguished team of researchers, representing Duke, Harvard, Maryland, and other universities, strives to better define touch as it promotes health and contributes to the treatment of disease. **Their research indicates that North Americans are among the world's least tactile people and suffer from "touch hunger."** Males may be particularly vulnerable to touch hunger. Right from birth, boys are held for shorter periods and caressed less often than girls. My experience is that men need and want to be touched just as much as women, but we often don't know how to ask for it and feel frightened that our need to be held will be seen as unmanly.

Men are often accused of being preoccupied with sex. Well, we are, let's face it. Our hunger for sex is not only a desire for the sensual pleasure leading to orgasm. We also crave the skin-to-skin touch we rarely receive. For many men, sex is the only time we are touched and held. I get a regular massage every two weeks, and I love it when Carlin touches me. I think the world would be a more joyful, less violent place if men were touched more lovingly and more often.

True Connection: Using Your Attachment Love Tool

Thich Nhat Hahn, a Vietnamese Zen Buddhist monk, is an internationally known author, poet, scholar, and peace activist who was nominated for the Nobel Peace Prize by Martin Luther King Jr. His view of love is not based on scientific study, but he offers simple practices that fit well with what Sue Johnson and other attachment clinicians and researchers have found.

In a wonderful little book, *True Love: A Practice for Awakening the Heart,*[213] he offers a simple yet powerful process for expressing the emotional heart connection that can help us express our true love for our partner. "In Buddhism, we talk about mantras," says Hahn. "A mantra is a magic formula that, once it is uttered, can entirely change a situation, our mind, our body, or a person. But this magic formula must be spoken in a state of concentration, that is to say, a state in which body and mind are absolutely in a state of unity." He offers three love mantras that we can use every day.

Mantra #1: **Being present for your loved one**

When you are thinking about your loved one, or when you are in their presence, you say this simple phrase: "Dear one, I am really here for you." When I say this simple phrase and think of Carlin, I can feel my heart open to her. It makes us both feel wonderful. Even when she's not physically present, this works. *"Dear one, I am really here for you."* Of course, we can say these little mantra's out loud in our own words. I've often said with deep feeling when I see Carlin is hurting, "Hey, babe, I'm really here for you" and give her a hug.

Mantra #2: **Recognizing the presence of the other**

When you are really present for a loved one, you have the ability to recognize and "see" your partner in all their beauty. One of the greatest gifts we can give another person is to recognize and appreciate who they really are. As Thich Nhat

Hanh says, "To love is to be; to be loved is to be recognized by the other."

When we are loved, we wish the other to recognize our presence. You must do whatever is necessary to be able to do this. Take a deep breath in and release it. Do this several times. Then say the second mantra: *"Dear one, I know that you are here, and it makes me very happy."* Again, we can put this in our own words. I've often looked at Carlin with tears in my eyes and told her, "I'm so glad to be married to you. Having you in my life makes me feel warm and safe."

***Mantra #3:* Being there when someone is suffering**

We've all experienced how good it feels when someone is there for us when we're in physical or emotional pain. We also know how awful it is when we're hurting and our partner is not there for us. I know I'm not a very good patient. When I'm sick in body, mind, or spirit, I often get irritable and angry. It isn't easy for Carlin to be there for me when I'm like that, but that's when I need her most.

"When you are living mindfully," says Hahn, "you know what is happening in your situation in the present moment. Therefore it is easy for you to notice when the person you love is suffering." At such a time, you go to him or her with your body and mind unified, with concentration, and you offer the third mantra: *"Dear one, I know that you are suffering, that is why I am here for you."* Recently, Carlin found out she had a small breast tumor that was found early and removed. During the months of testing, preparation, and having the surgery, I repeated this mantra many times.

I've expanded on these mantras and use a simple set of attachment love practices that allows us to connect deeply with our needs for love and support in our intimate relationships. If you have a love partner, you can use it deepen your connection. If you don't have one, you can imagine the kind of person you would like to be in love with, or you can remember a time when you felt intimate and close to another person. This tool draws on what I've learned in my own love life, as well as what I've learned from Sue Johnson, Thich Nhat Hahn, and others.

1. Accept that we are deeply dependent on the love of our partner.

2. Close your eyes and take in a number of deep breaths. Slowly let them out. Allow yourself to feel your emotional need for your loved one. Say to yourself, "I know you love me, and I need your love and support." Remember a time when you were deeply and completely loved. If you don't remember ever having felt loved so completely, imagine what it would feel like.

3. Remember that our partner is deeply dependent on our love.

4. Take in and release a few deep breaths. Remember that your partner needs your love and support. Say to yourself, "I love you deeply and know how much you need my love and support." Remember a time when you allowed yourself to be totally open and loving with your partner. If you don't remember ever having been so completely loving, imagine what it would feel like.

5. Allow your partner to respond to you when you are hurting.

6. Take in a few deep breaths and release them. Remember that we often need our partners the most when we

are hurting inside. Recall a time when you were feeling scared, hurt, or wounded and your partner responded with warmth and support. If you don't remember ever allowing a partner to see your hurts and offer support, imagine what it would feel like.

7. Allow yourself to respond to your partner when she or he is hurting.

8. Take a number of deep breaths and let them out. Remember that your partner may need you the most when they are hurting, but their hurt may come across as irritability, anger, or some other emotion that may cause you to become more distant. Recall a time when you were totally there for your partner when they were hurting, or if you haven't had that experience, imagine what it would feel like.

The attachment love tool is simple and effective, but it isn't easy to use. Many of us don't have a lot of experience being emotionally supportive to our partners. We often feel inept and don't reach out to them. We may also have a difficult time allowing ourselves to be vulnerable to our partners.

Part of my "manly" training was that real men keep their pain to themselves. We grin and bear it, and we don't complain or let others know we are suffering. I've learned that I don't want to continue living with those unhealthy beliefs. I often remind myself of the mantra from the Eagles song "Desperado": **"You better let somebody love you, before it's too late."** I'm much better now at allowing Carlin to nurture me when I'm hurting, and it increases the emotional bond between us.

For most of us, it's easier to use these tools of love and be there for our partner when they are there for us. The most difficult time for me is when I'm feeling my needs aren't being met, when Carlin seems angry or withdrawn. It's much easier for me to give back what I'm getting. It's much more difficult to be understanding and tuned into her pain when she's angry or to reach out to her when she seems to be putting up a barrier to any contact. Remember, the universe gives us back what we put out. **If we want more love and understanding, we have to give more love and understanding, especially when we don't feel loved and understood.**

These simple tools for love are powerful and effective. Like all the tools I describe in the book, anyone can learn them and apply them in their lives. I guarantee that if you do, your life will improve. Because relationships are such a key part of who we are, learning these relationship skills can be particularly helpful. I've learned a lot from reading Thich Nhat Hahn's *True Love* and Sue Johnson's *Hold Me Tight*. If you'd like additional help and support, Johnson notes that there are therapists all over the world trained in using her methods. You can learn more by contacting the International Centre for Excellence in Emotionally Focused Therapy (ICEEFT). [214]

CHAPTER 8:
EMOTIONAL FREEDOM
TECHNIQUES (EFT)

Traditional Psychotherapist Meets Energy Medicine Maven

David Feinstein wasn't the first man to have his world turned upside down by a woman. But he may be the first to have such an encounter revolutionize the field of psychology and health care. Here's how he describes his journey in the book *The Promise of Energy Psychology: Revolutionary Tools for Dramatic Personal Change*,[215] which he wrote with his wife, Donna Eden, and Gary Craig, the founder of Emotional Freedom Techniques (EFT):

> My personal voyage into the perspective reflected here occurred over many years and with much resistance. I happened to marry a woman, Donna Eden, who was destined to become one of the world's most renowned natural healers. For the first nineteen years or so of our relationship, I did not know what to make of her work.

I had early in my own career served for seven years on the faculty of the Johns Hopkins University School of Medicine, a fount of innovation in heath care, but I'd never seen anything like this. As I witnessed people coming to see her from all over the world with serious illnesses report improvement after a session or two, I explained to myself that these outcomes were a product of Donna's empathy, charisma, belief in the power of her methods, and perhaps a peculiar healing presence. I certainly did not think it was a system that could be taught or replicated, and the "subtle energy" explanations that were bandied about by alternative healers seemed more confusing than clarifying.

For her part, Donna was confident in her methods and didn't even try to back them up with research support. When hard-pressed, she might cite an occasional quote by an authority, such as Nobel Laureate in Medicine Albert Szent-Györgyi's observation that, "In every culture and in every medical tradition before ours, healing was accomplished by moving energy."

"What energy?" I'd ask. "Electrical energy? Not in any studies I've seen! Kinetic, thermal, magnetic, chemical, nuclear?" Donna responded by talking about the "subtle energies" of meridians and chakras. I was unconvinced. You can imagine the dinner-table discussions.

When Donna was asked to do a book, she asked David to help her write it. He agreed, and he spent the next two years interviewing her day after day, trying to understand how she was able to heal and how they might teach the process to others. David continues with his description:

I eventually realized from the discussions with Donna leading to her book that she operates according to principles that are highly empirical, a fact that eluded me for nearly two decades. Her approach is based on observation (though through an unusual lens) and experimentation. She sees and feels where energies are not flowing or not in balance or not in harmony, uses her hands or other means to try to correct the problem and, based on what happens, figures out the next step. Everyone's hands actually have an electromagnetic field extending beyond the fingers, so simply holding one's hand over an affected part of the body can have a therapeutic effect, as can massaging, tapping, or holding specific energy points on the skin.[216]

Now I understood my first encounter with energy healing so many years ago, when the woman held her hands over her son's wound and he was okay by the time we got to the hospital. There really was something helpful in what she was doing. As I learned more about this kind of healing, I became more and more convinced that it was real.

As David delved more deeply trying to understand how Donna was able to bring about such powerful healings in the people she worked on, he developed a new understanding of *energy*. "Energy is the blueprint, the infrastructure, the invisible foundation for the health of your body," he says. "Your body is composed of energy pathways and energy centers that are in a dynamic interplay with your cells, organs, moods, and thoughts. **If you can shift these energies, you can influence your health, emotions, and state of mind.**"[217]

In the foreword to *The Promise of Energy Psychology*, neuroscientist Candace Pert says, "*The Promise of Energy Psychology* is a synthesis of practices designed to deliberately shift the molecules of emotion. These practices have three distinct advantages over psychiatric medications. They are noninvasive, highly specific, and have no side effects."[218] This is the kind of medicine that makes sense to me.

Energy Healing and Emotional Freedom Techniques (EFT)

Energy Medicine[219] was published in 1999 and has become one of the most important books in the field, translated into fifteen foreign languages and selling more than 250,000 copies. Eden says, "Energy medicine is safe, natural, and accessible. It is both contemporary and ancient. The term is being used in many ways today, ranging from the introduction of shamanic healing practices in modern cultures to the use of powerful electromagnetic and imaging technologies in modern hospitals."[220] Eden goes on to say that "energy medicine" is the "best term I know for describing the growing number of approaches in which an understanding of the body as a system of energies is being applied for promoting health, healing, and happiness."[221]

It was becoming clearer to me why even a mainstream doctor, heart surgeon Mehmet Oz, would say in 2007 that **the next big frontier in medicine is energy medicine.**[222] Eden recognized it much sooner. "The return of energy medicine is one of the most significant cultural developments of the day, for the return of energy medicine is a return to personal authority for health care, a return to the legacy of our ancestors in harmonizing with the forces of nature, and a return to practices that are natural, friendly, and familiar to the body, mind, and soul."[223]

With the book taking off and requests for talks and trainings coming in daily, Feinstein reluctantly closed what had been a deeply satisfying clinical practice in psychology to support this new turn in his wife's career. Like many men at midlife, Feinstein found that ending a career can open a man to a deeper calling. But we often have to experience the grief associated with endings before we can feel the joy of new beginnings.

"While these were exciting developments," he remembers, "I also mourned the loss of my practice and recognized that I might be leaving forever a career I loved. I was already in my fifties, and I had no idea where energy medicine would lead me. Many of Donna's students turned out to be therapists who were interested in energy psychology (EP). After years spent grudgingly accepting that seemingly ephemeral energies could impact physical conditions, this new wave of therapists was now asking me to believe that tapping on the body, supposedly to move these questionable energies, produces desired *psychological* changes."[224]

Energy psychology, energy medicine, and energy healing are closely related. Feinstein sees energy psychology as a subset of energy medicine, much as psychiatry is a subset of conventional medicine. Energy healing, as I use it in this book, includes practices that could fall under the category of energy psychology, energy medicine, or other systems of health care. As mind/body healing practices come together, so too will energy medicine, energy psychology, and energy healing. As Feinstein learned more about energy psychology, the experts in the field continually talked about Gary Craig, who had developed emotional freedom techniques (EFT).[225] He reached out to Craig and found him a great source of information and experience.

"The person with by far the most experience in bringing energy psychology methods to the general public was Gary Craig," says Feinstein. "Gary is not a psychotherapist by training, yet he has personally, or through his home-study programs, trained more professionals and nonprofessionals in the basic methods of energy psychology than anyone else, and his training manuals, videos, e-newsletter, and website constituted a significant portion of the field's evolving literature."[226]

"What excites me most about EFT," says Craig, "is its application to physical health and wellness. I'm convinced more than ever that modern medicine has walked right by a major contributor to chronic and acute diseases. Our unresolved angers, fears, and traumas show up in our physical bodies and manifest not just as back pain but as rheumatoid arthritis, cancer, multiple sclerosis, Parkinson's disease, and hundreds of other illnesses.[227]

"In essence, EFT is an emotional version of acupuncture wherein we stimulate certain meridian points by tapping on

them with our fingertips," says Craig. "This addresses a new cause for emotional issues (unbalanced energy meridians). Properly done, this frequently reduces the therapeutic process from months or years down to hours or minutes. And because emotional stress can contribute to pain, disease, and physical ailments, we often find that EFT provides astonishing physical relief."[228]

This is my kind of medicine—men's medicine—with no needles, no drugs, no long talks about the past and healing that gets to the core of our physical and emotional stresses, and gets there quickly. Of course, these are aspects that make it attractive to women as well. Like so many things that are simple, we often neglect doing them because they just seem so easy we can't believe they really work. In today's complex, money-driven world, we distrust solutions that are simple, easy to use, and inexpensive.

According to the website EFT Universe,[229] which hosts a wealth of resources useful to both experienced and new EFT users, EFT (emotional freedom techniques) is a simple yet remarkable healing system that reduces the stress underlying much disease. When I first tried EFT, I was surprised how easy it was to learn, yet how effectively it helped deal with the pain I was experiencing.

EFT: Acupuncture Without Needles

EFT has been called "acupuncture without needles." The early theories of how EFT worked drew on theories from acupuncture. According to Traditional Chinese Medicine, a form of bodily energy called chi is generated in internal organs and systems. This energy combines with breath and circulates throughout the body, forming paths called meridians.

The meridians form a complex, multilevel network that connects the various areas of the body to each other, including the surfaces with the internal. All of the meridian systems work together to assure the flow and distribution of chi throughout the body, thus controlling all bodily functions. The interwoven meridian systems and the possibilities for diagnosis and treatment they offer are called *meridian theory.*

When an organ or system is not balanced, related acupuncture points may become tender or red, allowing for diagnosis. For treatment, a point on the skin is stimulated through pressure, suction, heat, or needle insertion, affecting the circulation of chi, which in turn affects related internal organs and systems.

How EFT Works

Dr. Feinstein learned a lot about energy healing from living and working with his wife, Donna Eden, and also from his experiences with one of the most widely researched and accepted forms of energy healing, emotional freedom techniques or EFT. He has expanded on the theories of how acupuncture works and developed a ten-point theory of how EFT and other "tapping" therapies can heal:[230]

1. Energies—both electromagnetic energies and more subtle energies—form the dynamic *infrastructure* of the physical body.

2. The health of those energies—in terms of flow, balance, and harmony—is reflected in the health of the body, mind, and spirit.

3. Conversely, when the body, mind, and spirit are not healthy, corresponding disturbances in our energy fields can be identified and treated.

4. Flow, balance, and harmony can be noninvasively restored and maintained within an energy system by tapping specific energy points on the skin.

5. Tapping specific energy points while holding fearful or anxiety-provoking memories can permanently change the way these memories are processed and stored in the brain.

6. When you bring to mind an anxiety-provoking memory, thought, or related cue, an alarm response is activated in the amygdala. (The amygdala is an almond-shaped group of nuclei located deep within the brain that helps in the processing and memory of emotional reactions.)

7. The simultaneous stimulation of acupoints sends deactivating signals to the amygdala, initiating an opposing process.

8. The signals sent by the acupoint stimulation turn off the alarm response, even though the trigger is still present.

9. With a few repetitions, the trigger no longer evokes fear, and this innocuous experience, which becomes

the defining memory about the trigger, is stored in the long-term memory banks of the brain.

10. We still remember the event or situation that triggered the negative emotional response, but it no longer causes us problems.

I'm sure there will be other theories of how EFT and other therapies can heal the body, mind, and spirit. The nature of science is that theories are continually tested and updated as more knowledge becomes available. But you don't have to wait until all the data is in before you get the benefits of this useful healing tool. Learn it now, and try it out. Like me and millions of others, you'll find it very helpful for many of the stress-related issues we face today.

Emotional Freedom Techniques (EFT): The Most Widespread and Easy to Use Meridian Tapping Technique

I learned about EFT from an acupuncturist I had gone to for shoulder pain. I liked what EFT founder Gary Craig said about pain. "EFT often relieves pain where nothing else will," he said. "Further, it brings relief in 80 percent of the cases in which it's tried, and in the hands of a skilled practitioner, its success rate can exceed 95 percent."[231]

Craig teamed up with David Feinstein and Donna Eden to write a most helpful book on how to use this powerful tool. In the book *The Promise of Energy Psychology*, they offer these insights about using EFT:

1. This technique and healing art is based on the oldest, safest, most organic, most accessible, and most affordable medicine there is.

2. It teaches you how to participate more fully and knowledgeably in your own healing, health, and well-being.

3. It is both an empowering system for self-help and a powerful tool in the hands of competent health care practitioner.

4. Your emotional health, your success in the world, and your level of joy can all be dramatically enhanced by shifting the energies that regulate them.

5. Anger can be managed more reliably.

6. Many cases of depression can be alleviated without drugs.

7. Achievements in sports, school, music, and business can be given a powerful boost.

8. Stubborn anxieties, worries, and fears often fade in minutes.

9. Even elusive physical problems respond where other treatments have failed.

Using Energy Healing Tool Element #1: Basic Instructions for Using EFT

Energy psychology experts David Feinstein, Donna Eden, and Gary Craig offer a simple yet effective set of instructions for addressing a range of problems. I think of the process as having four simple steps: Get Ready. Get Set. Go. Review. The following description will show you how to use this powerful tool. If you'd like to see it demonstrated, you can follow along with me at: http://MenAlive.com/TappingDemo.

Take a picture of this tag with your smartphone to see Dr. Diamond demonstrate EFT tapping techniques.

Get Ready: Understand that changing your energy field can change the discomfort you are feeling.

Those of us who work in the health profession agree that negative, self-limiting emotions can often be traced back to emotionally damaging early life experiences. A current stressor may activate an earlier experience which triggers a defensive emotional response and leads to increased stress and dysfunction.

The new idea in energy healing is that there is a step between the memory and the emotion, and that step is a ***disturbance in your body's energy field.*** Conventional psychotherapy focuses on the memory and often goes back in time to address the issues surrounding the earlier trauma. Energy healing focuses on the energy disturbance as well as the memory, and it works quickly and easily.

Get Set: Focus on the problem and rate your discomfort.

The problem you pick to work on could cover a range of issues, as we'll discuss in later chapters. But they can be summarized as follows:

- **Emotional reactions** such as "resentment toward my father" or "anger because my spouse is treating me insensitively."
- **Physical reactions** such as "the stress headaches I get at work" or "my back pain when I try to sleep."
- **Habits of thought** such as "seeing other's negative qualities rather than what they do well" or "getting irritated each time my wife is the least bit late."
- **Patterns of behavior** such as "alcohol use" or "overeating."

Once you have selected the issue or memory you wish to work on, the next step is to rate it on a scale of zero (no distress) to ten (extreme distress, or the worst it has ever been), based on the amount of discomfort you experience when you think about it.

Go: Create the setup, tap, do the "eye movements," tap again.

The setup is a way of establishing a psychological and energetic receptiveness for change. Whenever you decide to change a habit of thought, behavior, or emotion, the part of you that initially established the pattern may resist your efforts. To do this, you state a precisely worded affirmation while stimulating certain energy points. One of the easiest methods is to say the affirmation while tapping the "karate chop" area on the fleshy part of the outside of either hand with the fingers of the other hand. Self-acceptance in the face of our problem allows change to occur.

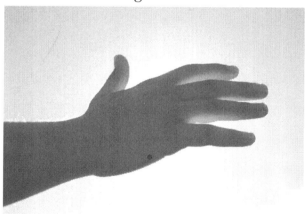

The affirmation statement has two parts:
1) *Even though I have this* _____,
2) I deeply love and accept myself.
You fill in the blank with a brief description of the problem being addressed. Here are a few examples:
- *Even though I have this anger toward my wife, I deeply love and accept myself.*

- *Even though I have this chronic back pain, I deeply love and accept myself.*
- *Even though I feel frustrated and depressed, I deeply love and accept myself.*

Although some approaches advise us to ignore negative thoughts and feelings and state positive affirmations, this approach encourages people to state the problem while tapping. The affirmation is best stated out loud, with feeling and emphasis. If the affirmation doesn't feel quite right to you, it's okay to use alternative wording as long as you acknowledge the problem while at the same time affirming your worthiness even though you are having a problem.

I think of the next step as an ice-cream sandwich: two chocolaty wafers surrounding a big slab of tasty ice cream. Have the picture. The top wafer is the first tapping sequence. The tapping sequence is designed to restore an optimal flow of energy through our body's "meridians," or energy pathways. There are fourteen major meridians, and each is associated with acupoints on the surface of the skin that, when tapped or otherwise stimulated, move energy through the entire meridian system. It turns out that the meridians are interconnected, so stimulating one meridian can affect others. This also means that working with only a subset of meridian points is all that is usually necessary to get the entire energy system into enough of a flow to resolve the issue you are addressing.

Various specific subsets have been used with good results. The sequence you will learn includes nine points found to be an effective combination (I think of my wafer as having nine little holes in it to remind me of the nine places to tap. The diagram below will show you where to tap). **Tap about seven**

times on each of the tapping points described below, while repeating a reminder phrase. The reminder phrase can be the same as the one used in your initial setup or a shortened version. The idea is to just keep your mind focused on the problem. For instance, you could say, "Anger toward my wife" or shorten it to "This anger." You could say, "Chronic back pain" or just "Back pain."

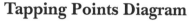

Tapping Points Diagram

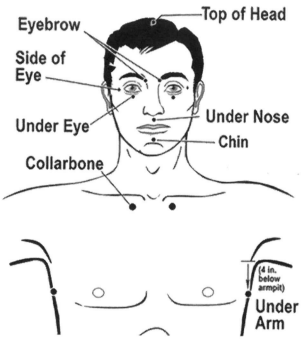

1. Beginning of the eyebrows—inside edge of the eyebrows, just above and to one side of the nose.
2. Sides of the eyes—on the bone bordering the outside of each eye.
3. Under the eyes—on the bone under each eye, about one inch below the pupil.

4. Under the nose—on the small area between the bottom of the nose and the top center of the upper lip.

5. Under the lower lip—midway between the point of the chin and the bottom of the lower lip.

6. The two points immediately below the "collar-bone corners. To locate these points, place your forefingers on your collarbone and move them toward the U-shaped notch at the top of your breastbone (about where you'd knot a tie). Move your fingers through the bottom of the U. Then go to the left and right about an inch and tap.

7. Under the arm—about four inches beneath the armpit, about even with the nipple in men.

8. Karate-chop points—in the middle of the fleshy part on the outside of either hand, between the top of the wrist bone and the base of the little finger.

9. Top of the head—tap the top of the head with all your fingers.

Tapping can be done with either hand, both hands simultaneously, or in sequence. You can tap with the fingertips of your index finger and middle finger, or make a "three-finger notch" by including your thumb. Tap solidly but never so hard as to hurt or risk bruising yourself.

After we've done a round of tapping (top wafer of my ice-cream sandwich), we then do the "eye thing," or as thought-field therapy founder, Roger Callahan, calls it, **The Nine-Gamut Procedure.**

The "gamut point" (on the back of either hand between the pinkie and ring fingers, about one-half inch beyond the knuckles, towards the wrist) is continuously tapped while nine simple steps are carried out.

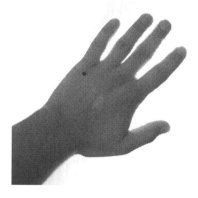

1. Close your eyes.
2. Open your eyes.
3. Move your eyes down and to the left.
4. Move your eyes down and to the right.
5. Circle your eyes, rotating them 360 degrees in one direction.
6. Circle your eyes 360 degrees in the other direction.
7. Hum a tune for a few seconds ("Happy Birthday" or "Row, Row, Row Your Boat" or something easy to remember).
8. Count to five.
9. Hum again.

When you are finished, bring your eyes down to the floor and then slowly and very deliberately bring them up to opposite wall, projecting your sight and the "old" energy out into the distance as your eyes move up the arc.

Now repeat the tapping procedure again (the second wafer of our ice-cream sandwich), just as you did the first time round.

Review: Revisit the problem, repeat if necessary, challenge the healing.

When you have completed the second sequence of tapping, assess the intensity of the problem again. Close your eyes, bring the original memory to mind, and give it a rating from zero to ten on the amount of distress it causes you *now*, as you think about it. The rating will almost always go down. If it isn't down to zero, you can go through the sequence again. Once you've learned the techniques, each round should take about three or four minutes.

Sometimes you will resolve a problem after a single tapping sequence. More often, you will get only partial relief, and you will need to repeat the whole sequence a number of times. You will need to make a simple adjustment for these rounds to acknowledge that you still are experiencing some degree of pain.

Change the setup phrase slightly:

"Even though I still have some of this_____"

For instance, you might begin with "Even though I still have some shoulder pain, I still deeply love and accept myself."

Continue going through the above sequence until your discomfort rating goes down to zero or one.

Once you get the subjective distress level down to zero or near one, the final step is to "challenge" it. Try to recall or visualize the situation in a manner that evokes the earlier experience of distress. If you can remember the experience, but there isn't any emotional distress, you know you've taken care of it. Here's how David Feinstein, Donna Eden, and Gary Craig describe this final step: "If the disturbed energy pattern and neurological sequence have been corrected—that is, if the earlier memory, thought, or situation is now paired to a stable response in your brain and energy system—you will not be able to activate your earlier feelings. **The speed with which this can often be accomplished is among the most striking benefits of energy psychology.**"[232]

When I first experienced how quickly I was able to heal long-standing traumatic memories and even physical pain in my body, I couldn't quite believe it. Even after using EFT for many years, I still have to remind myself that it really does work. Men, particularly, are conditioned to believe "No pain, no gain." We often *want* to experience pain because we are convinced that's the only way to we can improve our lives. It requires a radical change in our belief systems to accept that we can heal quickly and easily.

When I first read the description of the "basic recipe," I thought, "This is really complicated." But it's a lot more complicated to explain for the first time than to do it. **Once you've practiced it a few times, you'll find that it is quick and easy.** As you read more, you'll get other examples and opportunities to practice. For now, become familiar with the directions and try it on some issue that may be troubling you. Don't worry about "getting it right." The more you practice, the more you'll hone in on what works for you.

Making a Good Thing Even Better

According to EFT experts, David Feinstein, Donna Eden, and Gary Craig, "In the hands of a relatively proficient newcomer, the basic recipe seems to produce effective results about 80 percent of the time when applied to reducing the emotional charge on specific difficult memories."[233] These are great results by any standard, but you can do even better if you address these potential blocks to progress:

1. Unresolved *aspects* of the problem
2. Psychological reversals

Unresolved *Aspects* of the Problem

If you didn't get results, first go back and make sure you followed the directions. If you're like me, you sometimes speed ahead because you want to *do* something and may miss an important part of the practice. If you did follow the directions, the most common reason your distress rating doesn't go down to zero or close to zero is that another aspect of the problem is involved and was not focused upon during the energy intervention.

Likewise, when an issue seems resolved during your practice, but returns later, there are often aspects of the real-life situation that weren't fully addressed. For instance, when I was dealing with irritation when my wife was late coming home, I found many other aspects relating to fears that she had been injured, fantasies of her meeting some other guy, and old feelings of abandonment stemming from childhood experiences.

While many problems are straightforward and do not have multiple aspects, some have a number of physical or psychological aspects that need attention if full healing is to occur. The *physical* aspects of a problem include the look, sound, smell, taste, or feel of the situation. When I worked on my irritation over my wife's being late, I focused first on the time and remembering her words that "I'll be home by 9:00." I was able to get my irritation down to three or four, but it wouldn't go further. When I then tuned to my fear of her getting in an accident and used the reminder phrase, "Fear of Carlin's being hurt," my distress rating went down to two. When I tapped on the aspect of my fear that she was seeing another guy, it went down to one. And finally, when I tuned into my memory of being left alone as a child, my distress level went down to zero.

Feinstein, Eden, and Craig offer a helpful metaphor. Think of the issue you are addressing as a table. If the emotional problem such as fear, anxiety, or shame is the top of the table, the legs are its aspects, particularly specific events that produced similar emotions. By chipping away at the legs, the tabletop will eventually fall away. They point out that it isn't necessary to remember and treat every aspect involved with the problem in order to overcome it. Just as the brain generalizes out from one trauma and gets triggered when there is a related experience, so too can healing be generalized. When we heal some key aspects, others go away by themselves.

They conclude by saying, "While many issues can be overcome by using the basic recipe directly on a general statement about the obvious problem, for other issues you need to be as specific as possible about their aspects. Particularly with an amorphous condition, such as anxiety, it is often necessary to identify specific events. These may be memories from your childhood, more recent incidents, or current situations. If you neutralize their emotional charges, one by one, the relief will eventually generalize to the larger issue."[234]

Psychological Reversals

We've all experienced *psychological reversals* when one part of us wants to change and another part of us, on the energetic or subconscious level, is resistant to change. I've found there are three common reasons why we resist changes we know consciously are good for us.

1. We don't think we deserve to have a positive change in our lives. Most of us are raised with messages that there is something wrong with us and we don't deserve to be joyful in our lives. That's why EFT begins with a setup phrase that says, "Even though I have this problem, I still love and accept myself." While the standard phrase resolves most psychological reversals, there may need to be a modification for some people.

2. Although we believe we want to make a change, there may be hidden drawbacks to our letting go of the problem. I've been working with a successful attorney who says he wants to cut back on his work so he can enjoy life more fully, "smell the roses," and have more time with his family. But when the basic sequence didn't create the results he wanted, we looked more deeply. We found that he believed that if he cut back on his hours, his clients would go elsewhere for services and his twenty-five-year practice would collapse.

   We changed the setup phrase to acknowledge this fear. "Even though I have a fear of losing my practice if

I cut down on my hours, I choose to have clients who stick with me." We talked about the reality of his fears, and he concluded that he might lose a few clients if he wasn't immediately available, but most of his clients were loyal and would stick with him even if he worked a little less. When we used EFT with this revised phrase, his anxiety decreased even more, and he found he could enjoy his time off.

3. There may be hidden benefits to keeping the problem. Many of the "problems" we say we want to eliminate actually have benefits that may be held in our unconscious or less conscious minds. When I worked with the attorney described above, he found some of these hidden benefits.

As we talked, he had an additional insight: "I realize I like being seen in the firm as the top dog, the guy who works the hardest. It boosts my ego. I'm not really sure I want to let go of that feeling." As we discussed this further, he realized there were only two people in the firm who really boosted his ego when he worked long hours, and he didn't really care that much about what these two thought of him. So we tapped with this setup phrase, "I choose to leave at 5:00 p.m. and still feel I'm giving my best to my clients." With this adjustment, his level of anxiety and worry went to zero and he was able to take off at a reasonable time each day without feeling guilty.

You can do your own detective work if the basic sequence doesn't bring your discomfort level down to zero. But if you're still having difficulty, it helps to work with another person. Sometimes family and friends can help you discover other aspects of the problem you had not considered. They can also help you discover psychological reversals that may be unconscious. You can also work with a counselor who is skilled at using EFT. Some guys like to work things out themselves. Others find it's very helpful to get input from others.

PART III:
COMBATING STRESS WHERE MEN LIVE

CHAPTER 9:
WHO'RE YOU CALLING IRRITABLE! WHAT MAKES YOU THINK I'M DEPRESSED?

Although I did my best to believe that I had not inherited any of my father's tendencies toward anger and depression, I finally had to accept that I was wrong. Over the years, I have gotten good counseling and used the energy healing tools I describe. I've heard from thousands of men and women who are dealing with these issues, and I learn something new from each one.

"For about a year now (it could be even longer, it's hard to know exactly), I have gradually felt my husband of twenty-two years pulling away for me and our family," Martha told me in an anguished phone call. "He has gradually become more sullen, angry, and moody. His general life energy is down and his sex drive has really dropped off.

"He blames me for everything these days. If his socks or underwear are missing, I must have put them somewhere or done something with them to piss him off. I'm not kidding, that's what he tells me. The thing that bothers me the most is how unaffectionate he has become. I don't even get the hugs and kisses I used to get, and when he does touch me, I feel grabbed rather than caressed. **My husband used to be the most positive, upbeat, funny person I knew. Now it's like living with an angry brick!"**

I found I was hearing from more and more women like Martha, who were hurt and confused about the changes they were seeing in their husbands. I was also hearing from the men.

Rick is a fifty-two-year-old married man with children aged twenty-two and twenty-six. Here's how he described the anger and irritability that nearly cost him his marriage. His responses are typical of many men who have spoken out:

"I think my irritability is related to the time of life I am in and to the stresses that seem to be mounting both at work and at home. I'm an electrical engineer and work for a large company in the Midwest. There has been a great deal of 'consolidation' over the last few years, and many people have been let go or forced into early retirement. Even though I have been here a long time and don't think I am vulnerable to losing my job, I still worry.

"There is always so much to do, and there never seems to be enough time to do it all. I have trouble staying on top of it all. I don't have much physical or mental energy these days. All of this is affecting my sleep. My wife keeps asking me what's wrong. I don't know what to tell her. I usually answer that nothing is wrong. When she persists, I often snap at her.

"Although I love my wife, I feel we have grown apart over the years. We used to be very close, but now we often seem like opposites, and that creates its own kind of stress. I often feel unappreciated, unheard, uncared for. She expresses the same feelings. Even though we are aware of it, we don't seem to be able to do anything about it. It's very discouraging and depressing.

"For me, depression and irritability are closely linked. I don't really lash out that often. I mostly hold the feelings in. I don't want to fight, but sometimes things erupt, and I blow up at her or our children. I can tell she's hurt. I feel guilty and that makes me angrier. It seems to be a vicious cycle.

"I know I lack a sense of general wellbeing much of the time. I have come to doubt my ability to be a reliable, dependable, likeable person. My confidence in myself is low. When I feel hateful or annoyed with everyone, I just want to isolate myself. That way, I don't have to deal with them, and I won't do things I'll regret later. As a result, I have become estranged from my wife and children. Even at work, which used to be a place I felt comfortable and where I had a lot of friends, I feel cut off and isolated.

"This 'anger/depression thing,' or whatever it is, affects EVERYTHING in my life. I feel that I have achieved very little of what, as a young man, I had hoped to achieve. I long to be much more confident and competent, much more relaxed, much more self-sufficient, and much more successful. I guess I feel like a failure."

This kind of anger can go from being repressed into a stony silence to becoming extreme and explosive. "Wrath is extreme anger," says Caroline Myss, author of *Defy Gravity: Healing Beyond the Bounds of Reason,* "a passion that is destructive, cruel, and merciless. Wrath is a dark passion capable of destroying lives, or of destroying you....We all have anger running through our veins; wrath goes deeper than anger, however, because it is anger with permission to destroy. Anger can flare up in a moment, vent itself verbally, and then be gone. In a loving relationship, partners say they just can't stay angry at each other. But wrath begins to speak in a self-righteous voice, building a case within your mind—your reason—that you are 'right' and therefore action is justified. Your reason refuses to relent, stoking the fire of anger constantly, because it takes a great deal of fuel to keep the fires of self-righteousness burning. Wrath eventually consumes you on your own pyre.

"An angry heart is a tragic, dangerous heart, one that becomes unforgiving," says Myss. "An angry heart turns love into a torment, punishing those who we think do not love us enough or in the right way. But there is not a right way to love an angry heart, so love is always futile when mixed with anger. Ultimately anger pushes love away, again and again."[235]

We've all had the experience of feeling love mixed with anger and how corrosive and destructive it can be.

Irritable Male Syndrome: A Problem for all Male Mammals?

As a psychotherapist specializing in men's health, I have always had patients who were irritable and angry. For many of these men, this seems to be a life-long response to feelings of insecurity, stress, and fears of failure. Now I was seeing more men who rather suddenly were changing from "Mr. Nice" to "Mr. Mean." There was no diagnostic label for what was troubling these guys, so I started calling it the Jekyll and Hyde Syndrome, after the Robert Louis Stevenson story of the guy who suddenly changes from a well-respected doctor to an out-of-control madman.

Over the years, I have treated a lot of these men and the women who loved them, but I still felt like I was missing something essential about what was going on. I got my first clue to what that missing thing might be when a colleague sent me copy of an article by Dr. Gerald A. Lincoln, a researcher in Edinburgh, Scotland. Dr. Lincoln had recently published the results of his studies on animals in the journal *Reproduction, Fertility, and Development*. He titled the paper, "The Irritable Male Syndrome" and described what he observed in the animals following the withdrawal of testosterone.

In the introduction, he said that the "irritability-anxiety-depression syndromes associated with withdrawal of sex steroid hormones are well recognized in the female." They are, he noted, connected with changes associated with the ovarian cycle and include premenstrual syndrome, postnatal depression, and menopause. "The occurrence of a potentially similar behavioral syndrome in males following withdrawal of testosterone (T) has received less attention. A clear behavioral response to T withdrawal is predicted, however, because T has well-defined psychotropic effects in relation to sexuality, aggression, performance, cognition, and emotion.[236]

My wife and I visited Dr. Lincoln in Edinburgh and found he had been studying irritable male syndrome (IMS) in a number of animals, including Soay rams, red deer, reindeer, and Indian elephants, and concluded that IMS occurs in all male mammals following the withdrawal of testosterone. While he believes that IMS is a problem that all male mammals experience some time in their lives, he hasn't worked with human males. I told him I thought he might be right. I was seeing the effects he described in the mammals I know best: *Homo sapiens.* When we returned home, I began an extensive research project to determine the key symptoms and causes of IMS in men. I created an IMS questionnaire,[237] and more than thirty thousand men and ten thousand women have responded to it.

The Core Symptoms of Irritable Male Syndrome (IMS)

Men suffering from IMS often exhibit the following core symptoms: hypersensitivity, anxiety, frustration, and anger. Let's look at the four core symptoms in more detail:

The first core symptom is *hypersensitivity.*

The women who live with these men say things like:

- "I feel I have to walk on egg shells when I'm around him."
- "I never know when I'm going to say something that will set him off."
- "He's like time bomb ready to explode, but I never know when."
- "Nothing I do pleases him."
- "When I try to do nice things, he pushes me away."
- "He'll change in an eye-blink. One minute, he's warm and friendly. The next, he's cold and mean."

The men don't often recognize their own hypersensitivity. Rather, their perception is that they are fine, but everyone else is going out of their way to irritate them. The guys say things like:

- "Quit bothering me."
- "Leave me alone."
- "I told you, nothing's wrong. I'm fine." (Said while there's steam coming out of his ears.)
- "Why do you do that? You know I don't like it."

Or they don't say anything. They increasingly withdraw into a numbing silence.

One way to understand this concept is to think of a person who is hypersensitive as having *emotional sunburn*. Picture a man who is extremely sunburned and gets a loving hug from his wife. He cries out in anger and pain. He assumes she knows he's sunburned, so if she "grabs" him, she must be trying to hurt him. Since the sunburn is not visible, she has no idea he is sunburned and can't understand why he reacts angrily to her loving touch. You can see how this can lead a couple down a road of escalating confusion.

The second core symptom is *anxiety*.

Anxiety is a state of apprehension, uncertainty, and fear resulting from the anticipation of a realistic or fantasized threatening event or situation. Often, men will appear confident and self-assured to others but actually be living with a great deal of worry and fear. There are many real threats they are dealing with in their lives: sexual changes, job insecurities, relationship problems. There are also many uncertainties that cause a guy to get lost in his thoughts and to ruminate and fantasize about problems that don't even exist.

These kinds of worries usually take the form of "what ifs." What if I lose my job? What if I can't find a job? What if she leaves me? What if I can't find someone to love me? What if I have to go to war? What if something happens to my wife or children? What if my parents die? What if I get sick and can't take care of things? For most of us, this list is infinite.

The third core symptom is *frustration.*

Princeton University's WordNet offers two definitions that can help us understand this in the context of IMS:

1. The feeling that accompanies an experience of being thwarted in attaining your goals. Synonym is defeat.
2. A feeling of annoyance at being hindered or criticized.

The dictionary offers an enlightening example to illustrate the use of the word: "Her constant complaints were the main source of his frustration."

IMS men feel blocked in attaining what they want and need in life. We often don't even know *what* we need. When we do know, we often feel there's no way we can get it. We often feel defeated in the things we try to do to improve our lives. We feel frustrated in our relationships with family, friends, and coworkers. The world is changing, and we don't know where, how, or if we fit in.

Author Susan Faludi captures this feeling in her book *Stiffed: The Betrayal of the American Man.* The frustration is expressed in the question at the center of her study of American males. "If, as men are so often told, they are the dominant sex, why do so many of them feel dominated, done in by the world?"[238] Most men I know understand and feel confused by the discrepancy between being told they are "top dog" and their sense they are weak little puppies.

The forth core symptom is *anger.*

Anger, simply defined, is a strong feeling of displeasure or hostility. Yet anger is a complex, often confusing emotion. Anger can turn into aggression and violence when outwardly expressed. When we turn our anger inward, it can lead to depression and suicide. Anger can be direct and obvious, or it can be subtle and covert. Anger can be loud or quiet. It can be expressed as hateful words, hurtful actions, or stony silence.

Anger is the only emotion many men allow themselves to express. Growing up, we are taught to avoid anything that is seen as the least bit feminine. We are taught that men "do" while women "feel." We learn to keep all emotions under wraps, to see them as unmanly. We cannot show we are hurt, afraid, worried, or panicked. The feeling we are allowed to express without being called feminine is anger. When men experience IMS, anger is often the primary emotion.

Many of us try to suppress our anger. Instead, we are on a constant simmer of irritability. Whereas feelings like anger, anxiety, and frustration can start quickly and end quickly, irritability can develop into a mood that lasts over a long period of time. Irritability often has a major impact on our whole lives. "When we're in a mood, it biases and restricts how we think," says Paul Ekman, professor of psychology and director of the Human Interaction Laboratory at the University of California Medical School in San Francisco.[239]

Dr. Ekman is one of the world's leading experts on emotional expression. He says these negative emotional moods "make us vulnerable in ways that we are normally not. So the negative moods create a lot of problems for us, because they change how we think. **If I wake up in an irritable mood, I'm**

looking for a chance to be angry. Things that ordinarily would not frustrate me do. The danger of a mood is not only that it biases thinking but that it also increases emotions. When I'm in an irritable mood, my anger comes stronger and faster, lasts longer, and is harder to control than usual. It's a terrible state…one I would be glad never to have."[240] This statement summarizes a lot of what I've experienced dealing with Irritable Male Syndrome in my own life.

The Underlying Causes of Irritable Male Syndrome (IMS)

Along with the four common symptoms of IMS—hypersensitivity, anxiety, frustration, and anger—there are four common causes: hormonal fluctuations, biochemical changes in brain chemistry, stress, and loss of male identity and purpose.

The first cause of IMS is hormonal fluctuations.

To understand how hormonal fluctuations cause IMS in men, we need to review what we know about testosterone. Theresa L. Crenshaw, MD, author of *The Alchemy of Love and Lust*, describes testosterone this way: "Testosterone is the young Marlon Brando—sexual, sensual, alluring, dark, with a dangerous undertone." She goes on to say, "It is also our 'warmone,' triggering aggression, competitiveness, and even violence. *Testy* is a fitting term."[241] We know that men with high testosterone levels can become angry and aggressive. Yet, research shows that most hormonal problems in men aren't from high levels, but rather testosterone levels that are *too low.*

Dr. Gerald Lincoln, who coined the term Irritable Male Syndrome, found that declining levels of testosterone in his research animals caused them to become more irritable, biting their cages as well as the researchers who were testing them. Larrian Gillespie, MD, an expert on male and female hormones says, "Low testosterone is associated with symptoms of Irritable Male Syndrome."[242]

The second cause of IMS is change in brain chemistry.

Changing hormones can also have an impact on brain chemistry and vice versa. Most people have heard of serotonin, the brain neurotransmitter. When we have enough flowing through our brains, we feel good. When there isn't enough, we feel bad. Siegfried Meryn, MD, coauthor of *Men's Health and the Hormone Revolution*, calls serotonin "the male hormone of bliss." Women have the same hormone in their brains, and it has an equally positive effect on them. "The more serotonin the body produces," says Dr. Meryn, "the happier, more positive, and more euphoric we are. Low serotonin can contribute to a man's irritability and aggression."[243]

Our drinking and eating habits have a major impact on our serotonin levels. Research has shown, for instance, that protein consumed in excessive quantities suppresses central nervous system serotonin levels. Many men are (or have been) taught to believe that eating lots of meat is manly. But too much meat is not good for us. Not only are hormones injected into the meat to make the animals fatter, but the protein contained in the meat can be harmful as well.

Judith Wurtman, PhD, and her colleagues at the Massachusetts Institute of Technology found that a high-protein, low-carbohydrate diet can cause increased irritability in men.

They found that men often mistake their cravings for healthy carbohydrates, like those found in potatoes, rice, corn, squash, with cravings for meat. "Eating protein when we need carbohydrates," says Wurtman, "will make us grumpy, irritable, or restless."[244]

Wurtman's team also found that alcohol consumption increases serotonin levels initially. However, chronic use dramatically lowers serotonin, resulting in depression, carbohydrate cravings, sleep disturbances, and a tendency to be argumentative and irritable. It may be that our propensity to eat too much meat and drink too much alcohol is contributing to lower serotonin levels in brain chemistry, which leads to Irritable Male Syndrome.

The third cause of IMS is stress.

In my experience as a psychotherapist, I have found that stress underlies most of the psychological, social, and medical problems people face in contemporary society, including IMS. For most of us, stress is synonymous with worry. If it is something that makes us worry, then it is stressful.

However, our bodies have a much broader definition of stress. To our body, stress is synonymous with change. It doesn't matter if it is a "good" change or a "bad" change, they are both stressful. The truth is that we are living in a society that is undergoing change that is so rapid that our bodies, minds, and spirits can't keep up.

Futurist Alvin Toffler was one of the first people to recognize the effect of stress produced by rapid change on society as a whole. "I coined the term 'future shock' in 1965," says Toffler, "to describe the shattering stress and disorientation that we induce in individuals by subjecting them to too much change in too short a time."[245] As Toffler describes soldiers who break down under the pressures of combat, it is easy to recognize what happens to all of us under the constant stresses of a rapidly changing world. "Mental deterioration often began with fatigue. This was followed by confusion and nervous irritability. The man became hypersensitive to the slightest stimuli around him. He became tense, anxious, and heatedly irascible. His comrades never knew when he would flail out in anger, even violence, in response to minor inconveniences."[246]

The fourth cause of IMS is loss of male identity and purpose.

For most of human history, our role was clear. Our main job was to "bring home the bacon." We hunted for our food and shared what we killed with the family and tribe. Everyone had their role to play. Some were good at tracking animals. Others were good making bows and arrows or spears. Some men were strong and could shoot an arrow with enough strength to kill a buffalo. Others were skilled at singing songs and doing dances that invoked the spirit of the animal and made the hunt more effective.

That isn't today's reality, though. Today, many of us work at jobs we hate, producing goods or services that contribute little of value to the community. We've gotten farther and farther away from the basics of bringing home food we've hunted or grown on our own. The money we receive is small compensation for doing work that is meaningless. As the economy continues to change, more and more men are losing their jobs and can't easily find new ones.

Any one of the four causes mentioned above could have a major impact on a man and contribute to IMS. Each cause often interacts with the others, and the impact is amplified. When a man doesn't feel he has meaningful work, for instance, his stress levels go up, and his testosterone levels go down. When men are stressed, we often drink too much, which lowers our testosterone as well as our serotonin levels.

The good news is that by affecting one cause, we can impact all of them. Here are a few things you can do now to improve your life and protect against IMS. Have your hormone levels checked. Find out if your testosterone is low. Eat healthy food with a good balance of carbohydrates, fats, and proteins. Exercise every day. Look for work that is meaningful for you, and don't take it personally if our dysfunctional economy pushes you out of your job.

IMS and Male-Type Depression

"Sadness isn't macho...this Eric Weaver knew," wrote Susan Freinkel in an article titled "The Secret Men Won't Admit" in the January 2007 issue of *Reader's Digest*. "When depression engulfed the Rochester, New York, police sergeant, it took a different guise: anger. To the former SWAT team leader and competitive bodybuilder, it was manly, and easy, to be mad."[247]

The father of three, then in his early thirties, stewed in a near-constant state of anger. "One minute I'd be okay, and the next minute I'd be screaming at my kids and punching the wall," he recalls. "My kids would ask, 'What's wrong with Daddy? Why's he so mad all the time?' I probably heard that a thousand times." For years, Weaver didn't know what was wrong. "I just thought I was a jerk." **The possibility that he was depressed never occurred to him—until the angry facade began to crumble, leaving him with no feelings except utter despair.** The tears finally came one night when he admitted to his wife a painful truth: "I've thought about committing suicide every day."

Weaver's confusion about what afflicted him is not unusual. Though millions of men suffer from depression, many don't recognize the symptoms or seek help. "Men don't find it easy to ask for help," says Thomas Insel, MD, director of the National Institute of Mental Health (NIMH). "That's a gene that must be on the Y chromosome," he says, tongue in cheek.

I believe one of the reasons men don't ask for help with depression is that professionals who diagnose depression are asking them the wrong questions. In order to help men like Eric, and the millions of other depressed men in the U.S. and throughout the world, I think we need a new questionnaire focused on male-type depression.

Research I have conducted on gender and depression convinces me that men often experience depression quite differently than women. Women often "act in" their pain and focus on internal judgments of their own inadequacies. Men, on the other hand, are conditioned to "act out," and thus men's depression is more likely to be expressed through chronic anger, self-destructiveness, drug use, gambling, womanizing, and workaholism.

I developed a new tool for assessing depression in men (the Diamond Male Depression Scale). [248] It draws on the research I have done on Irritable Male Syndrome and other recent research that shows that IMS and male-type depression overlap. The results convince me there are actually three types of depression in men:

1. Emotionally acting-in depression
2. Emotionally acting-out depression
3. Physical acting-out depression

Emotionally acting-in depression is indicated when respondents agree with the following statements:

- "I feel that I need to get away from it all."
- "I feel like things are stacked against me."
- "People I count on disappoint me."
- "I feel emotionally numb and closed down."
- "I feel powerless to improve things in my life."
- "I feel sorry for myself."
- "I have little interest or pleasure in doing things."

Emotional acting-out depression is indicated when respondents agree with the following statements:

- "I flare up quickly."
- "I have trouble controlling my temper."
- "I am easily annoyed, become grumpy, or impatient."
- "Other people often drive me up the wall."
- "When others disagree with me, I get very upset."
- "It doesn't take much to set me off."
- "I have difficulty maintaining self-control."

Physical acting-out depression is indicated when respondents agree with the following statements:

- "I have hit someone when I was provoked."
- "I work longer hours because going home is stressful."
- "I gamble with money I have set aside for other things."

- "I drive fast or recklessly as a way of letting off steam."
- "If I am feeling low, I'll use sex as a pick-me-up."
- "I have felt that I should cut down on my drinking or drug use."
- "I get so jealous or possessive I feel like I could explode."

These are not the typical questions to assess depression in men, but I believe they are statements that many depressed men identify with. Which of these statements do you agree with? Hopefully, as more men face these issues and realize there is help available, there will be will have fewer men suffering in silence or committing suicide.

The Despair of the American Male

In his Pulitzer Prize–winning play *A Long Day's Journey into Night*,[249] Eugene O'Neill captured the hopelessness and powerlessness so many men experience in their lives. He describes a family (generally viewed as autobiographical) that many of us recognize. I remember seeing the play as a young man. There were so many reverberations of the dysfunction I saw in my own family and the families I knew growing up that it was difficult for me to watch. The family in *Long Day's Journey*, like many families, constantly conceals, blames, resents, regrets, accuses, and denies in an escalating cycle of conflict. There are only occasional, desperate, and half-sincere attempts at affection, encouragement, and consolation.

Toward the end of the play, Edmund, the youngest son, confesses to his father that he feels desperately lonely and cut off from himself and everyone else. He describes the grief and despair of millions of men with these chilling words: *"It was a great mistake, my being born a man. I would have been much more successful as a sea gull or a fish. As it is, I will always be a stranger who never feels at home, who does not really want and is not really wanted, who can never belong, who must always be a little in love with death!"*[250]

For most of my life, I haven't felt totally comfortable in my own body. Like Edmund, I wondered if my life would be better if I were someone else. It's taken me a long while to gather the tools I've needed to feel the power of my own inner knowing. I've benefited from seeing an excellent psychiatrist who understood that I needed more than drugs to deal with my emotional issues. She provided a caring relationship where we could act as equal partners in finding ways that enabled me to learn to love and accept myself more fully. She was also supportive of my using the tools I describe in this book.

Depression Can Be Deadly, and Drugs May Not Be the Answer

Depression is one of the most destructive diseases of modern life. According to Dr. Stephen S. Ilardi, author of *The Depression Cure,* "Depression is a devastating illness. It robs people of their energy, their sleep, their memory, their concentration, their vitality, their joy, their ability to love and work and play, and—sometimes—even their will to live."[251]

Not only does depression take away our spiritual and emotional health, it also undermines our physical health. Recent research reported by Johns Hopkins Medical Center indicates that depression increases the risk of heart disease and aggravates chronic illnesses like diabetes, arthritis, back problems, and asthma, all of which lead to more work absences, disability, and doctor visits.

With all the modern pharmacological treatments, it might seem like depression would be cured by now. It is, in fact, on the rise. According to Dr. Ilardi, "About one in four Americans—over seventy million people—will meet the criteria for major depression sometime in their lives." And the rates of depression and suicide are going up and up. "It's roughly ten times higher today than it was just two generations ago," says Ilardi.[252]

Yet we continue to take antidepressant drugs in record numbers. More than 170 million prescriptions for these drugs have been written in the last few years. In fact, antidepressants have become the most prescribed category of drugs in the United States. But drugs may not be the best answer to the problem.

In his excellent book, *Rethinking Depression: How to Shed Mental Health Labels and Create Personal Meaning*, Eric Maisel says, "We are seduced by the medical model, in which psychiatrists dispense pills and psychotherapists dispense talk. It is very hard for the average person, who suffers and feels pain because he is a human being, but who has been trained to call his unhappiness depression, to see through this manipulation."[253]

After dealing with depression in my family, in my own life, and with thousands of clients, I've come to believe that medications are overprescribed. They can be helpful for some. I was glad I had a doctor who prescribed them when I needed them. But they don't treat the underlying causes of depression, and a number of the tools I describe in the book can do that.

A note of caution here: If you are seriously depressed or your symptoms are not improving, you should consult a clinician with expertise in treating depression and other emotional problems.

Using Emotional Freedom Techniques to Treat Irritable Male Syndrome and Male-Type Depression

Emotional freedom techniques (EFT) have proven very effective in addressing irritability, anger, and depression. I frequently use EFT along with other, more conventional interventions, including medications. Dr. Patricia Carrington is a clinical psychologist and a pioneer in the field of meridian tapping and EFT. She is one of a handful of practitioners worldwide to have been awarded the title master. She says, "I am reluctant to use tapping as the *sole* treatment for serious depression however, although I use it by itself with some mild or transient depression. I will typically ask a *seriously* depressed client to use medication *along with meridian tapping* until such time as they are feeling substantially better." Carrington goes on to say, "The dual use of antidepressive medication and tapping can often facilitate the tapping process so markedly that the client can eventually taper off the medication and rely on tapping alone."[254]

This was the case with Robert, a fifty-four-year-old construction worker who was feeling depressed and having difficulty with his relationship with his wife. His doctor had prescribed medications, but he felt it wasn't helping as much as he wished. "My wife, Donna, keeps trying to cheer me up, but it just makes me angry. In the down economy, I'm working less than I'd like, and I'm terrified I won't have enough money to support Donna and our son Josh."

I suggested trying EFT, and he agreed. We began with him thinking about the last time he got angry with his wife. As he recalled a recent incident where they had gotten into a fight about his pessimistic attitude toward life, he rated his distress level on a scale of one to ten at a nine. (See Chapter Eight for a more complete description of how to use EFT).

I had him tap the karate-chop area of his right hand with the fingers of his left hand while he repeated the setup phrase three times: "Even though I have this anger toward Donna, I deeply love and accept myself." After we completed this initial phase, I could see him lighten up a bit. "I'm glad to be able to acknowledge my anger. Usually I try to keep it suppressed," he told me. "But I have to tell you, it's difficult to say the words, 'I love and accept myself.' I realize how down on myself I am."

I introduced the next part of the process, what I call the ice cream sandwich. I explained that the top wafer of the sandwich was a sequence of tapping along each of nine meridians. The ice cream in the middle was a series of eye-movement exercises that help balance the brain. The bottom wafer was another series of tapping. While doing the tapping, he repeated the phrase "this anger with Donna."

After we completed the sequence, I asked him to remember the fight with his wife and rate his level of discomfort again. He took a moment, looked surprised, and said, "Wow, it's down to about a three." We repeated the tapping sequence until he was down to a zero or one. In subsequent sessions, we tapped on "my fear of losing my job and not being able to support my family." That triggered memories from childhood about his father being out of work and his mother having to leave the kids with a sitter while she went out to work.

After each session, he felt better and his mood improved. His relationship with his wife got better, and he worked with his doctor to decrease and finally stop his antidepressant use. We continued working together, combining EFT and more traditional "talk therapy" that explored other ways to improve his life. His depression fully lifted, and two years after our sessions ended he reported that things were going well. "Donna and I still have our ups and downs, and we fight occasionally," he told me, "but we resolve things quickly, and I don't get depressed. I feel better than I ever have in my life. I have to admit, I thought that 'tapping stuff' was weird at first, but it really did work."

Treating Irritable Male Syndrome and Male-Type Depression by Connecting to the Earth

There are many good reasons to exercise. It helps us lose weight, decreases the risk of heart disease and diabetes, and improves many other conditions. Evidence continues to mount that exercise, including simple walking and jogging, helps treat depression. "Over a dozen clinical trials now show that exercise can effectively treat depression," says Stephen S. Ilardi, PhD, author of *The Depression Cure: The 6-Step Program to Beat Depression without Drugs.* [255]

Beginning in the early 1990s, Dr. James Blumenthal at Duke University began to study exercise as a treatment for depression. The initial study involved 156 depressed patients—mostly middle-aged and extremely out of shape—who were randomly assigned to treatment with either Zoloft (a commonly prescribed antidepressant medicine) or exercise. Surprising to many, they found an exercise regime was more effective in treating depression than the antidepressant drug. What exercise proved so effective? *A brisk half-hour walk, three times a week.* "The two treatments worked about equally well for the first few months, but by ten months into the study, the exercisers were much more likely than those taking Zoloft to remain depression-free."[256]

And there are many different exercises to choose from. Over the years, I've enjoyed jogging, swimming, basketball, racquetball, football, and rowing. But I always come back to walking. It doesn't require any special equipment. I can do it anywhere and at any time. Plus, when I walk, particularly in nature, I feel like I'm in touch with an ancient practice. We know that our hunter-gatherer ancestors had to walk, on average, ten miles a day to feed themselves. Our bodies, minds, and spirits are designed to move.

Dr. Ilardi notes that modern-day hunter-gatherer bands, such as the Kaluli people of the New Guinea highlands, have been assessed by Western researchers for the presence of mental illness. "Remarkably," he says, "*clinical depression is almost completely nonexistent among such groups.*"[257] Take a page from our ancestors: get out and walk. It doesn't take walking ten miles a day to get the antidepressant benefits. Studies show walking for just half an hour, three times a week, can work wonders. "The hunter-gatherer lifestyle," says Ilardi, "is profoundly antidepressant."[258]

When I'm feeling irritable, depressed, or stressed, I remember the words of the philosopher Soren Kierkegaard: "Above all, do not lose your desire to walk. Every day I walk myself into a state of wellbeing and walk away from every illness. I have walked myself into my best thoughts, and I know of no thought so burdensome that one cannot walk away from it."

Walking with Someone You Care About Can Produce Even Greater Health Results

There are times when walking alone is very healing for me. I walk vigorously, get my blood flowing, feel the healing endorphins surging through me as I pick up the pace, and enjoy my unique and individual connection to the rest of the world. There are also times when I don't want to be alone. I've found that having a walking buddy can be very helpful. Not only is it easier to commit to getting out and walking when you walk with someone else, it is also more fun because we can talk with a friend. This socializing provides additional health benefits. In his excellent book *Dying to be Men: Psychosocial, Environmental, and Biobehavioral Directions in Promoting*

the Health of Men and Boys, Dr. Will Courtenay details important research about the health benefits men get from having
social supports in their lives.[259]

Men with the fewest social relationships are two to three
times more likely to die from all causes. **In one study of heart
disease patients, 50 percent of those without a confidant were
dead after five years, compared to only 17 percent of those
with a spouse or confidant.** Those of us with more social support tend to maintain more positive health practices. We are
likelier to modify unhealthy behaviors and adhere to medical
treatment. Our immune systems function better and react to
stress more efficiently. So if you don't have a friend to walk
with, find one and enjoy some time together.[260]

Walk to Improve Your Love Life

Early on in my counseling work with both men and women,
I noticed something seemingly obvious that I didn't understand. Women seem much more comfortable talking about
their problems in therapy than men do. I used to assume it
was just part of men's denial and resistance to getting help.
But I'd always felt I was missing something.

The missing piece fell into place when I began counseling adolescent boys at the local group home. I found they
couldn't sit still long enough to do counseling. They were
restless and active and needed to be moving. So I went with
the flow and moved with them. Instead of sitting in my office

talking, we would walk and talk or throw a football around and talk.

To my great surprise, I found that these guys talked rather easily once we got moving. This seems to be true for men generally. It seems particularly true when the topic of discussion is something that is anxiety producing, like "How's your relationship doing?" Most guys remember that uncomfortable, pit-of-the-stomach feeling when our spouse says, "Honey, we need to talk." We sit down in front of her, and it seems like all our poise, wisdom, understanding, and brains just seem to disappear out the nearest window. We stammer and stutter, act like fools, and then we often get angry and walk away in disgust.

She's hurt, we're confused, and the pattern can repeat endlessly. This may not happen with all men and women, but I've heard the story from so many of my clients and even experienced it enough times in my own life that I am convinced the experience is pretty nearly universal. As a student of anthropology and human origins, I wondered why this should be. I've read a lot about our early hunter-gatherer ancestors and how things worked for them. I came to the conclusion that the traditional way men communicated was side-by-side while they were on the trail of animals. It wasn't a great idea to talk much or they'd scare supper away, so they communicated in short, quiet grunts or hand gestures (the exact kind of communication women often accuse us of using).

While men's preferred style of communicating was often side-by-side, women like to communicate face-to-face. In the relative safety of the camp, the women could talk more loudly. Eye contact was essential, and words were important to communicate the subtleties of feelings needed to raise small children and communicate their needs to friends and families. When men were out hunting, the only time they had eyes looking directly at them was when they were being stalked by a wild animal.

We can build on these ancient ways of relating to improve the communications between men and women. Walking and talking in nature seems to work good for men and women. Men enjoy being able to communicate without the intense eye contact that can feel uncomfortable, and women can enjoy being able to talk while her man listens to her.

Until I began using this wonderful Earth-connecting element of walking, I didn't realize what a valuable and versatile tool it could be. Here are a few quotes about walking that I find particularly insightful:

"The best remedy for a short temper is a long walk."
—Jacqueline Schiff

"Of all exercises, walking is the best."
—Thomas Jefferson

"To live in the present moment is a miracle.
The miracle is not to walk on water.
The miracle is to walk on the green Earth
in the present moment."
—Thich Nhat Hanh

CHAPTER 10:
I HAVEN'T GOT
TIME FOR THE PAIN

More than seven hundred men gathered at the Scottish Rite Masonic Center in San Francisco to hear poet Robert Bly, storyteller Michael Meade, and psychologist James Hillman share their expertise about what it means to be a man in today's society. In one of the exercises, red strips of cloth were passed out to all the men. We were asked to tie the strips around any part of our bodies where we had been seriously injured and where we still experience pain.

I reflected on my own wounds and began tying the cloth strips around my left shoulder where I had dislocated my clavicle (a football accident), both my ankles (playing basketball), and my back (a wrestling accident). When I looked up, I was shocked to see the whole room turning red with seven hundred men acknowledging their wounds. These were just the serious physical injuries. We weren't yet talking about the emotional pain we each carried.

Pain is a Major Problem for Many People

Pain affects more Americans than diabetes, heart disease, and cancer combined. The chart below depicts the number of chronic pain sufferers compared to other major health conditions.[261]

Condition	Number of Sufferers	Source
Chronic Pain	116 million people	Institute of Medicine of The National Academies
Diabetes	25.8 million people (diagnosed and estimated undiagnosed)	American Diabetes Association
Coronary Heart Disease (includes heart attack and chest pain) Stroke	16.3 million people 7.0 million people	American Heart Association
Cancer	11.7 million people	American Cancer Society

Pain by the Numbers[262]

- The total annual cost of health care due to pain ranges from $560 billion to $635 billion (in 2010 dollars) in the United States, which combines the medical costs of pain care and the economic costs related to disability days and lost wages and productivity.
- An estimated 20 percent of American adults (42 million people) report that pain or physical discomfort disrupts their sleep a few nights a week or more.

- When asked about four common types of pain, respondents of a National Institute of Health Statistics survey indicated that lower back pain was the most common (27 percent), followed by severe headache or migraine pain (15 percent), neck pain (15 percent), and facial ache or pain (4 percent).
- Adults with lower back pain are often in worse physical and mental health than people who do not have lower back pain: 28 percent of adults with lower back pain report limited activity due to a chronic condition, as compared to 10 percent of adults who do not have lower back pain.[263]

"Pain is the classic example of a double-edged sword," says journalist John Scott. "It's a very clever system for warning us that something is wrong with the body—think of it as the dog that barks in the night to warn you of a robber entering your home. But once you have the message, you want the dog to stop barking. Except pain does not come with an on/off switch. Like a dog that lacks training, it will not obey your commands. If the cause of the pain is an accidental injury, it will most likely heal and the pain will fade of its own accord. But if the pain persists, you have to make an emotional adjustment."[264]

What Is Chronic Pain?

According to the American Academy of Pain Medicine, there is a difference between acute pain and chronic pain.

"While acute pain is a normal sensation triggered in the nervous system to alert you to possible injury and the need to take care of yourself, chronic pain is different. Chronic pain persists. Pain signals keep firing in the nervous system for weeks, months, even years. There may have been an initial mishap—sprained back, serious infection—or there may be an ongoing cause of pain—arthritis, cancer, ear infection—but some people suffer chronic pain in the absence of any past injury or evidence of body damage." [265]

Chronic pain affects people of all ages, races, and occupations. Severe chronic pain is a devastating health problem that affects as many as one in ten Americans (more than twenty-five million people).[266] For every person who must deal with chronic pain, many others are affected, including wives, children, employers, coworkers, and friends. Chronic pain costs the U.S. economy more than $90 billion per year in medical costs, disability payments, and productivity.[267]

Chronic pain shatters productive lives. Chronic pain almost always is accompanied by depression, anxiety, frustration, fatigue, isolation, and lowered self-esteem. Pain makes it hard to work, hard to play, and hard to ask for help or get support from others.

"Medicine has made great inroads into the control of acutely painful conditions using medications and anesthetic techniques," says chronic pain specialist Chris Stewart-Patterson, MD. "It has also had some success with the types of pain associated with terminal cancer, using morphine and related drugs. But the long-term pain that attends nonfatal conditions—such as injuries or lower back maladies—often responds poorly to standard medical treatments."[268]

Understanding the True Nature of Chronic Pain

Most of us accept, often without thinking, the common belief that all our pain has a physical cause. **"I have never seen a patient with pain in the neck, shoulders, back or buttocks who didn't believe the pain was due to an injury,"** says John E. Sarno, MD, author of *Healing Back Pain: The Mind-Body Connection.* Sarno describes the common causes his patients offer in their attempt to understand their pain. "I hurt myself while playing basketball/ tennis/bowling," "The pain started after I lifted my little girl/ when I tried to open a stuck window," or "Ten years ago I was involved in a hit-from-behind auto accident, and I have had recurrent pain ever since."[269] It seems so evident that pain is caused by some injury that we don't often give it a second thought.

Since 1973, Dr. Sarno has conducted research and clinical practice on disorders relating to musculoskeletal pain. **Dr. Sarno was one of the first researchers to recognize that chronic back pain, so pervasive in our culture, could not be adequately treated without acknowledging the emotional aspects of pain.** Through his groundbreaking experience, Dr. Sarno has identified the cause of most common back, neck, shoulder, and limb pain, and in doing so he has changed the way we can look at pain and its treatment.

"The idea that pain means injury or damage is deeply ingrained in the American consciousness," says Sarno. "Of course, if the pain starts while one is engaged in a physical activity, it's difficult not to attribute the pain to the activity.... But this pervasive concept of the vulnerability of the back, of ease of injury, is nothing less than a medical catastrophe for the American public, which now has an army of semidisabled men and women whose lives are significantly restricted by the fear of doing further damage or bringing on the dreaded pain again."[270]

Sarno points out that modern medicine's preoccupation with looking for physical causes for body pain rises from conventional medical philosophy and training of most medical doctors. "Modern medicine has been primarily mechanical and structural in orientation. The body is viewed as an exceedingly complex machine, and illness is a malfunction in the machine brought about by infection, trauma, inherited defects, degeneration, and of course, cancer."[271]

Based on his years of experience treating physical pain of all kinds, Sarno has concluded that "the majority of these pain syndromes are the result of a condition in the muscles, nerves, tendons, and ligaments brought on my tension."[272] Although still not accepted by the majority of mainstream medicine practitioners, this mind/body connection is increasingly being recognized in the complementary and alternative medical communities and by more and more people who are in pain.

In the 2007 National Health Interview Survey, back pain was by far the most common condition cited as a reason for using complementary and alternative medical (CAM) treatments, followed by neck pain, joint pain/stiffness, and arthritis. Another survey of more than four hundred patients at a chronic pain clinic found that almost 40 percent used at least one form of CAM.[273]

Eric Robins, MD, a Los Angeles–based physician, found Sarno's research and clinical work treating pain compelling. "For decades, Sarno has seen the worst chronic pain patients in the world," he says, "and most lived with severe pain in the neck, back, shoulder, or buttocks for ten to thirty years. Most received multiple epidural injections, one or more surgeries, and years of physical therapy."[274] Robins goes on to say that most of Sarno's patients had good reason to be in pain, having had such things as a forklift truck fall on them or a 747 jet roll over them.

Robins describes what most of us experience when we go to our doctor complaining of chronic pain. "Typically, when a pain patient goes to a physician for help," says Robins, "the doctor orders an MRI scan, which invariably shows some sort of anatomic abnormality like a slipped disc. The doctor concludes that the disc is causing the pain and prescribes symptom-suppressing drugs or therapies." Robins goes on to share the experience he has had with this kind of treatment philosophy. "Unfortunately, this approach usually has poor long-term results," he says. "The pain may disappear for a while, but it soon comes back, often worse than before."[275]

Although it might seem reasonable to assume that the cause of the pain is the physical abnormality that was found through medical testing, it turns out to be wrong. Dr. Sarno looked at the medical literature and found an interesting study in the *New England Journal of Medicine.* It showed that if you take one hundred middle-aged people who have *NO* back pain and do MRI scans on them, 65 percent will have a slipped disc or spinal stenosis. In other words, these people who have no back pain have conditions that are blamed for most of the world's back pain.[276]

Sarno pondered this finding, "If the disc isn't causing this pain, then what is?" He discovered that his patients had chronic tension and spasm of the muscles of the neck, back, shoulder, or buttocks. Then Dr. Sarno asked himself, "Why would someone have chronically tensed muscles to begin with?" He added to this knowledge something he knew from observation: that many of us grow up learning, on an unconscious level, that it's not okay to feel or express our anger or anxiety.

I realize it may be a stretch for some men to accept that their pain may be caused by their emotions, rather than the physical injury. But this is in fact what more and more practitioners are finding, and here is the good news about this. **You have the power to treat your own pain, and you can do it without surgery, drugs, or other invasive interventions.**

Dr. Sarno has discovered that simply becoming aware of our unexpressed feelings of anger or anxiety can help heal chronic pain. Dr. Robins notes that Sarno was able to achieve amazing results by having his patients listen to two lectures. In the first lecture, he'd tell them, "It's not the disc or spinal stenosis or any other anatomic abnormality that's causing your pain. Most people your age that have no pain have a slipped disc or spinal stenosis or other conditions that are abnormally blamed for back pain. What is causing your pain is chronic tension and spasm of the muscles."[277]

In the second lecture, he'd tell them, "Whenever you have pain, I want you to notice what you're angry or anxious about." Dr. Sarno then had his patients write in a journal, enroll in group therapy sessions, or engage in psychotherapy. Robins points out that Dr. Sarno's treatment methods are important breakthroughs, but the methods he recommends to handle emotional issues are archaic compared to the speed and efficiency of energy healing techniques.

Using Emotional Freedom Techniques (EFT) for Pain Relief: My Own Experiences

I first heard about EFT when I was looking for help treating chronic pain from a football injury I had suffered many years previously. I still remember the day it happened. A group of six or eight of us met to play a pick-up football game in our neighborhood. One of our favorite places to play was the local elementary school. It had a wide expanse of grass that made a perfect football field after we marked off the boundaries. We were all kids ranging in age from twelve to sixteen. Even at fourteen, I was one of the smallest kids there, but I was quick and I never gave up on a play.

On one of the plays, two of the bigger boys jumped on my back to bring me to the ground. I refused to buckle. At fourteen, I needed to show I was macho and imagined I would score the winning touchdown and carry these guys with me into the end zone. What actually happened was that I carried them for two steps before my legs gave way and they fell on top of me, driving my left shoulder into the ground.

I was in serious pain that day and the next. My mother finally took me to the doctor over my protests: "I'm fine, Mom, let me be." I was determined to show my manly ability to "tough it out." The doctor said it wasn't broken, but the shoulder was dislocated. He did some manipulations and said to come back if I had more problems. Of course, I didn't go back. It continued to hurt, but I saw it as a badge of courage that I could live with the pain. Later on, the pain would come and go. I took pain medications for a while and saw various doctors, chiropractors, and physical therapists. Nothing really helped.

On one of my regular physical checkups, my doctor noticed I was in pain and asked me about it. I gave her a brief rundown on the injury and the attempts I had made to relieve the pain over the years. She suggested I see an acupuncturist. "You mean those people who stick needles into you?" I asked. "Yes, I've found it has worked well for many of my patients." Well, I don't like needles, so I jokingly asked if there was some kind of acupuncture without needles. I was surprised when she told me there is. She had heard of a treatment called EFT that might be helpful, though she had no experience with it herself.

I thanked her and went home to Google EFT. I found a person who was certified to practice EFT. At that first appointment, he told me that EFT is an energy healing process developed by Gary Craig that with the mind/body energy system to eliminate all kinds of emotional, mental, physical and spiritual discomfort. He described it as "acupuncture without needles."

I was skeptical, I admit. I thought I knew what was causing the pain. I was sure it was caused by the long-ago football injury and only surgery could really fix it. But I didn't want surgery so was willing to give this a try.

He began by asking me to rate the level of discomfort I was feeling on a scale of one (no discomfort) to ten (excruciatingly painful). I told him it was about seven, but if I tried to lift my shoulder, it went up immediately to ten. He took me through a tapping sequence at different points on my face, chest, and arms while holding the memory of the injury in my mind. (See Chapter Eight for details.) After one round of tapping, I was truly amazed because the pain level had gone down to a five. I was overjoyed and was about to thank him and leave when he said, "We're not through yet. We want to get the level down to zero if we can."

It took some additional tapping that day and two additional weekly sessions to get the rating down to zero, but we got there. Some problems can be resolved in a single session. More often, there are additional issues related to the pain that need to be addressed. With the guidance of the counselor, I was able to tap while exploring the following related issues:

- The anxiety I felt over having boys I didn't know joining our game.
- The intense excitement of competition to win at all costs.
- The fear of being seen as a loser.
- The worry that I would let down my team if I showed weakness.
- The rage when I felt I was being disrespected.
- Irritation at my mother for fussing over me.
- Anger at various doctors and practitioners for not fixing me.

As I delved more deeply into the emotional issues and tapped them away, the pain level continued to go down, eventually reaching zero. The pain in my left shoulder has never returned, though I know the shoulder is still "dislocated" because I continue to feel the gap where my collarbone connects with the shoulder, and the bone continues to protrude. This is the bone the surgeon suggested he could cut off. I shudder to think I might have done that or when I think of how many other men go under the surgeon's knife when they can avoid it with energy healing.

EFT Works for All Kinds of Pain

If you are suffering from chronic pain, you are not alone. According to the Institute of Medicine of the National Academies of Science, 116 million people suffer from chronic pain.[278] The most common chronic pain is back pain. According to *Men's Health* magazine, "America is in the midst of a back-pain epidemic. There's an 80 percent chance that, at some point in your life, you'll suffer from severe back pain. Treating back pain costs about $26 billion annually and it currently accounts for 2.5 percent of our country's total health care spending. If worker compensation and disability payments were taken into account, the cost would be even higher."[279]

Many of us have back problems and assume that the pain and discomfort results from an injury we suffered or from overdoing some activity. But more and more doctors are recognizing that emotions are the real culprit. "Again and again," says Dr. Eric Robins, "patients with chronic pain have unresolved emotional issues or anger that's tied to past traumas. Stress and negative emotions aren't just in our heads; they are stored in our bodies, often in skeletal or smooth muscles. It's hard for blood to flow through chronically tensed muscles."[280]

In his book *EFT for Back Pain*, Gary Craig says, "What excites me most about EFT is its application to physical health and wellness. I'm convinced more than ever that modern medicine has walked right by a major contributor of chronic and acute diseases. Our unresolved angers, fears, and traumas show up in our physical bodies and manifest not just as back pain but as rheumatoid arthritis, cancer, multiple sclerosis, Parkinson's disease, and hundreds of other illnesses."[281]

A number of men who used EFT share their experiences. Alan was skeptical at first. "Three years ago, I had a bad fall resulting in a minor fracture on my spine. The healing was complete, but I could not sit upright for any length of time without my back hurting. I have been struggling with this for more three years, making traveling and sitting for any length of time difficult.

"While traveling on a bus, reading through the EFT success stories, my back started hurting as usual. The skeptic in me challenged me to try EFT. I began with the setup and worked through the different points and the gamut pressure points. I did both sides of the body and waited. Like ice cream melting silently in room temperature, the pain eased off and completely vanished. I sat still, disbelieving, waiting for the pain to come back as the bus swayed along for another half an hour. It did not.

"It has been a few days, and the pain has not returned. The conclusion is simple: EFT works! No gimmick! Thanks for this new way of working with mind and body."[282]

Andy learned about EFT in a workshop with Gary Craig. "I had been in constant pain for over a decade due to sports injuries and car accidents. I have broken my MCL and ACL in my left knee, and I had a pinched nerve and damaged discs in my neck. I tapped on 'this pain in my knee' for about five minutes, including the gamut point, and the pain receded immediately. Since then, if I ever have pain in the knee, I tap a round or two and it goes away."

Andy goes on to recount his experience with his family doctor. "My GP had suggested a dozen pain killers a day for the pain, but after EFT, I don't use any medication at all. He suggested that I might need surgery, but when I spoke to a surgeon I was told that even if I had surgery, I would still have pain in my knee, so I declined the surgery."

In addition to physical pain, Andy tried EFT on some of the emotional pain he was experiencing and found it worked for that as well. "I have also used EFT to deal with the death of my father and my beloved dog and the loss of my twelve-year marriage and my ten-year job as a youth counselor, all of which occurred in about a year and a half."[283]

I've found EFT is a very useful tool for dealing with both physical and emotional pain. In the conclusion to his book on back pain, Gary Craig says, "Whether you're working with yourself, your spouse or partner, your children, a friend or relative, a client, a patient, or a favorite pet, EFT is a powerful tool for the relief of all types of pain and discomfort."[284]

Earthing Helps Us Eliminate Pain, Sleep Better, and Reduce Inflammation

Another tool I have found to be helpful in eliminating pain is *Earthing* (See Chapter Five for details). Throughout my life, I have enjoyed sports and have always had to deal with aches and pains. Stephen Sinatra, MD, who co-wrote the book *Earthing: The Most Important Health Discovery Ever?* remembers a phone call he received from Clint Ober. Ober had done the initial research on *Earthing* and teamed up with Sinatra to write the book. He felt he had learned some important things about how *Earthing* could help with pain.

"Clint called me one day, excited about having found another important explanation for how grounding was working in the body. It didn't 'just' normalize cortisol, improve sleep, and reduce stress, as if that weren't enough. If somebody is in direct contact with the Earth—barefoot or through one of the grounding pads—the free electrons flow into the conductive circuitry of the body and snuff out inflammation. Inflammation causes pain. People with pain who are grounded experience less pain.

For him, the connection was simple.

Get grounded.

Get well.

Get pain relief.

Heal."[285]

Dr. Sinatra tells us that everyone is susceptible to inflammation—from high-performance athletes to nonperformance couch potatoes. "It's an equal-opportunity hit man," he says. But initially the "hits" are positive. "Inflammation is the complex biological response of the body to harmful stimuli, such as pathogens, damaged cells, or irritants," Sinatra says. "It is a protective attempt by the system to remove injurious or threatening agents as well as start the healing process for the affected tissue. In the absence of inflammation, wounds and infections would never heal and progressive destruction of the tissue would compromise survival."[286]

When the Body Is Under Attack, Free Radicals Come to the Rescue

Here's how it works. Your immune system protects you from all kinds of nasty bugs and helps repair tissue that has been damaged by injury or surgery. When a problem develops somewhere, your body does the equivalent of calling 911. The alarm sounds, and the immune system springs into action. The first responders, the white blood cells, travel to the site of the problem. As weapons, some of the cells release a shower of powerful free radicals (called an oxidative burst) that aids in the destruction of invading microorganisms and damaged tissue.[287]

"Free radicals" is not a left-wing chant urging the release of political prisoners. Simply put, free radicals are positively charged molecules that are missing one or more electrons. This makes them unstable and causes them to constantly search for electrons to restore their balance. Normally, these free radicals get their missing electrons by stripping electrons away from pathogens and damaged tissue. This kills the bad bugs in our bodies and breaks down damaged cells for removal. We experience this process as the familiar signs and symptoms of inflammation: swelling, redness, heat and pain.

That all sounds positive, so what's the problem with inflammation? The problem is similar to the stress response that helps us when we are under attack, but fails to turn off when the danger has passed. "The good guys become bad guys on a rampage," says Sinatra, "ripping up innocent, healthy cells. Think of security dogs that snag the burglar and then go after the owner."[288]

In our modern world, where we feel continually under stress, inflammation runs wild and causes all kinds of disease. Dr. Paul Ridker, professor of medicine at Harvard Medical School, says, "We are witnessing evolutionary biology in action—an adaptive response (inflammation) in the past is now maladaptive in our current modern environment."[289]

Enter Earthing—The Missing Link

Clint Ober's creative genius is that he understood that the increase of inflammatory diseases could be related to our disconnection from the Earth. He did his own experiments, and then he got scientists interested in looking more deeply. Here's their theory of how Earthing works to reduce pain:

- The Earth is negatively charged. It has a nearly endless supply of negatively charged electrons.
- Anytime two conductive objects make contact—like your bare feet (one conductive object) and the ground (another conductive object)—electrons will flow from where they are abundant to where there are fewer of them.
- The electrical potential of both objects tends to equalize. That's grounding.
- If you have a lot of positively charged free radicals running around your body and you connect to the Earth, your body can equalize.[290]

Dr. James Oschman, a world authority on energy and complementary medicine and author of *Energy Medicine: The Scientific Basis,* summarizes what happens this way: "The moment your foot touches the Earth, or you connect to the Earth through a wire, your physiology changes. An immediate normalization begins. And an anti-inflammatory switch is turned on. People stay inflamed because they never connect with the Earth, the source of free electrons, which can neutralize the free radicals in the body that cause disease and cellular destruction."[291]

Eliminating Pain Using Earthing Technology

In Chapter Five, I discussed three ways to use Earthing in our lives:

1. Take your shoes off. Walk barefoot on the Earth to get the benefits of all those negative electrons.

2. When you do wear shoes, wear leather-soled shoes. Be a rebel. Resist rubber soles and get back to wearing shoes that don't insulate you from the healing energies of the Earth.

3. When you're at home and work, get "barefoot substitutes."[292] Learn about the simple pads, sheets, and mats designed to keep you grounded in the comfort of your own home.

Earthing Relieves the Pain of Rheumatoid Arthritis

Howard Runion, PhD, a retired professor of neurophysiology, has lived with the pain of rheumatoid arthritis. The seventy-six-year-old Runion has arthritis is in his hands, shoulders, back, and lower extremities. "There is nothing going to remove this disorder. It is progressive and degenerative." He remembers a friend telling him about Earthing, so he ordered the sheets to see if it would help him sleep better. "I tried it," said Runion, "and noticed there was a tremendous difference. I thought at first it was my imagination. I stopped using it. The condition got worse again. So I tried it again, and I felt better.

"On a scale of one to ten, where ten is so bad that you wish you had something to blow your brains out, my pain level without sleeping grounded is often around eight. Sleeping grounded, the level may be about five. This is not a cure. But it certainly helps, and the difference makes it worth doing. For anyone who suffers from rheumatoid arthritis, I recommend this simple, effective procedure of sleeping on a grounded sheet as an aid to significant pain reduction. It works."[293]

Earthing for Back Pain, Neck Pain, Carpal Tunnel Pain, and Other Pains of Living

Jim Bellacera is a fifty-one-year-old business motivational speaker. "Six years ago," says Bellacera, "I first heard about sleeping on a bed pad that was grounded. I thought I would be a great test case because for more than twenty plus years I had had chronic pain from my days in construction and cabinetmaking.

"My pain problems started around age twenty-six. I had back pain, neck pain, and carpal tunnel pain. During one job, I jumped off a trailer while carrying one of my cabinets, and I crushed my back. Nothing I did ever seemed to help, from seeing doctors and getting regular back treatments to taking 800 mg of ibuprofen two or three times a day and sometimes other anti-inflammatories as well.

"And, son of a gun, I woke up in disbelief the morning after the first night I slept grounded. 'No, this can't be,' I said. 'My back doesn't hurt.' Not only didn't it hurt, but after a day or two, I didn't have to reach for my daily dose of big ibuprofen horse pills.

"Anybody who's in business for themselves is feeling a lot of different types of stresses. There are a lot of things going around in your mind 24/7. You're never really turned off. So for me, one of the hardest things to do was just actually going to sleep. It used to be where I would just toss and turn all the time and my head would go back and forth, until at some point I would fall asleep. Besides the pain, I also noticed from the start that I went to sleep really fast, and I'd wake up in the morning really refreshed and with more energy."[294]

Earthing for the Pains of Aging

Arnold Belden, a ninety-year-old retired clinical psychologist, has found that Earthing helps him deal with the pains of aging. "I've been sleeping grounded pretty regularly for more than eight years. Within a year, I realized that I wasn't going to doctors like I used to do. My hands and hip hurt me less from arthritis. I also noticed that my mind seems clearer, and I seem to have more energy and stamina.

"After a year, I had a checkup with my doctor, and he commented that he was amazed at my excellent health given my age.

"I still do a lot of yard work, including tree pruning, and I've had my share of cuts, scrapes, and even falls. I was out a few weeks ago on my recumbent three-wheeler bike, and I took a fall. I banged myself up but didn't break anything, and I healed up nice and quick. Same thing with the yard work. None of the cuts ever gets infected, even though I don't put any topical medicine on them.

"My sleep has definitely been better ever since I started this. If I wake up at night, it seems like after a minute or so, I am back sleeping again.

"Now after all these years of continued Earthing, I can't say I've reversed the aging process. I still have the arthritis, but I don't need to take any medication for it. In fact, I don't take a single medication for anything. I feel darn good for somebody who is ninety. My energy is great."[295] For more details about Earthing, please refer to Chapter Five.

CHAPTER 11:
THE LION IN WINTER:
ANDROPAUSE AND MIDLIFE SEX

When my book *Male Menopause* was first published in 1997, most people had never heard of "male menopause," also known by the more scientific term "andropause." But I knew the impact on family members who loved these men. Common symptoms of male menopause, including erectile dysfunction, loss of sexual desire, irritability, weight gain, and low energy, impact the men as well as their families. More men and women are recognizing that male menopause is real. It affects all men as they move through their forties (though it can start as early as thirty or as late as fifty-five). We can now do a lot to prevent and treat the problems associated with this major change of life.

While many in the mainstream medical community still question whether men go through a hormonally based change of life, increasing numbers of health care profession-als are convinced as they study the research.[296]

- Marc R. Blackman, MD, former chief of endocrinol-ogy and metabolism at Johns Hopkins medical center, says, "The male menopause is a real phenomenon, and it does similar things to men as menopause does to women, although less commonly and to a lesser extent."[297]

- Ronald Klatz, MD, DO, president of the American Academy of Anti-Aging Medicine says, "One of the best-kept secrets is that men go through a male form of menopause called andropause."[298]

- Robert S. Tan, MD, fellow of the American Geriatrics Society and pioneer researcher, says, "The andropause is the time in a man's life when the hormones naturally decline. *Mosby's Medical Dictionary* **defines the andropause as 'a change of life for males that may be expressed in terms of career change, divorce, or reordering of life. It is associated with a decline in androgen levels that occur in men during their late forties or early fifties."[299]**

- Theresa Crenshaw, MD, expert on male and female hormones and author of *The Alchemy of Love and Lust*, says, "In the case of male menopause, we are still in the Dark Ages. Men have fewer guideposts to help them today than women had a generation ago. Only recently have we begun to understand the biochemistry of these events, tilting the scales toward a physiological explanation."[300]

- Author Gail Sheehy says, "If menopause is the silent passage, male menopause is the unspeakable passage. It is fraught with secrecy, shame, and denial. It is much more fundamental than the ending of the fertile period of a woman's life, because it strikes at the core of what it is to be a man."[301]

My colleague, Malcolm Carruthers, MD, one of the world's experts on the male change of life captures the essence of what men go through: "Andropause is a critical health concern for men and the women who love them. It's often insidious onset can be at any time from the age of thirty onward, though typically it is in the fifties. One of the reasons it's often missed is that it is usually more gradual in onset than the menopause in the female, although it is more severe in its long-term consequences. **It is a crisis of vitality just as much as virility, even though it's most obvious sign is loss both of interest in sex and of erectile power.**"[302]

Andropause/Male Menopause: What Is This Thing We're Going Through?

The term "male menopause" is obviously technically inaccurate. The term "menopause" was introduced by French doctors in the 1870s, combining two Greek words—*menses* ("periods") and *pausis* ("stop"). Men don't have a period, so they don't stop having one. I chose to use male menopause because there are more similarities than differences. In both men and women, there is a change in hormone levels, as well as physical and emotional changes that impact our health and wellbeing.

This important life transition has had several names: male menopause, andropause, the male climacteric, and ADAM (androgen deficiency in the aging male). What they have in common is they all indicate a change or ending that occurs in male functioning. Increasingly, I use the term andropause (*andro* from the Greek word meaning "male" and *pausis* from the word meaning "stop").

The name implies an ending of a certain aspect of maleness. It also focuses on the drop in male hormones, particularly the androgens (*andro*, "male" and *gen* "to give") like testosterone during this time of life.

What Are the Most Common Signs We Are Moving Into the Andropause?

The most common signs of andropause include:
1. Reduced libido or sex drive
2. Reduced potency or ability to obtain and maintain an erection
3. Irritability and "grumpiness"
4. Fatigue or loss of vitality
5. Aches, pains, and stiffness
6. Depression, which often manifests as anger or boredom
7. Night sweats or "hot flashes"
8. Dryness and thinning of the skin
9. Restlessness and longing to break free and start over
10. Weight gain, especially acquiring a "pot belly"

Do Men Experience Hormonal Cycles?

Lowered levels of hormones at midlife are central to the changes associated with andropause. Testosterone is one of the significant hormones that decrease as men age, but there are also testosterone cycles that occur throughout a man's life. We now understand that men, like women, experience complex hormonal rhythms that affect their sexuality, mood, and temperament. Researchers have found five different testosterone cycles in men: [303]

- Rhythmic fluctuations, three to four times an hour. (Could this account for research that shows men think about sex every fifteen minutes?)
- Daily changes, with testosterone higher in the morning and lower in the afternoon.
- Fluctuations throughout the year, with levels higher in October and lower in April.
- Decreasing levels associated with andropause that occur as we age.
- Monthly fluctuations that are rhythmic, but different for each man.

"The morning highs, daily fluctuations, and seasonal cycles whip men around," says Dr. Theresa Crenshaw, author of *The Alchemy of Love and Lust.* "Think about the moment-to-moment impact of testosterone levels firing and spiking all over the place during the day and what this must be doing to a man's temperament."[304]

Some clinicians and researchers believe that andropause is primarily the result of our loss of testosterone. It is clear to me that it is much more than that. **Andropause is a multidimensional change of life with hormonal, physical, psychological, interpersonal, social, sexual, and spiritual aspects.** All aspects are equally important, and all must be understood and treated. They are all present with men during andropause, though they may not all be of equal intensity or equally obvious.

Andropause and Adolescence: Similar Life Stages?

I often describe andropause as "adolescence the second time around" or "puberty in reverse." During puberty, male hormones (like testosterone) surge mightily. Most of us remember those times. "This is the familiar period of hormonal madness, when nature prepares both sexes to reproduce," says Dr. Crenshaw. "The body's chemicals start issuing orders at a dizzying pace. Girls bloom and bleed as they begin menstruating and developing breasts and curvaceous hips. Boys' voices crack and their penises swell at the most unwelcome times. At the height of the testosterone onslaught, they swagger aggressively, obsess about girls, and masturbate relentlessly, regardless of repercussions."[305] Our penises didn't fall off, as we were warned they would, but it felt like we may have been getting close.

Do any of the things listed below sound familiar to you? Think about what we're seeing at this time of life:

- Mood swings
- Hormonal shifts
- Confusion about sexuality
- Desire to break away from family while at the same time clinging tightly to family for support
- Obsession with the latest toys and gadgets
- Need for intimacy side by side with fears about getting close
- Physical changes in the body
- Questioning identity and direction in life

I think we all recognize these as signs of transition. But are we looking at a fifteen-year-old or a fifty-year-old? The similarity between adolescence and andropause is one of the reasons that midlife parents have such a difficult time dealing with their teenage kids. They are both working through the same issues. When Dad freaks out thinking about his daughter's emerging sexuality, it is often because he is also dealing with changes in his own sexuality. When father has difficulty setting reasonable limits on his son's behavior, it is often because he is having trouble setting limits for himself.

Double Menopause: His Change, Her Change, Our Change of Life

When my wife started going through "the change," it was hell on our relationship. She was moody, irritable, and difficult to talk with. She would be warm and approachable one minute. The next, she was hostile and withdrawn. I never knew which woman I would see when I came home. Sometimes she was amorous and interested in sex. More often, her interest seemed to be everywhere except on our sex life.

I'll admit, I blamed a lot of our problems on her and longed for the wife I remembered to return. She gradually got through to the other side, but to my dismay, things between us didn't get better. We were still fighting like crazy, all the joy had gone out of our relationship, and our sex life had gone south and left us behind. After one of our fights, Carlin had the audacity to suggest that maybe *I* was going through "male menopause." I was insulted. What did she mean *male menopause?* There was no such thing. But I'd heard similar stories from many of my friends and clients I counseled. So I started doing research that would become the books *Male Menopause* and later *Surviving Male Menopause: A Guide for Women and Men.*

In *Surviving Male Menopause,* I described what it's like when both the man and woman are going through "the change." We either empathize with our partner and work together or we are pulled apart by the stress, tension, and sexual problems. Nancy Cetel, MD, author of *Double Menopause: What to Do When Both You and Your Mate Go Through Hormonal Changes Together,* was seeing a similar problem with couples she counseled. She said it was common to see a well-established midlife couple with everything to be grateful for—a beautiful family, cozy home, a comfortable lifestyle—and a divorce proceeding heatedly under way.[306]

Dr. Cetel details some of the perceptions men and women have as they go through these changes:

His perceptions include:

- "She seems edgy, tired, and irritable."
- "She doesn't seem to be as interested in me as she used to be."
- "Sex isn't as spontaneous. What happened to the excitement?"
- "Am I still as capable as I used to be?"
- "Our relationship is changing in uncomfortable ways."
- "It's her menopause, and I better not mess with her."

Her perceptions include:

- "He seems edgy, tired, and irritable."
- "He doesn't seem to be as interested in me as he used to be."
- "Sex isn't as enjoyable. I've lost my interest, and he is embarrassed that he is having trouble in that department."
- "Is he depressed or having a midlife crisis?"
- "Our relationship is changing in uncomfortable ways."
- "He doesn't find me attractive anymore."[307]

With so many similarities, you'd think it would be easy to be sympathetic to each other's needs. This doesn't happen, though, because we often see the changes in the other person, but not in ourselves. When we do recognize our own perceptions, we often believe we are simply responding to the other person.

Many times I have felt that my own irritability and anger was simply a response to my wife's withdrawal and lack of interest in sex. It didn't occur to me that her lack of interest may have been caused by my irritability and anger. And of course, it didn't occur to her that my irritability and anger may have been triggered by her withdrawal.

"Acknowledging and becoming knowledgeable about each other's hormonal changes is a necessary first step to avert a hormone-induced breakup," says Cetel. "When a man becomes educated about the hormonal changes a woman experiences during menopause, he is transformed from a helpless mate to a helpmate." She goes on to say, "When a woman becomes educated and aware that her man is not immune from a midlife hormonal transition, she, too, becomes empowered to be a better helpmate and can tune into the subtle changes."[308]

How Women Shame Men and Men Frighten Women

One of the most common yet destructive patterns I see occurring with midlife men and women is how shame and fear get triggered. Here's an example from my own life. My wife, Carlin, and I were returning late from a visit to see our children and grandchildren in the Bay Area. I was driving, and we were both tired. The last ten miles of the drive from Willits to our home is along a windy highway road. I'd driven it hundreds of times before, so I wasn't aware that I was driving faster than usual.

I had a vague sense that Carlin was repeatedly bracing herself every time we went around a curve. For no reason I could express, that made me increasingly agitated. By the time we got home, we had gotten into a fight about something that was so inconsequential I don't remember what it was. We both went to bed angry but neither of us understood why.

A month later, we had another encounter that helped me make sense of what had happened. I came home one day after work to find a note from my wife: "Jed, you forgot to lock the door again when you went out the other day. Love, Carlin." I read the note, briefly tried to remember when else

I forgot to lock the door when I left, and quickly forgot the whole thing.

The next morning Carlin wanted to know why I hadn't responded to the note.

"I don't know, I didn't think it needed a response," I said. I could feel my discomfort rising.

"Well, usually when I leave you a note, you at least acknowledge it. I'm upset about your leaving the door unlocked, but even more upset that you just ignored my note," she said.

I thought to myself, "Damn, what's the big deal here? Why's she getting on my case?" but I bit my tongue and didn't say anything even though, as usual, I felt like I was a kid being chastised by the school principal. These exchanges lead to an emotional chill that comes over our relationship, and both of us end up feeling hurt and misunderstood.

But Carlin continued and said something that broke the ice and led to a greater connection between us. "It's really scary for me when I come home to find the door open," she told me. I could hear the fear in her voice. "I go around the house wondering if there might be an intruder inside. It's really creepy."

As soon as Carlin talked about her fear, I was able to feel my shame. "Protecting you and keeping you safe is one of the most important things in my life," I thought.

"When I feel I've let you down, I feel ashamed," I told her. "I realize the way I often handle shame is to block out the incident and erase it from my mind. I really *do* understand your fear and will be sure to lock the doors before I leave for the day."

I immediately remembered the incident driving home and recognized a similar dynamic. When I was driving faster than was comfortable for Carlin, she felt afraid. I didn't register her fear, but felt her bracing herself as a negative comment on my driving. Her fear triggered shame in me. When I feel ashamed, I often cover it with anger, which makes her even more afraid.

For most of us, there are thousands of little hurts that can undermine a relationship over time. Like me, most men are not aware of the ways their behavior can frighten women. And most women are not aware of the things they do that trigger shame in men. **Throughout their lives, but particularly at midlife, women are particularly sensitive to fears of abandonment. Throughout their lives, but particularly at midlife, men are particularly sensitive to feelings of shame.**

This creates a vicious cycle that often torpedoes even a good relationship that's lasted for twenty-five years or more. Without being aware of it, women's fear causes them to subtly demean and trigger shame in the man in her life. When a man feels ashamed, he questions his self-worth and begins to withdraw emotionally. The more he withdraws, the more fearful the woman becomes, and the more she says and does things that make him feel inadequate.

If we could eavesdrop on what was going on in their subconscious minds, we might hear something like this:

Him: *I want more than anything to be the good man my wife needs, but it feels like I can't do anything right. She spends more time with friends and family than she does with me. I feel like I'm on the bottom of her priority list. Sometimes I feel like breaking down and crying because I feel so lonely. But she'd just see what a wimp I am* *and have even less respect for me than she has already. The only way I can survive is to withdraw.*

Her: *I want more than anything to be the loving woman my husband needs, but it feels like he's pulling away from me. He spends more time at work or on his computer than he does with me. I feel like I'm on the bottom of his priority list. Sometimes I feel like screaming at him to get his attention because I feel so lonely. But he'd just think I'm a raving bitch and withdraw even more. At least with my friends I feel like I'm cared for. The only way I can survive is to withdraw into my own world.*

Do you recognize these feelings in yourself or your partner? I see too many men and women at midlife who want essentially the same things, but misinterpret each other's behavior, and they both withdraw instead of coming together just when they need each other the most. **I often think of midlife men and women as porcupines caught in the snow. They desperately want to get close together to ward off the freezing winds of winter, but as soon as they draw together, they injure each other with their sharp barbs and then quickly pull away again.** They hunger for the warmth of love and connection, but fear the other person will hurt them, which causes them to keep their distance.

Using Energy Healing Tools to Improve Your Midlife Relationship

This is a wonderful time to use your energy healing tools. One that I often find useful is the attachment love tool.

Close your eyes and take a number of deep breaths. Slowly let them out. Remind yourself that you are dependent on your partner and your partner is dependent on you to meet your needs for safety, security, and love. Recall a memory in which you felt deep love and affection for your partner. Imagine that you enclose them in your arms and whisper in their ear, "I love you deeply, and I am here for you." Now recall a time when your partner reached out to you when you needed them. Imagine your partner enclosing you in their arms and whispering in your ear, "I love you deeply, and I am here for you."

Let yourself feel the warmth and gratitude of feeling cared for and loved. If you don't have a partner, imagine a partner you might like to have and feel yourself being held and holding a partner. Or think of a time in your life when you felt love for someone else. It could be an old lover or friend or even a child. Imagine holding them, seeing them, and feeling them. Or think of a time when you were loved, cared for, and protected. Let yourself be filled with the light of unconditional love.

Another energy healing tool that I often use is the Heart-Math Quick Coherence Technique. Close your eyes and take a number of deep breathes and let yourself relax. Focus your attention on the area around your heart. Breathe deeply but normally and feel as if your breath is coming in and going out through your heart area. As you maintain your heart focus and heart breathing, activate a positive feeling. Remember a time when you felt strong and sure of yourself, a time when your partner or someone important in your life let you know what a good man you were. Hold that thought as you continue to imagine your breath coming in and out of your heart area.

I'm always amazed that shifting my internal energy from a state of anger, agitation, hurt, or shame to one of joy, peace, and self-acceptance can turn things around when they seem out of control. Midlife, like adolescence, is a difficult time for most of us. Using these energy healing tools can make our midlife passage smoother and more joyful.

The Perils and Pitfalls of Midlife

If you're feeling your change-of-life years are difficult, you're not alone. Researchers from Great Britain and the U.S. have analyzed data spanning more than thirty-five years on depression, anxiety, mental wellbeing, happiness, and life satisfaction. The findings show that men and women in their forties are more likely to be depressed and aren't as happy as other ages. **Middle age is such a low point for wellbeing; it's at the bottom of a U-shaped curve that shows greater happiness among the younger and older people.** "It's midlife per se," says coauthor Andrew Oswald, an economist at the University of Warwick in Coventry, England. "It's something deep beyond all the controls in our equation. It's a developing midlife low. It doesn't just happen one year and go away another."[309] **For both sexes, the probability of depression peaks around age forty-four.**

A study by Oswald and fellow economist David Blanchflower of Dartmouth College published in the journal *Social*

Science & Medicine found the same U-shape by age for seventy-two of eighty countries studied. "You can be almost certain you will follow this U-shaped curve," Oswald says. "If you are finding life tough in your forties, maybe it's useful to know this is completely normal."[310]

Although this time of life is difficult for men and women, the statistics on suicide indicate that men have a more difficult time as we age. We know the suicide rate for men increases significantly as we age, while it stays about the same for women. Males commit suicide at higher rates than females throughout their lifespan, but the difference increases as we age. The rate for men between the ages of forty-five and fifty-five is 350 percent higher than for women. Between age fifty-five and sixty-five, the rate jumps to 425 percent higher. For men between the ages of sixty-five and seventy-five, it is 610 percent higher. And for men over seventy-five, the rate is 1,220 percent higher than the rate for women of the same age.[311]

Not only is aging a particularly difficult thing for men, but the times we live in make it even more difficult. *Newsweek* recently did a cover story titled "Dead Suit Walking" in which reporters looked at the impact unemployment has on men. More middle-aged, middle-management men are losing their jobs. "The same guys who once drove BMWs, in other words, have now been downsized to BWMs: beached white males," the article says.[312]

I was quoted in the article saying, "I call it the double whammy. The first is a hormonally based change of life affecting our sexuality, psychology, and emotions. The second is unemployment. It's devastating. The extreme reaction is suicide, but before you get there, there's irritability and anger, fatigue, loss of energy, withdrawal, drinking, more fights with their wives."[313]

Most of us would agree with Sigmund Freud's summary of our basic needs: **"Love and work are the cornerstones of our humanness."** For most men, love has been intimately connected to our ability to achieve rock-hard erections that last, if not forever, at least long enough to have intercourse for many hours. Likewise, we believe that to be successful at work, we should continue moving up the ladder and have a better and better job each year that pays ever-higher wages. Plus, success meant we would never be unemployed. But the economic climate is changing, and it's hitting men hard.

Male Menopause: The Passage to the Most Powerful, Passionate, and Productive Time of a Man's Life

Just as adolescence is a transition period that ideally prepares us to move from childhood to adulthood, male menopause helps men to move from first adulthood to second adulthood. For those who have the courage to make the full, complete journey, the second half is often even more fulfilling than the first. I'm reminded of this every time our men's group meets.

We began meeting in 1979. We meet four times a year for a four-day retreat. One man recently died at age eighty-five. For the last fifteen years of his life, he was involved in a variety of community activities and spent a good deal of time mentoring young men. Now our oldest member is seventy-five and the youngest is sixty-three. Although we're all still working full-time or part-time, we have more time for creative endeavors. One man has taken up woodworking, another is doing small-scale farming. All of us are active volunteering in our communities. We also have more time for our relationships with our spouses and partners and with family and friends. Getting older has its challenges, but we all feel blessed to be alive each day and very grateful to have hung in there with each other through all these years.

My friend, author and philosopher Sam Keen, who described his own experiences with men in the book *Fire in the Belly: On Being a Man,* decided to take up flying trapeze two months shy of his sixty-second birthday. In Keen's view, flying trapeze is more than a mere recreational sport. Like archery, flower arranging, and motorcycle maintenance, it serves as a vehicle of profound inner discovery and transformation. Learning to fly involves cultivating equanimity, trust, and the willingness to let go—in the real sense of the term, he says. The challenge and the thrill of trapeze lie in overthrowing our resistances and becoming what he calls *connoisseurs of fear.*

What a great image and challenge. Stress can be overwhelming, and our fears can immobilize us physically and emotionally, causing us to become cold-hearted and angry. Imagine what it would be like to embrace fears, rather than trying to ignore them or make them go away? It turns out this is a particularly important skill to develop in the second half of our lives when everything changes, including our sex and love lives.

Imagine that you're on the trapeze. You swing out, holding the bar. At the height of the swing, you let go and "fly." If you're skilled and your timing is right, the other bar is wait-ing for your outstretched hands. It isn't possible to play it safe hanging on to one bar until the other bar is grasped. I find it useful to think of the old view of love and work as the first bar. We have to let it go completely before we can reach for something else.

How might that look? Well, I'll tell you what it was like for me. In the area of love, I was preoccupied with sex. When my wife and I weren't having good sex, I felt like our love life was going down the tubes. As we both went through our own changes of life, there were long periods of time when sex was difficult and at times nonexistent. I raged and withdrew and masturbated and fumed and longed for the old days when sex was free and easy. Over the years, I finally learned that love really *is* more about connection, friendship, and trust than it is about hot sex. Don't get me wrong—hot sex and love are wonderful, but as we get older they are not a great ideal to always shoot for, so to speak.

Long talks, soft touches, and smiles really form the back-bone of our love. I used to think that was "women's love." Of course, a woman wants all that "romantic" stuff. But real men want real love, and for me that meant sexual intercourse. I now realize the purpose of sex when we are young is to make babies, or at least have the kind of sex that has the potential to make babies. As we get older and our baby-making years are behind us, I see the purpose of making love is, well, to make *love*. Success now is less about erections and more about con-nections, less about orgasms and more about pleasure.

I've found there are benefits to our love life when we learn that losing an erection is not like losing one of our children.

It is not the end of the world, really. It may be frightening, but if we embrace the fear, new possibilities begin to open up. We learn that being rock hard on demand is not necessarily the best way to be as we move into our sixties, seventies, and beyond...even if we could keep it up. What would our lives be like if we didn't buy into the pharmaceutical sales pitch that says we all have the new disease of "erectile dysfunction" for which we can buy a $10-a-pop pill that promises to cure us? Perhaps we would find a new level of ease and intimacy in our lives.

Using Energy Healing Power Tools to Achieve Real Success as We Age

Energy healing power tools give me the edge I need to keep on track as my stress levels continue to increase. We live on a finite planet. That means key resources required for life such as water, good soil to grow food, and nutrients are also limited. As our world population increases, we feel the pressure. In 1800, the world population stood at about one billion. By 1930, it had doubled to two billion. Only thirty years later, in 1960, it had doubled again to four billion. Globally, we are adding about seventy million new "consumers" every year. Currently, we are on track to achieve a third doubling, to eight billion humans, in 2025.

We all know we won't live forever. Midlife signals the end of our upward climb and the beginning of our turn toward home as we look forward to life in the second half. Similarly, we are reaching the limits to human growth. We live on a finite planet, with limited resources. We can either accept our limits and begin to reverse our present trends or keep on using more and more of the earth's resources and wait for the crash. A few of the energy healing tools can help us stay calm and keep our hearts open during these difficult times.

I use emotional freedom techniques regularly to tap my intensions with setup phrases like these:

- "Even though I feel the pressures of increased population, I unconditionally love and accept myself."
- "Even though I feel the fear and pain of people around me, I accept myself fully and completely."
- "Even though I'm concerned about my children and grandchildren, I accept myself fully and completely.

I use heart coherence techniques to keep my love open and feel the positive energies of hope, peace, and reconciliation. As I write this, it is September 11, 2011, and I'm awaiting the worldwide Peace Intention Experiment[314] that is being led by Lynne McTaggart, a visionary peace activist. The world can't afford our continuing wars and conflicts. We can make a difference by keeping our minds, hearts, and souls focused on peace.

I practice attachment love and recognize how critical those close to me are to my survival and wellbeing, particularly as I get older. I also recognize how important I am in the lives of my family and friends. Being in a men's group that has been meeting regularly for more than thirty years, I have learned to ask for help and support when I'm afraid, to allow myself to be held and nurtured. When one of our members died last year, I realized how much we need each other. I'm also more willing to ask my wife to hold me when I'm afraid and to rub my back for comfort. In the past, I would have felt those kinds of needs weren't manly.

I use Earthing techniques to keep my connection to this beautiful planet we all share. As I walk on the Earth and stay connected through grounding, I picture the Earth's healing energies filling my being, and I relax and am embraced. I remember and repeat a poem I first heard in a workshop for men and women led by Clarissa Pinkola Estes and Michael Meade. I'm still moved to tears when I think of Clarissa's poem, "Father Earth":

There's a two-million-year-old man no one knows.

They cut into his rivers,

They peeled wide pieces of hide from his legs,

They left scorch marks on his buttocks.

He did not cry out.

No matter what they did to him, He did not cry out.

He held firm.

Now he raises his stabbed hands and whispers that we can heal him yet.

We begin the bandages, the rolls of gauze, the gut, the needle, the grafts.

Slowly, carefully, we turn his body face up,

and under him, his lifelong lover, the old woman,

is perfect and unmarked.

He has lain upon his two-million-year-old woman

all this time, protecting her with his old back, with his old scarred back.

And the soil beneath her is fertile and black with their tears.[315]

This poem never fails to bring tears to my eyes. It reminds me that the male spirit is alive and well as an integral part of the Earth. Women learned to reclaim the feminine spirit when they recognized that the image of "God, the Father," left them out. Images of the Goddess were empowering and enlivening. Men are also learning to tap into the male soul when we identify with "Father Earth." We're learning to let go of our notion that the male spirit is destructive. I so love the image of the two-million-year-old man protecting his lover, the old woman. May the images of this wonderful poem infuse our lives with love.

CHAPTER 12:
MEN'S WORK AT
THE TRANSITION FROM EMPIRE
TO EARTH COMMUNITIES

I have never considered myself part of a "men's movement," but I've been drawn to men's work since 1969. Like many men, I was drawn to men's work because of changes going on in my relationship to my wife and our family. That year, my wife was pregnant with our first child, and I had spent the previous nine hours coaching her in the Lamaze breathing techniques we had practiced together. When I began the classes, I wasn't sure I wanted to be part of the birth process. In truth, I was afraid I might pass out at the sight of the blood or become overly concerned with her pain and be more of a problem than a support.

When she was wheeled into the delivery room, the doctor asked me to leave. I experienced a mixture of sadness and relief. Following doctor's orders, I dutifully squeezed my wife's hand, turned, and walked down the long hallway toward the exit sign leading to the waiting room to sit with the other expectant fathers. Yet in the eternity of those few moments it took to make the journey out, something shifted in me. I felt a call from some deep part of myself—or maybe it was from the life preparing to come into the world. It was a call that could not be denied.

I turned around and walked into the delivery room and took my place at the head of the table. There was no question of asking permission, no chance I would leave if asked. I was simply there. I felt a wonderful calm come over me and a sense of unbelievable wonder as my son, Jemal, came into the world. My tears flowed freely as I joined in the magic of life and silently made a commitment to myself and my son that our relationship would be different than my father's had been with me and that I would do everything in my power to create the kind of world where men, women, and children were honored, understood, and supported.

In the early years of Jemal's life, I was busy learning to be a father, struggling to earn a living, and trying to be a good husband. In 1976, I attended my first "Men and Masculinity" conference at Pennsylvania State University, sponsored by the National Organization of Men Against Sexism (NOMAS). We explored many issues including ways to end male violence, sexism, homophobia, sexual harassment, and sexual abuse.

It's somewhat ironic that as I write this, Penn State is involved in a major scandal. The *New York Times* is reporting that Jerry Sandusky, a former defensive coordinator under legendary football coach Joe Paterno, was charged with sexually abusing eight boys across a fifteen-year period. Paterno had been widely criticized for failing to involve the police when he learned of one alleged assault of a young boy in 2002. He was fired from Penn State and died shortly afterwards from complications due to lung cancer.[316]

Child sexual abuse has always been shrouded in secrecy. It's important that these issues come to light and that all of us address them. Too many have kept silent for too long. Many victims keep silent out of fear of reprisals or shame over what happened to them. Perpetrators keep silent to protect their deeds. Those who know what is going on but keep silent have a variety of reasons for not protecting the child. Many don't recognize the seriousness of abuse or are afraid to confront those in power who are the abusers. Most of us have such a hard time even imaging molesting a child that we close our hearts and minds to the reality of abuse even when we are confronted with it in our own lives. "He's such a good man or she's such a wonderful woman," we say to ourselves. We can't imagine they could do something horrible to a child. But child abuse has happened, is happening, and will continue to happen until we all increase our awareness and stand up for those who need our love and support.

The Men's Movement Collides with the Titanic

One of the most important things the men's movement can do is recognize that the old system of domination is going under and a new system of partnership is emerging. I had my first experience of this transition in 1993 when I attended the Fourth Annual Men's Leaders' Conference in Indianapolis, Indiana, sponsored by *Wingspan Magazine*. It started off like many other conferences I had attended. We shared stories, read poetry, talked about our children, our wives, lovers, friends, and neighbors. We caught up with old friends and heard about what was going on with men and their relationships in other parts of the country.

But this gathering had something new to offer: a sweat lodge ceremony. I've had asthma since I was a kid and worried about being in a hot, enclosed space, but I joined others who wanted to experience this ancient healing ceremony.

The sweat lodge is a small structure made of a frame of saplings and covered with animal skins and blankets. A depression is dug in the center into which hot rocks are positioned. Water is thrown on the rocks to create steam, and a small flap opening is used to regulate the temperature.

As we touched the earth and made a prayer for "all our relations," we crawled naked through the doorway and took our positions around the stone pit. We were told there would be three "rounds" where we would chant and pray. In between rounds, the flap would be opened to allow us to cool down. With each round, more stones were added, the lodge became hotter, and the experience became more intense. As it turned out, I was at the back of the lodge where it was the hottest. In the third round, it became so hot that many of the men crawled out. I was one of the few men left inside, but I didn't feel the heat. I felt transported to another time and another place, where I experienced this vision. In the vision I "saw" the ending of our dominator culture and the emergence of a new way of life based on connection and cooperation:

We are all on a huge ocean liner. Everything we know and have ever known is on the ship. People are born and die. Goods and services are created, wars are fought, and elections are held. Species come into being and face extinction. The ship steams on and on, and there is no doubt that it will continue on its present course forever.

There are many decks on the ship, starting way down in the boiler room where the poorest and grimiest toil to keep the ship going. As you ascend the decks, things get lighter and easier. The people who run the ship have suites on the very top deck. Their job, as they see it, is to keep the ship going and keep those on the lower decks in their proper places. Since they are at the top, they are sure they deserve to acquire more and more of the resources of all those below them.

Everyone on the lower decks aspires to get up to the next deck and hungers to get to the very top. That's the way it is. That's the way it has always been. That's the way it will always be. However, there are a few people who realize that something very strange is happening. What they come to know is that the ship is sinking. At first, like everyone else, they can't believe it. The ship has been afloat since time before time. It is the best of the best. That it could sink is unthinkable. Nonetheless, they are sure the ship is sinking.

They try to warn the people, but no one believes them. The ship cannot be sinking, and anyone who thinks so must be out of their mind. When they persist in trying to warn the people of what they are facing, those in charge of the ship silence them and lock them up. The ship's media keeps grinding out news stories describing how wonderful the future will be. Any problems that are occurring will surely be solved with the wonders of our civilized lifestyle.

The leaders of the ship smile, wave, and they promise prosperity for all. But water is beginning to seep in from below. The higher the water rises, the more frightened the people become and the more frantically they scramble to get to the upper decks. Some believe it is the end and actually welcome the prospect of the destruction of life as we know it. They believe it is the fulfillment of religious prophesy. Others become more and more irritable, angry, and depressed.

But as the water rises, those who have been issuing the warnings can no longer be silenced. More and more escape confinement and lead the people toward the lifeboats. Though there are boats enough for all, many people are reluctant to leave the ship. Many questions are asked. "The old stories tell us that we've been on this ship for more than six thousand years, isn't it safer to stay aboard? Could things really be this bad that we have to leave? Where will we go? Who will lead us? What if this is all there is? What if we all die?"

Nevertheless, the ship is sinking. Many people go over the side and are lowered down to the boats. As they descend, they are puzzled to see lettering on the side of the ship, T-I-T-A-N-I-C. When they reach the lifeboats, many are frightened and look for someone who looks like they know what to do. They'd like to ride with those people.

However, they find that each person must get in their own boat and row away from the ship in their own direction. If they don't get away from the ship as soon as possible, they will be pulled down with it. When everyone, each in their own boats, rowing in their own direction, reaches a certain spot, a new web will be formed. It will be the basis for a new way of life that will replace the life that was lived on the old ship.

I slowly came back to the present and found myself alone at the back of the sweat lodge. I wasn't quite sure what had happened, but the vision was clear in my head and has remained so. Since that fateful day in 1993, I have been trying to understand what I had been given in the vision and how to best share it with others. Here's what I understand so far.

Seven Truths I Have Learned from the Vision

1. **Working to achieve success in a "business-as-usual world" is like getting a better deck chair on the *Titanic*.** When the ship sinks, it doesn't matter which deck you've managed to reach. "The world we have created is not sustainable," says Ervin Laszlo, the editor of the international periodical *World Futures* and two-time nominee for the Nobel Peace Prize. "Whether we realize it or not, we have entered a state of global emergency."[317]

2. **The ship of civilization is a six-thousand-year-old way of life that has been based on extracting more and more resources from the earth.** In the last 150 years, fossil fuels have been critical. But this way of life is coming to an end.[318] In his prescient 2003 book, *The Party's Over: Oil, War and the Fate of Industrial Societies*, Richard Heinberg says, "The world is changing before our eyes—dramatically, inevitably, and irreversibly. The change we are seeing is affecting more people, and more profoundly, than any that human beings have ever witnessed. I am not referring to war or terrorist incident, a stock market crash, or global warming, but to a more fundamental reality that is driving terrorism, war, economic swings, climate change, and more: the discovery and exhaustion of fossil energy resources."[319]

3. **We have reached the end of growth and everything is changing.** Our whole way of life has been based on the idea of continued growth. Once we accept that in

many areas of our lives growth is coming to an end, the way we look at the world will change dramatically.

"Economic growth as we have known it is over and done with," asserts Heinberg in his recently published book, *The End of Growth: Adapting to Our New Economic Reality.*[320] He defines growth as being the expansion of the overall size of the economy, with more people being served and more money changing hands, with increasing quantities of energy and material goods flowing through it. Endless growth can no longer continue.

4. **Indicators of a failing system are increasingly evident and hard to ignore.**

    *   Prices of commodities essential to our present way of life are increasing.
    *   Our economic system is chaotic and vulnerable.
    *   Unrest in North Africa, the Middle East, and Europe continues to spread.
    *   The devastation in Japan and damage to nuclear power plants is causing us to look more closely at our use of energy to power our lives and the necessary trade-offs that accompany the use of nuclear power.
    *   Our government seems gridlocked and can't deal with the changes we face.

Rebecca D. Costa, author of *The Watchman's Rattle: Thinking Our Way Out of Extinction,* helps us understand why civilizations such as the Mayans, the Romans, and others grew ever larger and more complex and eventually collapsed. [321] She says the first sign of impending collapse is gridlock. "Gridlock occurs when civilizations become unable to comprehend or resolve large, complex problems, despite acknowledging beforehand that these issues may lead to their demise."[322]

Costa shares her ideas on complexity and "the greatest discovery you've never heard of" in this TED talk.[323] Take a picture of this tag with your smartphone to see and hear Rebecca Costa address the stresses of modern life.

5. **The three *Es*—energy, economy, and environment— are intimately related.**

In his web course and book,[324] *The Crash Course*, Chris Martenson offers a clear understanding of how these three key factors relate to each other and what we can do to ensure that we get off the sinking ship and into the lifeboats. "It's time to face the facts," he says. **"A dangerous convergence of unsustainable trends in the economy, energy, and the environment will make the 'twenty-teens' one of the most challenging decades ever.** *The Crash Course* explains this predicament and provides sufficient context to support the idea that it is well past time to begin preparing for a very different future."[325]

6. **Men are the "canaries in the coal mine" alerting us to worldwide changes.**

Canaries were once used in coal mining as an early warning system. Toxic gases such as carbon monoxide and methane in the mine would kill the bird before affecting the miners. Male illness and breakdown are the world's early warning signs of impending catastrophe. Things like irritable male syndrome, male depression and aggression, and high suicide rates are alerting us to the toxic nature of our current lifestyles. Comedian Elayne Boosler understood something significant about the different ways men and women act when they are depressed. **"When women are depressed, they either eat or go shopping," she said. "Men invade another country."**

7. Personal healing and social justice must go together.

In the vision, each person had to get into their own boat and get off the sinking ship. We each have to do our own personal healing if we are going to succeed during these times of change. But personal healing isn't enough. We have to band together with other like-minded people to bring about the social change that is necessary for us to survive and thrive. Those who have gotten the most economic benefit from the old ship of state will try to take possession of as many planetary resources as possible. We must link together to stop them and protect ourselves, our communities, and our planet.

"At first I thought I was fighting to save rubber trees," said environmental activist Chico Mendez before he was murdered in Brazil, "then I thought I was fighting to save the Amazon rain forest. Now I realize I am fighting for humanity."[326]

Using Energy Healing Tools to Deal with the Stresses of Transition

The changes we are experiencing are like nothing else we've ever gone through. As a result, the stress levels will continue to rise. I've found that in order to combat the stress, I have to increase my energy healing practices. Here are some of the specific things I have found to be helpful.

1. I walk more in nature. I always like walking in nature, but in times of stress I find it wonderful to walk among the big trees and remind myself that they have been here for hundreds of years. I recently walked among the redwood trees, one of which was more than three feet in diameter and fourteen hundred years old. I think of what these trees have survived and I feel more confident in my own future.

2. I keep my heart tuned to the beauty of what I have.

3. I often use the HeartMath techniques to keep my heart open and to bring positive thoughts to mind. Although there may be a lot of chaos and uncertainly in the world, there is also security and predictability. As I breathe through my heart, I picture beautiful sunrises and sunsets or snow falling gently through the trees. I breathe and picture the things I'm grateful for, including my wife and kids, good health, friends, and community.

4. I remember my attachment to those I love.

5. When there is a lot of change going on, I often feel cut-off from others and alone. I get lost in my own thoughts and concerns. When I practice the meditations of attachment love, I feel reconnected with loved

ones and feel their care and support. It also reminds me that others need me, and just my presence in the world is a source of support for my family and friends.

6. I practice EFT for worry and anxiety.

7. I often tap using setup phrases such as "Even though the world is changing, I deeply love and accept myself" or "Even though the old system is coming apart, something new and better is being born." I've found that fears and anxieties are always in the future. If I ask myself how am I doing *now,* the answer will always be okay. It's only when I fret about what could happen in the future that I get worried. Tapping helps me come into the present and allows me to take action.

Men of Courage Can Help Lead the Way Home

The world of my sweat lodge vision is in a transition period—away from the sinking ship of the old system into a new one that is smaller, more sustainable, and more interdependent. David C. Korten describes the process in his book, *The Great Turning: From Empire to Earth Community.* "I use the term, Empire with a capital E as a label for the hierarchical ordering of human relationships based on the principle of domination. The mentality of Empire embraces material excess for the ruling classes, honors the dominator power of death and violence, denies the feminine principle, and suppresses realization of the potential of human maturity." [327] This is the old ship that appears to be sinking.

He contrasts this way of being to Earth Community as a label for the egalitarian democratic ordering of relationships based on the principle of partnership (as described by Riane Eisler, author of *The Chalice and the Blade* and *The Real Wealth of Nations*).

"The mentality of Earth Community," says Korten embraces material sufficiency for everyone, honors the generative power of life and love, seeks a balance of feminine and masculine principles, and nurtures a realization of the mature potential of our nature."[328]

Although some believe men are inherently more hierarchical and dominating and women are inherently more democratic and partnering, this is not the case. All of us have suffered in cultures of Empire, and all of us will benefit as we move to Earth community. These changes impact all our lives. Men of courage can lead the way.

For most of human history, we lived as hunter-gatherers in small bands. In their role as hunters, it was the men who were first to become aware of ecological changes—to notice when the buffalo had moved or animals were dying. It was their job to protect their tribe and lead their people to safety.

As has been true throughout human history, males are genetically endowed to be the risk-takers. It is the role of modern men to lead their people away from the sinking ship of empire and move us into a world where humans don't attempt to dominate nature, but live in balance with nature.

Daniel Quinn has offered his ideas in books like *Ishmael, The Story of B,* and *Beyond Civilization: Humanity's Next Great Adventure.* "Hierarchy" and "domination" are key concepts in understanding "civilization," says Quinn. "Every civilization brought forth in the course of human history has been a hierarchical affair. You can have hierarchy without civilization, but you can't have civilization without hierarchy; at least we never have—not once, not anywhere, in ten thousand years of civilization building. To have a civilization is to have a hierarchical society."[329] But, as Quinn says, we can move beyond civilization.

Now is the time for men to step forward. We are called upon to lead our families and communities into a new world where all are respected. We must learn to love and respect ourselves in deeper and more meaningful ways. As we do that, we will find it easier to love and respect our wives, our families, our communities, and the fragile planet we all share.

Finding New Work In a World Turned Upside Down

Most of us wait until there is a crisis before we make a radical change in how we work and live. Chris Martenson, the developer of *The Crash Course* I mentioned earlier, stepped away from his career and made a radical change in his lifestyle just when it appeared he had it all. Here's how he describes the change:

"Not long ago, I was firmly seated on the American Dream bandwagon. I had done everything that you are supposed to do—and more. In the 1990s, I earned my PhD in pathology/toxicology from Duke University and did two years of postdoctoral research with the intention of becoming a full-time professor. But life takes its twists and turns; I went on to get an

MBA from Cornell and spent the next ten years working my way through and up the corporate ladder, ultimately becoming a VP at SAIC, a Fortune 300 company."[330]

When the economy began going south in 2002, Martenson wasn't satisfied with the answers he was getting from the "experts," so he used his scientific background and business skills to find answers for himself. Based on what he learned, he decided to quit his job, sell the house and the boat, and move with his family to a small town where they could develop more sustainable lifestyle. At age forty-two, his midlife crisis sent him in a new direction toward a new life, one that is much more satisfying than life he had been leading.

But Martenson, like many men at this stage of life, had an intuitive sense that he needed to make a break with the past, not just for himself, but for his family and community. "The reason I have chosen this path in life over others that may have been easier or cushier is to fulfill my one highest goal," says Martenson. **"I want to create a world worth inheriting. Everything else pales in comparison."**[331]

Preparing for the Transition and Living Well After the Crash

I also had a vision that things weren't right with the world, and I spent some years researching the problem and figuring out what we could do in face of major changes going on in the world. Unlike Martenson, I had to wait until there was a real crisis in my life, an actual medical emergency of an adrenal tumor, before I was able to fully commit to a new way of life. Here are a few of my thoughts that I believe will help us make the transition.

See yourself as a pioneer in a new world. We are not facing the end of the world, as some would have us believe, but the greatest adventure of our lives. We have the unique opportunity to write a new chapter in the history of humankind, to be active participants in shaping a new world. Daniel Quinn opened his book *Ishmael* with a description of a short ad in the Personals section of a newspaper: "TEACHER seeks pupil. Must have an earnest desire to save the world. Apply in person."[332]

In *Beyond Civilization: Humanity's Next Great Adventure*, Quinn elaborates and offers additional guidance. "Saving the world can only mean one thing: saving the world *as a human habitat,*" he says. "Accomplishing this will mean (*must* mean) saving the world as a habitat for as many other species as possible. We can *only* save the world as a human habitat if we stop our catastrophic onslaught on the community of life, for we depend on the community for our very lives."[333] We are the teachers we've been waiting for, and we are the pupils who will develop new skills and relearn old skills that will serve us well as we enter the world of the future.

Find your place, plant your flag. In times past, people had deep ties to a particular place. We had ancestral homes and communities where people knew their neighbors. In recent times, we have been on the move. Job requirements or job searches take us to different parts of the country, and in some cases, different parts of the world. But as we enter a new world where our economy is no longer growing, we will be drawn back to doing more in our local communities. This is the time to put down roots and make a commitment to a place. As nations and states continue to experience economic upheavals, the action will increasingly be at the local level. What we need to survive and thrive will be acquired closer to home. Some will put down their roots in the country, others in the city. Follow your intuition and find the place that is calling to you.

Create a support group and join a tribe. I've talked about my men's group that has been getting together since 1979. The group started with guys all living in the same general area, but over the years we've moved farther apart. We still get together three or four times a year and have developed deep and lasting bonds. But I've felt a need to have a local group of guys that I meet with more often and who I see frequently. My wife, Carlin, and I have also joined a mixed group of men and women we call "the village circle" that meets monthly for support, ritual, discussion, and a wonderful shared meal. Daniel Quinn reminds us that humans are meant to be members of a tribe, even if people often resist that notion. "If you note that hive life works well for bees, that troop life works well for baboons, or that pack life works well for wolves, you won't be challenged, but if you note that tribal life works well for humans, don't be surprised if you're attacked with an almost hysterical ferocity."[334]

It's not that tribal life is idyllic. People are people and can do mean and ugly things no matter what the structure of their society. "The tribal life doesn't turn people into saints: it enables ordinary people to make a living together with a minimum of stress year after year, generation after generation," says Quinn.[335] Having a support group and being part of a tribe is not just fun, but necessary. British novelist Elizabeth Jane Howard once said, "Call it a clan, call it a network, call it a tribe, call it a family: whatever you call it, whoever you are, you need one."[336]

Look for work worth doing. For most of my life I believed the American Dream—that I could grow up and do anything in life. Just as we seemed to have an economy that could continue growing forever, I believed that I had an endless choice of possible professions. In the new world, our choices will be more limited and also more expansive. We can't continue doing work that harms the planet, but there are millions of new jobs that can be good for us *and* good for the planet.

We can no longer do just any kind of work. Let's face it; some work is destructive to our souls or the wellbeing of the planet. The work we do must be in support of all life, starting with our own. People who follow their deepest calling find that even if they earn less, they are more joyful in their lives.

Join a network and expand your view of work. We all need to work, not just to make a living, but to feel good about ourselves. But the economy is changing from one based on growth and the overuse of nonrenewable resources to one based on sustainability and balance. If you want to find out about the jobs for the future, join BALLE.[337] The Business Alliance for Local Living Economies (BALLE) is fastest growing network of socially responsible businesses, comprised of over eighty community networks in thirty U.S. states and Canadian provinces and representing over twenty-two thousand independent business members across the U.S. and Canada.

BALLE believes that local, independent businesses are among our most potent change agents, uniquely prepared to take on the challenges of the twenty-first century with an agility, sense of place, and relationship-based approach others lack. They are more than employers and profit-makers; they are neighbors, community builders, and the starting point for social innovation, aligning commerce with the common good and bringing transparency, accountability, and a caring human face to the marketplace.

Think of work differently. I grew up thinking that working for someone else was safe and working for myself was risky. When I lost my job at age sixty, I returned to school and got my PhD in international health. I put more energy into private counseling. My wife and I cut back on buying things that caught our attention and only bought things we really wanted. It turns out a lot of what I bought was to deal with the stresses of being in a job I no longer enjoyed. When I was doing what I loved, I found I didn't need to earn as much money.

I realized that even if I worked for myself, the failing economy might still cause my income to drop. I always do some volunteer work in the community, but I am usually so focused on my career that I don't have a lot of free time. After losing my job, I understood that if I was going to be successful, I needed to find work that I could do no matter what was happening to the economy. I started teaching classes on reducing stress and losing weight, two things that I wanted to do and seemed to be needed in the community. They were free and well attended.

Along with a local physician, I started the Willits Healthy Action Team (WHAT) that offers community walks for men, women, and children (and well-behaved pets). Our logo says that we are committed to personal, community, and planetary healing. It is a big success and gives me a chance to do things I love and offer them free to the community. In a declining economy, the best "social security" may be the old-fashioned security of helping others, knowing they will likely help you in return.

Work less, live more. In her book *The Overworked American: The Unexpected Decline of Leisure,* economist Juliet Schor detailed the fact that we are working longer hours and enjoying our life less. She quotes a man who could easily be speaking for many of us. "Being a man means being willing to put all your waking hours into working to support your family. If you ask for time off, or if you turn down overtime, it means you're lazy or you're a wimp."[338] Call a man a wimp and you can get him to do anything, even work himself to death.

But times are changing. More men are realizing they can work less and enjoy their lives more. In a down economy, it may seem crazy to work less, but that's just what Schor's research suggests we do. "Work less in the declining market," she says, "but use those freed-up hours productively, to invest in new skills and activities."[339] Many men are going back to school, training for new jobs in the "green economy," or building up social capital by becoming more deeply connected with others in the community.

Get to the new good life. Twenty-one-year-old Baskin-Robbins heir John Robbins had it made. He was set to take over a thriving business selling unlimited flavors of ice cream. "I was born at the pinnacle of the old good life," he says, "with its promise of unlimited consumption, and I was poised to champion it into a new generation."[340] But he chose a different path, one with less money but more in line with his values. He went on to write best-selling books, including *Diet for a New America* and *Healthy at 100*, and over the years he accumulated his own money while doing the work he loved.

Living simply, but wanting to have secure income to pass on to their son Ocean and his family, Robbins and his wife followed the guidance of a wealthy friend and invested all their life savings with him. The friend invested his own money and theirs with a trusted friend, and they hoped to be set for life. But the friend turned out to be Bernard Madoff.

Robbins remembers the call that told them that Madoff had been arrested for perpetuating the most massive financial fraud in world history. "On that phone call, we learned that more than 95 percent of our net worth had been stolen. Every cent we had put into the fund was gone....At first, I felt such enormous shock that I genuinely wondered if it might kill me."

But Robbins did recover, and he went on to share his experiences in *The New Good Life: Living Better Than Ever in an Age of Less*. "Born into riches," says Robbins, "I've gone from there to chosen rags to self-made riches to unchosen rags to now recovering and once again creating sufficiency."[341] Most of us don't go through changes as dramatic as John Robbins', but we all must deal with our own challenges.

Use and Share Your Energy Healing Power Tool to Empower Yourself for the Challenges Ahead

Never before in human history have we been forced to deal with the massive disruptions brought about by changes in energy, environment, and the economy. Our energy healing power tool can help us keep our heads on straight while we navigate these difficult waters. Emotional freedom techniques, Earthing, heart coherence, and attachment love can help you deal with the winds of change as we move from empire to earth communities. I use mine every day and continue to practice so that I can enjoy life, even in these difficult times. But there's an old saying, "You can't keep it unless you give it away."

Once you recognize how valuable this tool can be, share it with those you care most about.

Share it with your spouse. I've found that my wife, Carlin, was dealing with many similar issues to the ones I was addressing. I showed her how to use the energy healing tools, and she has gotten similar benefits to what I have enjoyed. Tapping together, as well as using the other elements, can be great fun and can greatly improve your relationship.

Teach your children. Many people have told me they have used EFT, heart coherence, Earthing, and attachment love with their children. I've taught these simple techniques to my children and grandchildren. Children often learn them more easily than adults and can use them to deal with their own issues in a more constructive way.

Writing this section made me think of the song "Teach Your Children," by Crosby, Stills, Nash, and Young. It's been a favorite of mine since I first heard it on November 15, 1969, at a San Francisco rally against the Vietnam War, shortly after the album was recorded but before its release. The recording features Jerry Garcia on pedal steel guitar, probably the first time Garcia recorded with that instrument. The song has always reminded me of the importance of listening to our children and sharing the healing experiences that have been important in our own lives.

Share it with those you coach. Many of us are involved in coaching. I've found these tools to be very helpful for children and adults to improve individual and team success. Dr. Jack Rowe is a sports psychologist with an MBA degree in addition to his PhD. He uses EFT to improve athletic performance in everyone from weekend warriors to professional athletes.

Rowe has a particular interest in improving golf performance. He says, "Golf (and probably all sports) is at least 90 percent mental after the fundamentals are learned. Even learning the fundamentals is mostly mental. EFT is the most powerful tool available to allow athletes to control 90 percent of their performance—their mental game. It is readily used as a self-help tool in the middle of the game, in the moment when it is needed. In the hands of a trained EFT sport psychologist, it is the most effective tool for training athletes in mental game principles."[342]

I first learned about Greg Warburton's work when I saw a YouTube video of one of the pitchers he coached at Oregon State University using EFT to calm himself and focus his mind in a College World Series game. The ESPN announcers weren't sure what the young man was doing. "According to some of the players in the Beaver's dugout, what Jorge Reyes is doing with tapping is just kind of realigning the energy and so forth. He was told...actually a psychologist or consultant came in....kinda like a holistic approach....kinda realigning the energy." After years of working with athletes, Warburton has recently published a wonderful e-book[343] on how everyone can use energy healing techniques to improve their game.

But coaching can go way beyond sports. Carol Look is a success and abundance coach in the energy psychology field. Her specialty is inspiring clients to *attract abundance* into their lives by using EFT and the *Law of Attraction* to clear limiting beliefs, release resistance, and build "prosperity consciousness." Carol is one of the few EFT masters in the world trained by EFT founder Gary Craig between 2005 and 2007. To learn about Carol's work, visit her at www.attractingabundance.com/.[344] To learn about the work of other EFT masters, visit www.eftmastersworldwide.com/.[345]

Another EFT master and life coach is Lindsay Kenny. For over thirty years, Lindsay has been helping people lose weight, improve their health, increase their energy, improve their self-esteem, find their life partners, and become more effective in life. This helps people become happier, more confident, and more productive citizens. She can be reached at www.ProEFT.com/.[346]

All four elements—EFT, Earthing, heart coherence, and even attachment love—can be used in coaching of all kinds, whether we're helping improve athletic performance or life skills. Coaching others can be a wonderful way to pass on what you've learned, while improving your own skills.

Try it with your men's group. I've been in a men's support group for more than thirty years and have shared these tools with the guys in the group. Whether we're in a formal men's group or just have male friends, you'll find they are very receptive to this power tool. Most all men want to improve their lives. With so much stress going on in the world, we don't always have time to take care of ourselves properly or don't have the time or the money deal with the various problems we face. Having a tool you can use any time, one that is easy to learn, effective, scientifically sound, and well-tested, is something most guys are ready to embrace. They may just need to have someone tell them about it, show them how to use it, and share their results.

Share it with the world. It seems clear to me that we aren't going to be successful making the transition from empire to earth communities without a major change in world consciousness. We're not going to get there with small, incremental changes we can do on our own. It's also clear to me that changes of this magnitude can only occur on an "energy" level. I'm seeing a number of Internet-based programs that using energy healing to impact planetary consciousness. The Tapping World Summit[347] has brought together some of the best practitioners of meridian therapies in the world to teach these techniques to hundreds of thousands of people.

The Shift Network[348] aims to empower a global movement of people who are creating an evolutionary shift of consciousness that in turn leads to a more enlightened society, one built on principles of sustainability, peace, health, and prosperity.

The Intention Experiment[349] is a series of scientific, web-based experiments testing the power of thought to change the physical world. Thousands of volunteers from ninety countries around the world have participated in these rigorous, laboratory-controlled experiments.

The Global Coherence Initiative[350] is a science-based, creative project designed to unite people in heart-focused care and intention, to facilitate the shift in global consciousness from instability and discord to balance, cooperation, and enduring peace.

The Future Is Ours: Prepare for the Ride of Your Life

If our survival depended on what we were getting from corporate-controlled media, our prospects would seem to range from "extremely grim" to "totally hopeless." It's not surprising that millions of people are turning to *The Daily Show* and *The Colbert Report* to see the news through the eyes of comedians. But there is a more hopeful future available to those who take the time to dig a little deeper.

In his book *Blessed Unrest: How the Largest Movement in the World Came into Being and Why No One Saw It Coming*, Paul Hawken says, "The dawn of the twenty-first century has witnessed two remarkable developments in our history: the appearance of systemic problems that are genuinely global in scope, and the growth of a worldwide movement that is determined to heal the wounds of the earth with the force of passion, dedication, and collective intelligence and wisdom."[351]

Hawken is a world-renounced environmentalist, entrepreneur, journalist, and author. For the last thirty years, he has traveled throughout the world and seen this huge, but little recognized movement firsthand. At first, he estimated the number of organizations focused on social justice and the environment to be around one hundred thousand. By the time he had completed his research for *Blessed Unrest* in 2006 he says, **"I now believe there are over one—and maybe even two—million organizations working toward ecological sustainability and social justice."**[352]

Hawken helped create WiserEarth,[353] a global village for sharing and kinship-building among change-makers from around the world. As of November 11, 2011, WiserEarth provided a directory of more than 113,500 organizations worldwide, over sixty thousand registered members, and more than twenty-seven hundred groups with content organized in forty-six areas of focus and 379 subareas. WiserEarth is currently available in English, French, Portuguese, and Spanish. If you want to get involved and find kindred spirits in the area of social change that excite you, this is a great place to begin.

John Petersen is president and founder of The Arlington Institute and is considered by many to be one of the most informed futurists in the world. In his 2008 book *A Vision for 2012: Planning for Extraordinary Change*, he says, "I believe we are entering one of those punctuation points in the evolution of our species that will rapidly propel us into an unimaginable new era. This new world won't be at all like what we currently find familiar. Because this shift is so fundamental and acute, the most positive option will not make sense at all from this vantage so early in the transition. In the face of almost certain uncertainty, our job is to rise to the occasion, to evolve in our thinking, our perceptions, and in our commitment to make this transition as positive as possible."[354]

You can learn more about the work of The Arlington Institute[355] by visiting its website. One of the most helpful resources is its FutureEdition e-newsletter that offers regular updates on world events and ideas that we can use to help us get through the transition in the most positive way possible.

Lynne McTaggart, author of *The Bond: Connecting through the Space Between Us,* believes this movement is now reaching critical mass and has the possibility of uniting people throughout the world. [356] "An entirely new scientific story is emerging that challenges many of our Newtonian and Darwinian assumptions," she says, "including our most basic premise: the sense of things as separate entities in competition for survival. **The latest evidence from quantum physics offers the extraordinary possibility that all of life exists in a dynamic relationship of cooperation.**"[357]

I limit my time watching the news on TV or reading newspapers. There is really very little that is new. I'd rather join the energy revolution and have fun with those people working together to create a better future for us all. Lynne McTaggart[358] is one of the people I enjoy connecting with. "We need to adopt a new definition of what it means to be human," she says. "We need to look at our universe with a fresh pair of eyes. Applying these new discoveries to every aspect of our lives requires nothing less than making ourselves anew."[359]

When I had my vision in the sweat lodge in 1993, I had no idea what it meant to get off the sinking ship. In the intervening years, I've learned a great deal. This book is result of my journey thus far. I hope you'll join me for "the rest of the story."

LET'S STAY IN TOUCH

For more information about books and other resources or if you need help dealing with the stresses in your life, I invite you to visit me at http://MenAlive.com.

I'd enjoy hearing from you. Send an email to Menalive@menalive. com and sign up for Team MenAlive, which is a book owner list, so I can send you the latest information, videos, and updates.

Let's start a conversation. Say "hi" on Twitter @MenAliveNow or use the hashtag #MenAlive to join the discussion by sharing your insights and examples. Learn how others are using the concepts you've just read about.

You can also join us on Facebook at http://Facebook.com/MenAliveNow for more tips and ongoing dialogue.

The field of energy medicine is changing rapidly. New information becomes available nearly every week. As a special bonus for those purchasing this book, you can get the latest updates by going to www.MenAlive.com/updates or take a picture of this tag using your smartphone to visit the MenAlive updates site.

End Notes

Introduction

1   Feinstein, David & Eden, Donna. 2008. Six pillars of energy medicine: Clinical strengths of a complementary paradigm. Alternative Therapies, 14(1), 44-54.

2   Current research studies on energy healing and energy psychology, http://energypsych.org/displaycommon.cfm?an=1&subarticlenbr=296.

Chapter One

3   Joiner, Thomas. *Lonely at the Top: The High Cost of Men's Success.* New York: Palgrave/Macmillan, 2011.

4   Ibid.

5   National Institute of Mental Health Report, "Suicide in the U.S.: Statistics and Prevention," http://www.nimh.nih.gov/health/publications/suicide-in-the-us-statistics-and-prevention/index.shtml.

6   Goldberg, Herb. *The Hazards of Being Male: Surviving the myth of masculine privilege.* New York: Nash Publishing, 1976.

7   Farrell, Warren. *Why Men Are the Way They Are.* New York: McGraw-Hill, 1986.

8   Men's Health Network, http://www.menshealthnetwork.org/.

9   Kellermann, A. and A. Mercy. 1992. Men, women, and murder: gender-specific differences in rates of fatal violence and victimization. *Journal of Trauma* Jul;33(1):1–5.

10   Real, Terrence. *I Don't Want to Talk About It: Overcoming the Secret Legacy of Male Depression.* New York: Scribner, 1997.

11   Courtenay, Will. *Dying to be Men: Psychosocial, Environmental, and Biohavioral Directions in Promoting the Health of Men and Boys.* New York: Routledge, 2011.

12   Joiner.

13   Mason, Betsy. July 2002. Men die young, even if old. *New Scientist Magazine.*

14   Courtenay.

15   Ibid.

16   Dunlop, Boadie W. and T. Mletzko, 2011. Will current socioeconomic trends produce a depressing future for men? *The British Journal of Psychiatry,* 198, 167-168.

17   Ibid.

18   See studies cited by Lynne McTaggart. *The Bond: Connecting Through the Space Between Us.* New York: Free Press, 2011.

19   Diamond, Jed. The Irritable Male Syndrome: Understanding and Managing the 4 Key Causes of Depression and Aggression. Emmaus, PA: Rodale, 2004.

20   Joiner.

21   Ibid.

22   Courtenay.

23   Ibid.

24   McTaggart.

25   Sterling Institute, http://www.sterling-institute.com/.

26   ManKind Project, http://mankindproject.org/.

27   Michael Gurian, http://michaelgurian.com/.

28   Promise Keepers, http://www.promisekeepers.org/.

29   *Men's Health Magazine*, http://www.menshealth.com/.

30   *Wired Magazine*, http://www.wired.com/magazine/.

31   The Shift Network, http://theshiftnetwork.com/main/.

32   The Ultimate Men's Summit, http://ultimatemenssummit.com/.

33   The Shift Men's Initiation, http://shiftmen.com/MensInitiation.

34   Young Men's Ultimate Weekend, http://www.ymuw.org/.

35   Sacred Lifeboats, http://www.sacredlifeboats.com/.

36   Gift Communities, http://www.weneedeachother.net/.

37   Alpha Leaders, http://www.alphaleader.net/default.asp.

38   The Good Men Project, http://goodmenproject.com.

39   Tom Matlack, The Good Men Project, http://goodmenproject.com/author/tom-matlack.

40   Ibid.

41   Information on the Flexner report taken from Wikipedia, http://en.wikipedia.org/wiki/Flexner_Report.

42   Kessel, Reuben A. October 1958. Price Discrimination in Medicine Author. *Journal of Law and Economics* 1:20–53; The University of Chicago Press, http://www.jstor.org/stable/724881.

43   Larsen, Stephen. *The Healing Power of Neurofeedback: The Revolutionary LENS Technique for Restoring Optimal Brain Function.* Rochester, VT: Healing Arts Press, 2006.

44   Ibid.

45   Ibid.

Chapter Two

46   Robert Sapolsky film, "Killer Stress," http://www.pbs.org/programs/killer-stress.

47   Sapolsky, Robert. *Why Zebra's Don't Get Ulcers: A Guide to Stress, Stress-Related Diseases, and Coping.* New York: W.H. Freeman and Company, 1994.

48   Killer Stress, http://killerstress.stanford.edu.

49   O'Connor, Richard. *Undoing Perpetual Stress: The Missing Connection Between Depression, Anxiety, and 21st Century Illness.* New York: Berkeley Books, 2005.

50   Ibid.

51   Bremner, J. Douglas. *Does Stress Damage the Brain?* New York: W.W. Norton & Company, 2002.

52   Merrell, Woodson. *The Source: Unleash Your Natural Energy, Power Up Your Health and Feel 10 Years Younger.* New York: Free Press, 2008.

53   See American Institute of Stress website, http://www.stress.org/.

54   Merrell.

55   Myss, Caroline. *Defy Gravity: Healing Beyond the Bounds of Reason.* Carlsbad, California: Hay House, 2009.

56   "The End of Men," Hanna Rosin, *Atlantic,* July/August 2010.

57   Michael Moore, www.MichaelMoore.com.

58   Faludi, Susan. *Stiffed: The Betrayal of the American Man.* New York: William Morrow and Company, 1999.

59   Faludi, 1999.

60   Schor, Juliet P. *Plentitude: The new economics of true wealth.* New York: Penguin Press, 2010.

61   Faludi, 1999.

62   Personal communication from Mary Furlong, September 3, 2007.

63   Lipton, Bruce. *The Biology of Belief: Unleashing the Power of Consciousness, Matter & Miracles.* Carlsbad, California: Hay House, 2008.

64   Ibid.

65   Merrell.

66   Loyd, Alexander with Ben Johnson. *The Healing Code.* New York: Inter-media Publishing Group, 2010.

67   Loyd, Alexander. The nature of stress and its impact on our lives, http://www.youtube.com/watch?v=znFw8D_LzfM.

68   O'Connor, Richard. *Undoing Perpetual Stress: The Missing Connection Between Depression, Anxiety, and 21*st *Century Illness.* New York: Berkley Books, 2005.

69   Felitti VJ, Anda RF, Nordenberg D, et al. 1998. The relationship of adult health status to childhood abuse and household dysfunction. *American Journal of Preventive Medicine* 14:245–258.

70   Centers for Disease Control and Prevention. 2006 [cited April 9, 2007]. Adverse Childhood Experiences Study, available from: http://www.cdc.gov/nccdphp/ace/index.htm.

71   Quoted by David Cramer, MD, and Neville Cramer, MD, http://www.dnaremedies.com/index.php?option=com_content&view=article&id=66&Itemid=92.

72   Article "Memory is a No Brainer," http://www.redorbit.com/news/science/87598/memory_is_a_nobrainer/.

73   Loyd and Johnson.

74   Ibid.

75   Lipton, Bruce.

76   Keynote Address by Antonio Damasio, "The Science of Emotion," http://www.loc.gov/loc/brain/emotion/Damasio.html.

77   Loyd and Johnson, 123–133.

78   Ibid.

79   Ibid.

80   Ibid.

81   Ibid.

82   Merrell.

83   I read this in an article on stress by Bill Allin at http://www.scribd.com/ doc/60806986/Stress-Tolerable-Today-It-Could-Kill-You-Tomorrow.

Chapter Three

84   http://en.wikipedia.org/wiki/Ren%C3%A9.

85   Ibid.

86   Ransom Stephens, personal correspondence, November 29, 2011.

87   Hawking, Stephen and Leonard Mlodinow. *The Grand Design.* New York: Bantam Books, 2010.

88   Quoted by Normal Shealy and Dawson Church in *Soul Medicine: Awakening Your Inner Blueprint for Abundant Health and Energy.* Santa Rosa, California: Energy Psychology Press, 2008. See also Laszlo, Ervin. *Quantum Shift to the Global Brain: How the New Scientific Reality Can Change Us and Our World.* Rochester Vermont: Inner Traditions, 2008.

89   Rumi, Jalal Al-Din. Rumi: The Book of Love: Poems of Ecstasy and Longing, translated by Coleman Barks, http://quotesnack.com/rumi/ out-beyond-ideas-of-wrongdoing-and-rightdoing-there-is-a-field-ill-meet-you-there/.

90   Lipton, Bruce H. and Steve Bhaerman. *Spontaneous Evolution: Our Positive Future (and a Way to Get There from Here).* Carlsbad, California: Hay House, 2009.

91   Ibid.

92   http://www.spaceandmotion.com/Physics-Particle-Wave-Duality-Paradox.htm.

93   Lipton and Bhaerman.

94   Lipton, Bruce. *The Biology of Belief: Unleashing the Power of Consciousness, Matter, and Miracles.* Carlsbad, California: Hay House, 2008.

95   2002. Time to move beyond the mind-body split. *BMJ* 325, available at http://www.bmj.com/content/325/7378/1433.full.

96   Weil, Andrew. *Health and Healing.* Boston, Houghton Mifflin, 1983.

97   Ibid.

98   Ibid.

99   Ibid.

100   Goswami, Amit. *The Quantum Doctor: A Quantum Physicist Explains the Healing Power of Integral Medicine.* Charlottsville, Va.: Hampton Roads, 2011.

101   Lipton, Bruce. *The Biology of Belief: Unleashing the Power of Consciousness: Unleashing the Power of Consciousness, Matter & Miracles,* Carlsbad, California: Hay House, 2008. Lipton's evolution is described in the Introduction.

102   Ibid.

103   Ibid.

104   Ibid.

105   Ibid.

106   Lipton,   Bruce.   The   New   Biology,   http://www.youtube.com/watch?v=iB81L9zGLjE.

107   Loyd, Alexander, with Ben Johnson. *The Healing Code.* New York: Hachette, 2010.

108   The Healing Codes, http://thehealingcodes.com/, accessed November 26, 2011.

109   Ibid.

110   Lipton.

111   Ibid.

112   Church, Dawson, *The Genie in Your Genes: Epigenetic Medicine and the New Biology of Intension.* Santa Rosa, California: Elite Books, 2007.

Chapter 4

113   Schenk, Roy U. and John Everingham, eds. *Men Healing Shame: An Anthology.* New York: Springer Publishing Company, 1995.

114 Kaufman, Gershen. "Men's Shame" in Schenk and Everingham.

115 Ibid.

116 Gilligan, James. *Violence: Our Deadly Epidemic and its Cause.* New York: G.P. Putnam's Sons, 1996.

117 Ibid.

118 Feinstein, David and Donna Eden. 2008. Six pillars of energy medicine: Clinical strengths of a complementary paradigm. *Alternative Therapies* 14(1) 44–54.

119 National Center for Complimentary and Alternative Medicine. 2002. What is complementary and alternative medicine? Bethesda, MD: NCCAM, http://nccam.nih.gov/health/whatiscam.

120 Eden, Donna with David Feinstein. *Energy Medicine.* New York: Jeremy P. Tarcher/Putnam, 1998.

121 Feinstein, David, Donna Eden, and Gary Craig. *The Promise of Energy Psychology: Revolutionary Tools for Dramatic Personal Change.* New York: Jeremy P. Tarcher/Putnam, 2005.

122 Feinstein, David and Donna Eden. 2008. Six pillars of energy medicine: Clinical strengths of a complementary paradigm. *Alternative Therapies* 14(1) 44–54.

123 For a more complete description, see Feinstein's article noted above, which can be accessed at

http://www.energymed.org/hbank/handouts/six_pillars_em.htm.

124 Church, Dawson. *The Genie in Your Genes: Epigenetic Medicine and the New Biology of Intention.* Santa Rosa, CA: Elite Books, 2007.

125 See http://en.wikipedia.org/wiki/Medicine.

126 See http://en.wikipedia.org/wiki/Psychology.

127 Quoted in "The Power of Energy Healing," Sounds True, www.SoundsTrue.com.

128 Thomas, Linnie and Carrie Obry. *The Encyclopedia of Energy Medicine.* Minneapolis, Mn: Fairview Press, 2010.

129   Earthing, *http://www.earthinginstitute.net.*

130   Ober, Clint, Stephen T. Sinatra, and Martin Zucker. *Earthing: The Most Important Health Discovery Ever?* Laguna Beach, Ca.: Basic Health Publications, 2010.

131   Personal correspondence with Sam Keen, author *To A Dancing God,* September 6, 2011.

132   Heart Coherence, http://www.heartmath.org/.

133   Centers for Disease Control and Prevention, http://www.cdc.gov/heartdisease/.

134   Servan-Schreiber, David. *The Instinct to Heal: Curing Stress, Anxiety, and Depression Without Drugs and Without Talk Therapy.* Emmaus, PA: Rodale, 2004.

135   Attachment Love, http://www.iceeft.com.

136   Emotional Freedom Techniques, http://www.eftuniverse.com.

137   Dr. Oz on Complementary Medicine, interview by Lana Zak, August 31, 2009, http://abcnews.go.com/GMA/OnCall/story?id=8450292.

138   Ibid.

139   Myss, Caroline. *Defy Gravity: Healing Beyond the Bounds of Reason.* Carlsbad, California: Hay House, 2009.

140   See descriptions of his books and work at http://www.energyresearch.bizland.com/.

141   Pollack, William S. and Robert L. Levant. *New Psychotherapy for Men.* New York: John Wiley & Sons, 1998.

142   Ibid.

Chapter Five

143   Ober, Clinton, Stephen T. Sinatra, and Martin Zucker. *Earthing: The Most Important Health Discovery Ever?* Laguna Beach, California: Basic Health Publications, 2010.

144   Ibid.

145   Earthing Institute, http://earthinginstitute.net.

146   Ober, Clinton, Stephen T. Sinatra, and Martin Zucker. *Earthing: The Most Important Health Discovery Ever?* Laguna Beach, California: Basic Health Publications, 2010.

147   Ibid.

148   Ibid.

149   Ibid.

150   Ibid.

151   Ibid.

152   Ibid.

153   Ibid.

154   Ibid.

155   Ibid.

156   Ibid.

157   Ibid.

158   Ibid.

159   Ibid.

160   Ibid.

161   Ibid.

162   Ibid.

163   Ibid.

164   Barefoot Substitutes, http://www.earthenergies.net/

165   Ilardi, Stephen S. *The Depression Cure: The 6-Step Program to Beat Depression without Drugs.* New York: Da Capo Press, 2009.

Chapter Six

166   Servan-Schreiber, David. *The Instinct to Heal: Curing Stress, Anxiety, and Depression Without Drugs and Without Talk Therapy.* Rodale Press: 2004.

167   McCraty, Rollin. "Heart Coherence: The Key to Optimal Health, Intuition and Cognitive Functioning," Speaking at International Bioenergetic Conference, October 7–9, 2011, http://www.integrativelifesolutions.com/McCraty.html.

168   Servan-Schreiber, David. *Anti Cancer: A New Way of Life.* New York: Viking Penguin, 2009, http://www.amazon.com/Anticancer-New-Way-Life/dp/0670021644/ref=sr_1_1?s=books&ie=UTF8&qid=1304867237&sr=1-1.

169   Dr. David Servan-Schreiber's Remarkable Story, http://www.youtube.com/watch?v=xfddD6keYq0.

170   Institute of Heart Math, http://www.heartmath.org/.

171   Childre, Doc and Deborah Rozman. Sleep Better Now: Three Ways Your Heart Can Help, *Huffington Post,* January 18, 2010.

172   Emmons, Robert E. *Thanks! How Practicing Gratitude Can Make You Happier.* Boston: Houghton Mifflin, 2008.

173   Childre, Doc, and Howard Martin. *The HeartMath Solution.* 1999.

174   Ibid.

175   Science of the Heart: Exploring the Role of the Heart in Human Performance: An Overview of Research Conducted by the Institute of HeartMath, http://www.heartmath.org/research/science-of-the-heart.html.

176   M. Mittleman, et al. 1995. *Circulation* 92(7).

177   I. Kawachi et al. 1994. *Circulation* 89(5).

178   L. Kubzansky et al. 1997. *Circulation* 95(4).

179   T. Allison et al. 1995. *Mayo Clin Proc.* 70(8).

180   H. Eysenck. 1988. *Br J Med Psychol.* 61(Pt 1).

181   B. Penninx et al. 1997. *Am J Epidemiol.* 146(6).

182   Quick Coherence Technique. HeartMath, http://www.heartmath.com/personal-use/quick-coherence-technique.html.

183   Institute of HeartMath, http://www.heartmath.org/.

Chapter Seven

184   Johnson, Sue. *Hold Me Tight: Seven Conversations for a Lifetime of Love,* New York: Little Brown & Company, 2008.

185   Ibid.

186   Ibid.

187   Ibid.

188   Levine, Amir and Rachel Heller. *Attached: The New Science of Adult Attachment and How It Can Help You Find—and Keep—Love.* New York: Tarcher/ Penguin, 2010.

189   Ibid.

190   Gilmore, David. *Misogyny: The Male Malady.* Philadelphia: University of Pennsylvania Press, 2001.

191   Keen, Sam. *Fire in the Belly: On Being a Man.* New York: Bantam Books, 1991.

192   Ibid.

193   Johnson, Sue. *Hold Me Tight.*

194   Ibid.

195   Ibid.

196   Ibid.

197   Ibid.

198   Ibid.

199   Ibid.

200   Joiner, Thomas. *Lonely at the Top: The High Cost of Men's Success.* New York: Palgrave Macmillan, 2011.

201   Ibid.

202   Johnson, Sue.

203   Ibid.

204   Ibid.

205   Jaak Panksepp. *Affective Neuroscience: The foundations of human and animal emotions.* Oxford: Oxford University Press, 1998.

206 Ibid.

207 Sue Johnson. My, How Couple's Therapy Has Changed: Attachment, Love, and Science, http://www.psychotherapy.net/article/couples-therapy-attachment.

208 Johnson, Sue. *Hold Me Tight.*

209 Ibid.

210 Johnson, Sue. How Can I Tell if My Marriage is in Trouble, and How do I Prevent a Breakup, http://www.youtube.com/watch?v=VfFEhLagGFE &feature=related.

211 Ibid.

212 Touch Research Institute, http://www6.miami.edu/touch-research/.

213 Thich Nhat Hanh. *True Love: A Practice for Awakening the Heart.* Boston: Shambhala, 2006.

214 International Centre for Excellence in Emotional Focused Therapy, http://www.iceeft.com.

Chapter Eight

215 Feinstein, David, Donna Eden and Gary Craig. *The Promise of Energy Psychology: Revolutionary Tools for Dramatic Personal Change.* New York: Tarcher/Penguin, 2005.

216 Ibid.

217 Ibid.

218 Ibid.

219 Eden, Donna with David Feinstein. *Energy Medicine.* New York: Tarcher/Penguin, 1999.

220 Ibid.

221 Ibid.

222 Oz, Mehmet, *The Oprah Show,* November 20, 2007.

223 Eden, Donna, *Energy Medicine.*

224 Feinstein, David. November 2010. "The Case for Energy Psychology Snake Oil or Designer Tool for Neural Change?" *Psychotherapy Networker.*

225 Gary Craig has now retired, but his work continues. For updates on his work and EFT certification go to http://www.emofree.com/.

226 Feinstein, Eden, and Craig, *The Promise of Energy Psychology.*

227 Ibid.

228 Craig, Gary. EFT for Back Pain. Fulton, California: Energy Psychology Press, 2009.

229 EFT Universe, http://www.eftuniverse.com.

230 Eden, Donna and David Feinstein. Nov./Dec. 2010. *Principles of Energy Medicine,* www.innersource.net; and Feinstein, David. The Case for Energy Psychology: Snake oil or therapeutic power tool? *Psychotherapy Networker.*

231 Craig, Gary. *EFT for Back Pain.* Fulton, California: Energy Psychology Press, 2009.

232 Feinstein, Eden, and Craig, *The Promise of Energy Psychology.*

233 Ibid.

234 Ibid.

Chapter Nine

235 Myss, Caroline. *Defy Gravity: Healing Beyond the Bounds of Reason.* Carlsbad, California: Hay House, 2009.

236 Gerald A. Lincoln. 2001. "The irritable male syndrome." Reproduction, Fertility and Development, 13, 567-576.

237 http://theirritablemale.com/quiz.htm.

238 Faludi, Susan. *Stiffed: The Betrayal of the American Man.* New York: William Morrow, 1999.

239 Quoted in Daniel Goleman, *Destructive Emotions: How Can We Overcome Them? A Scientific Dialogue with the Dalai Lama.* New York: Bantam Dell, 2003.

240   Ibid.

241   Crenshaw, Theresa. *The Alchemy of Love and Lust: Discovering Our Sex Hormones and How They Determine Who We Love, When We Love, and How Often We Love.* New York: G.P. Putnam's Sons, 1996.

242   Gillespie, Larrian. *The Gladiator Diet: How to Preserve Peak Health, Sexual Energy and a Strong Body at Any Age.* Beverly Hills, Ca.: Healthy Life Publications, 2001.

243   Meryn, Siegfried, Metka Markus and Kindel George. *Men's Health & the Hormone Revolution.* Ontario, Canada: NDE, 2000.

244   Wurtman, Judith and Suffes Susan. *The Serotonin Solution: The potent brain chemical that can help you stop bingeing, lose weight, and feel great.* New York: Ballantine Books, 1996.

245   Toffler, Alvin. *Future Shock,* New York: Bantam, 1970.

246   Ibid.

247   Freinkel, Susan. January 2007. "The Secret Men Won't Admit." *Reader's Digest,* http://www.rd.com/health/the-under-reporting-of-male-depression-in-america/.

248   Diamond, Jed. *Male vs. Female Depression: Why Men Act Out and Women Act In.* San Francisco: Scribd, 2010. e-book http://www.scribd.com/doc/25714272/Male-vs-Female-Depression-Why-Men-Act-Out-and-Women-Act-In

249   O'Neill, Eugene. *A Long Day's Journey into Night.* New Haven: Yale University Press, 1956, 2002.

250   Ibid.

251   Ilardi, Stephen. *The Depression Cure: 6-Step Program to Beat Depression without Drugs.* New York: Da Capo Press, 2009.

252   Ibid.

253   Maisel, Eric. *Rethinking Depression: How to Shed Mental Health Labels and Create Personal Meaning.* Novato, California: New World Library, 2012.

254   Carrington, Patricia. *Discover the Power of Meridian Tapping: A Revolutionary Method for Stress-Free Living.* Brookfield, CT: The Tapping Solution, 2008.

255   Ilardi, Stephen.

256   Blumenthal, J. A, et al. 2007. Exercise and Pharmacotherapy in the Treatment of Major Depressive Disorder. *Psychosomatic Medicine* 69:587–596.

257   Ilardi, Stephen.

258   Ibid.

259   Courtenay. Will. *Dying to be Men: Psychosocial, Environmental, and Biobehavioral Directions in Promoting the Health of Men and Boys.* New York: Routledge/Taylor & Francis Group, 2011.

260   Ibid.

Chapter Ten

261   AAPM Facts and Figures on Pain, http://www.painmed.org/patient/facts.html.

262   Ibid.

263   National Center for Health Statistics. Health, United States, 2006, with Chartbook on Trends in the Health of Americans. Hyattsville, MD: 86.

264   Scott, John. Modern Pain Management, http://www.articlesbase.com/medicine-articles/modern-pain-management-1636972.html.

265   American Academy of Pain Medicine. Incidence of Pain, As Compared to Major Conditions, http://www.painmed.org/patient/facts.html.

266   http://www.chronicpain.org/.

267   Ibid.

268   Stewart-Patterson, Chris. Working with Chronic Pain, http://www.shambhalasun.com/index.php?option=com_content&task=view&id=2190&Itemid=0.

269   Sarno, John E. *Healing Back Pain: The Mind-Body Connection.* New York: Warner Books, 1991.

270   Ibid.

271   Ibid

272   Ibid.

273   National Center for Complementary and Alternative Medicine, http://nccam.nih.gov/health/pain/chronic.htm.

274   Interview with Eric Robins in *EFT for Back Pain* by Gary Craig. Fulton, Ca: Energy Psychology Press, 2009.

275   Ibid.

276   Jensen, M., et. al., 1994. Magnetic Resonance Imaging of the Lumbar Spine in People without Back Pain. *New England Journal of Medicine* 331:69-73.

277   Ibid.

278   AAPM Facts and Figures on Pain, http://www.painmed.org/patient/facts.html.

279   *Men's Health Magazine,* "The Psychology of Back Pain," *http://www.menshealth.com/health/chronic-back-pain.*

280   Pain Relief, New "Acupuncture without Needles" Technique Reports 80% Effectiveness, Often Out-Performing Drugs, http://eftuniverse.com/index.php?option=com_content&view=article&id=571&Itemid=528.

281   Craig, Gary. *EFT for Back Pain.* Fulton, California: Energy Psychology Press, 2009.

282   http://eftuniverse.com/index.php?option=com_content&view=article&id=574&Itemid=531.

283   http://eftuniverse.com/index.php?option=com_content&view=article &id=576&Itemid=533.

284   Craig, Gary. *EFT for Back Pain.*

285   Ober, Clinton, Stephen Sinatra and Martin Zucker. *Earthing: The Most Important Health Discovery Ever?* Laguna Beach, California: Basic Health Publications, 2010.

286   Ibid.

287   Ibid.

288   Ibid.

289   Ibid.

290   Ibid.

291   Ibid.

292   Barefoot Substitutes, http://www.earthenergies.net/Home.htm.

293   Ober, Clinton, Stephen Sinatra and Martin Zucker. *Earthing.*

294   Ibid.

295   Ibid.

Chapter Eleven

296   Diamond, Jed. *Male Menopause.* Naperville, Illinois: Sourcebooks, 1997.

297   Quoted in Ronald Klatz and Carol Kahn, *Grow Young with HGH: The Amazing Medically Proven Plan to Reverse Again,* New York: HarperCollins, 1997.

298   Ibid.

299   Tan, Robert S. *The Andropause Mystery: Unraveling Truths About the Male Menopause.* Houston, Texas: Amred Publising, 2001.

300   Crenshaw, Theresa. *The Alchemy of Love and Lust: Discovering Our Sex Hormones and How They Determine Who We Love, When We Love, and How Often We Love.* New York: G. P. Putnam's Sons, 1996.

301 Sheehy, Gail. April 1993. The Unspeakable Passage: Is There a Male Menopause. *Vanity Fair.*

302 Carruthers, Malcolm. *The Testosterone Revolution.* London: Thorsons, 2001.

303 Diamond, Jed. *The Whole Man Program: Reinvigorating Your Body, Mind, and Spirit after 40.* New York: John Wiley & Sons, 2002.

304 Crenshaw, Theresa.

305 Ibid.

306 Cetel, Nancy. *Double Menopause.* New York: John Wiley & Sons, 2002.

307 Ibid.

308 Ibid.

309 Jason, Sharon. January 29, 2008. Midlife Slump Finds People in Their 40s Down in the Dumps. *USA Today,* http://abcnews.go.com/Health/Depression/story?id=4208216&page=1.

310 Ibid.

311 Cochran, Sam and Fredric Rabinowitz. *Men and Depression: Clinical and Empirical Perspectives.* San Diego, California: Academic Press, 2000.

312 Martin, Rick and Dokoupil. April 28, 2011. Dead Suit Walking. *Newsweek,* 30–37.

313 Ibid.

314 Peace Intention Experiment, http://www.intentionexperiment911.com/.

315 Clarissa Pinkola Estes. Father Earth, spoken at Men's and Women's Conference, February 21, 1993, at the Palace of Fine Arts Theatre, San Francisco, California.

Chapter Twelve

316 November 8, 2011. Penn State Said to Be Planning Paterno Exit Amid Scandal. *New York Times,* http://www.nytimes.com/2011/11/09/sports/ncaafootball/penn-state-said-to-be-planning-paternos-exit.html.

317   Laszlo, Ervin. *WorldShift 2012: Making Green Business, New Politics & Higher Consciousness Work Together.* Rochester, Vermont: Inner Traditions, 2009.

318   Although some believe that "civilization" is synonymous with the rise of agriculture ten thousand to twelve thousand years ago, others such as James DeMeo in his book, *Saharasia: The 4000 BCE Origins of Child Abuse, Sex Repression, Warfare and Social Violence in the Deserts of the Old World,* believe that the these problems arose approximately six thousand years ago with environmental changes that created large areas of desert in what had once been a fertile part of the world. People reacting to environmental degradation become more aggressive, warlike, and abusive, both to themselves, the planet, and surrounding tribes.

319   Heinberg, Richard. *The Party's Over: Oil, War, and the Fate of Industrial Societies.* Gabriola Island, BC: New Society Publishers, 2003.

320   Heinberg, Richard. *The End of Growth: Adapting to Our New Economic Reality.* Gabriola Island, BC: New Society Publishers, 2011.

321   Costa, Rebecca. *The Watchman's Rattle: Thinking Our Way Out of Extinction.* New York: Vanguard Press, 2010.

322   Ibid.

323   Rebecca Costa. TED talk. The Greatest Discovery You Never Heard Of, http://tedxtalks.ted.com/video/TEDxSantaCruz-Rebecca-Costa-The.

324   The Crash Course book and course, http://www.chrismartenson.com/.

325   Martenson, Chris. *The Crash Course: The Unsustainable Future of Our Economy, Energy, and Environment.* New York: John Wiley & Sons, 2011.

326   Chico Mendez, quoted by Julian Burger in *The Gaia Atlas of First Peoples: A Future for the Indigenous World.* New York: Anchor Books, 2000.

327   Korten, David C. *The Great Turning: From Empire to Earth Community.* San Francisco: Berrett-Koehler, 2006.

328   Ibid.

329   Quinn, Daniel. *Beyond Civilization: Humanity's Next Great Adventure.* New York: Harmony Books, 2009.

330   Martenson, Chris. *The Crash Course: The Unsustainable Future of Our Economy, Energy, and Environment.* New York: John Wiley & Sons, 2011.

331   Ibid.

332   Quinn, Daniel. *Ishmael.* New York: Bantam, 1992.

333   Quinn, Daniel. *Beyond Civilization: Humanity's Next Great Adventure.* New York: Harmony Books, 1999.

334   Ibid.

335   Ibid.

336   *Washington Post,* http://views.washingtonpost.com/leadership/books/2010/04/summary-seth-godins-tribes-we-need-you-to-lead-us.html.

337   The Business Alliance for Local Living Economies (BALLE), http://www.livingeconomies.org.

338   Schor, Juliet B. *The Overworked American: The Unexpected Decline of Leisure.* New York; Basic Books, 1991.

339   Schor, Juliet B. *Plentitude: The New Economics of True Wealth.* New York: Penguin Press, 2010.

340   Robbins, John. *The New Good Life: Living Better Than Ever in an Age of Less.* New York: Ballantine Books, 2010.

341   Ibid.

342   Jack Eason Rowe, http://www.jackeasonrowe.com/sports.htm.

343   Greg Warburton, http://gregwarburton.com.

344   http://attractingabundance.com.

345   www.eftmastersworldwide.com.

346   Lindsay Kenny, www.ProEFT.com.

347   The Tapping World Summit, http://www.2011tappingworldsummit.com/tws_video/registration.php.

348   The Shift Network, http://theshiftnetwork.com/main.

349   The Intention Experiment, http://www.theintentionexperiment.com.

350   The Global Coherence Initiative, http://www.glcoherence.org.

351   Hawken, Paul. *Blessed Unrest: How the Largest Movement in the World Came into Being and Why No One Saw It Coming.* New York: Viking, 2007.

352   Ibid.

353   http://www.wiserearth.org.

354   Petersen, John L. *A Vision for 2012: Planning for Extraordinary Change.* Golden, Colorado: Fulcrum Publishing, 2008.

355   The Arlington Institute, http://www.arlingtoninstitute.org.

356   McTaggart, Lynn. *The Bond: Connecting Through the Space Between Us.* New York: Free Press, 2011.

357   Ibid.

358   http://www.lynnemctaggart.com.

359   Ibid.

ABOUT THE AUTHOR

Jed Diamond, PhD, is founder and director of the MenAlive, a health program that helps men live long and well. Though focused on men's health, MenAlive is also for women who care about the health of the men in their lives. Jed has been on the Board of Advisors of the Men's Health Network since its inception in 1992. He is also a member of the Association for Comprehensive Energy Psychology (ACEP) and the International Society for the Study of the Aging Male and serves as a member of the International Scientific Board of the World Congress on Gender and Men's Health. He is the only male columnist writing for the National Association of Baby Boomer Women.

His work has been featured in major newspapers throughout the United States including the *New York Times, Boston Globe, Wall Street Journal, Los Angeles Times,* and *USA Today.* He has been featured on more than 1,000 radio and TV programs including *The View* with Barbara Walters, *Good Morning America, Today Show, CNN-360 with Anderson Cooper, CNN with Glenn Beck,* and *To Tell the Truth.* He also did a nationally televised special on male menopause for PBS.

Diamond has been a licensed psychotherapist for over forty years and is the author of ten books, including the international best-selling *Male Menopause* and *Surviving Male Menopause,* that have thus far been translated into 22 foreign languages.

His PhD dissertation, *Gender and Depression,* broke new ground in creating a better evaluation system for diagnosing and treating depression in men and women.

He lives with his wife, Carlin, on Shimmins Ridge, above Bloody Run Creek, in Northern California. They are the proud parents of five grown children and twelve grandchildren.

To receive a copy of his free e-newsletter, visit Jed at his websites.

Websites:
www.MenAlive.com
www.TheIrritableMale.com

E-Mail: Jed@MenAlive.com
Mailing Address: Box 442, Willits, California, 95490
Phone: 707 459-5505

Index

12430914R00200

Made in the USA
Charleston, SC
04 May 2012